AF480701

A TEACHER'S ODYSSEY

A
TEACHER'S
ODYSSEY

A Memoir of Grit, Growth
& Global Adventures

TARIQUE CONNELLY

MONTEVISTA
PUBLISHING

Published in the United States by Montevista Publishing
Bala Cynwyd, Pennsylvania

MONTEVISTA PUBLISHING and its colophon are trademarks of Montevista Publishing LLC.

PUBLISHER'S CATALOGING-IN-PUBLICATION DATA
(Provided by Cassidy Cataloguing Services, Inc.)

NAMES: Connelly, Tarique, 1983– author.
TITLE: A teacher's odyssey : a memoir of grit, growth, and global adventures /
Tarique Connelly.
DESCRIPTION: Bala Cynwyd, Pennsylvania : Montevista Publishing, [2025]
IDENTIFIERS: LCCN 2025913993 |
ISBN 979-8-9985333-0-3 (hardcover) | 979-8-9985333-2-7 (paperback) |
979-8-9985333-1-0 (ebook) | 979-8-9985333-6-5 (audiobook)

SUBJECTS:
LCSH: Connelly, Tarique, 1983- | Teachers—United States—Biography. |
Education—Pennsylvania—Philadelphia—Social aspects. |
Public schools—United States. | Urban schools—United States. |
Educational change—United States. | Teaching—United States—Anecdotes. |
Teacher-student relationships—United States. | Resilience (Personality trait) |
Burn out (Psychology) | Travel—Psychological aspects. | Self-realization.

LCGFT: Autobiographies.

BISAC: BIOGRAPHY & AUTOBIOGRAPHY / Memoirs | EDUCATION / Urban |
TRAVEL / Essays & Travelogues | SELF-HELP / Personal Growth / Success

CLASSIFICATION: LCC LA2317.C656 A3 2025 | DDC 371.1/0092—dc23
Library of Congress record available at https://lccn.loc.gov/2025913993

Cover design by Tiago Pereira
Interior layout by Olivier Darbonville

Printed in the United States of America

montevistapublishers.com

Between stimulus and response there is a space.

In that space is our power to choose our response.

In our response lies our growth and our freedom.

— INSPIRED BY VIKTOR E. FRANKL

The illiterate of the 21st century will not be those

who cannot read and write,

but those who cannot learn, unlearn, and relearn.

— ALVIN TOFFLER

———

For my mother.
My greatest teacher.
Thank you for molding me into the man I am today.

———

CONTENTS

PART THREE

PART FOUR

PART ONE

Chapter 1

An Offer I Couldn't Refuse

———

I DRUM MY FINGERS ON THE DESK, WATCHING A STUDENT eye the door like it owes him money. He hovers at the edge of his seat, knee bouncing, body primed for launch. And he's not the only one. Half the room looks ready to bail, like the final bell is just a formality. I glance at the clock—just eleven minutes left, eleven minutes until freedom.

Oh, the joy of substitute teaching.

On the surface, the job is simple: show up, hand out busywork, keep the peace. That's it. It's not glamorous, but it's steady. And it pairs well with my airline gig, which lets me chase the horizon whenever the classroom walls close in. Still, a part of me wants more: to do more, to matter more, to be more than just a glorified babysitter.

The thought barely settles before the escape artist makes his move. He rises, bold and defiant, daring me to say something.

"Yo, chill! We 'bout to dip." I try to sound firm, like I'm in control. But we all know I'm not.

"I'm just throwing something out, bro," he says, strolling toward the trash can stationed right by the exit.

I see it coming, but before I can react, he's already gone—laughter trailing behind him while I pretend it doesn't bother me.

Moments later, someone else tries his luck.

I intercept him. "Wait! We've only got five minutes left!"

Geez Louise! Why is it so frigging hard for them to wait five minutes?

As the seconds tick by, the crowd inches forward, ready to burst out like steam from a tea kettle.

Then, at last, the bell rings.

Freedom.

The students scatter in every direction, and I'm right behind them. I turn off the lights, lock the classroom, and rush to the office to sign out. The hallway fills with students from various backgrounds—a beautiful microcosm of our country, and a glimpse of its future.

It's a far cry from the halls of my alma mater, Overbrook High, where nearly every face looked like mine. Still, the air smells the same: a pungent mix of cafeteria grease and adolescence. Funny how some things never change.

I follow the current of students down the hall and slip into the main office, where weary teachers exchange smiles of relief, their exhaustion mirroring my own. I make my way to the desk with the substitute log.

A friendly face greets me. "Thanks for covering," he says. "We really appreciate it."

"No problem!" I respond.

Just as I'm about to leave, he asks, "Do you have a second?"

Fudge! Why now?

"Sure," I reply in a tone that belies my eagerness to escape.

"John Oglesby," he says, reaching out for a handshake.

"Tarique Connelly. Pleasure to meet you."

"Likewise. I'm right across from the class you were covering, and I noticed how well you get on with the students. Have you ever considered teaching full-time? The district is desperate for new teachers, and I bet you would make a great candidate."

"Thanks, buddy. I appreciate that, but I'm not interested."

"Are you sure? You'd make a lot more than you are now, substituting."

"Facts! But I'm good. I like subbing. I can work as little or as much as I want. Plus, I can focus on my side hustles. Besides, I'm not taking out another dollar in student loans. Trust me, I have more than my fair share."

"Well, fortunately, you no longer have to. Have you heard about the new Teacher Residency Program?"

I shake my head nonchalantly.

"The district is paying for career changers with no teaching experience to get their license and master's degree. The only thing you need is a bachelor's, which I'm assuming you have. The best part is that they'll pay you forty thousand dollars to do it."

"That's unbelievable. Is the teacher shortage that bad? I've never heard of the district paying people to get their credentials."

"Well, they are now. It's just a two-year process. During the first year, you apprentice with a master teacher while earning your license. In the second, you manage your own class while earning your master's."

"Wow. That's a pretty sweet deal, but I'm good. I appreciate you sharing the info, though."

"Okay, no problem. Take care."

"You as well."

Yeah, right! Me, a certified hot mess during my entire public school journey, become a full-time teacher? That's absurd.

After my chaotic childhood, it's a miracle I even graduated from high school. In those four years alone, I was expelled twice, suspended too many times to count, held back once, and even dropped out for a bit. I only returned when the judge gave me an ultimatum: either go back to school or go to a group home.

Of course, I chose the milder form of institutional captivity.

Somehow—against all odds—I landed at New York University just two years later.

How, you might ask, does a total train wreck end up at the school of his dreams?

Well . . . that's a story for another time, my friends.

I step out the school building onto the bustling streets, welcomed by the cacophony of downtown life. The scene is frenetic, with traffic flowing steadily, creating a symphony of honks and hustle. Pedestrians stream down the sidewalk, the city's energy pulsing as students linger as if no one told them school's over. I dart across the street before the light changes.

As I head to my car, the conversation with Mr. Oglesby loops in my head like an earworm. I can't deny that the offer is enticing. I left my sales job two years ago because it filled my bank account but starved my soul. I vowed my next job wouldn't just be about a paycheck but about making a real difference in people's lives. Could this be the universe responding to that longing?

No way. I'm a free spirit. The thought of being locked in a classroom for nine straight months is unfathomable, especially if it means I can't travel whenever I want. Most people fall in love with other people. I fell in love with exploring—watching the sun rise over new landscapes, getting lost on purpose, feeling a quiet kinship with the earth and everyone drifting across it.

That kind of love only lasts if you keep traveling, and my airline gig makes that possible. From Philly alone, I can jet off to over three hundred places on any given day if I have the time and money. Becoming a full-time teacher will help with the latter, but it will likely monopolize the former.

After weaving through the streets for what feels like forever, I finally reach my car. I kick off my shoes and turn on the radio. I crank up the volume, but even Drake belting out "God's Plan" can't drown out the chatter in my brain about becoming a teacher. The stickiness of the conversation feels like a sign that I should explore this opportunity further. I've got nothing to lose and more than money to gain.

I reach home, run inside, and hop straight on the computer. I google "Philly Teacher Residency Program (TRP)." The first hit says: "Earn $40K a year while earning your license." I click on the link and discover that the School District of Philadelphia is partnering with the University of Pennsylvania (UPenn), Drexel University, Temple University, and a school I've never heard of before—the Relay Graduate School of Education—to help career changers earn their teaching credentials.

UPenn's and Drexel's TRPs cost about $60,000 and $80,000, respectively. *Hell to the no!* After graduating from New York University (NYU)burdened with over $100,000 in debt, I vowed never to borrow another dime in student loans, and I meant it. So, sadly, UPenn and Drexel are out. That leaves Temple and Relay.

Temple's program stands out because it's accelerated. I can earn a license and a master's degree in a year while receiving a salary. The best part? It won't cost me a dime. That's absolutely bonkers. Where does the city find all this dough? Earning my master's degree is ideal—it would give me an immediate salary boost. After the first year, I'll be making $60,000. Not bad.

Now it's not the big bucks I was pulling in from sales, but when you factor in the free license, the master's degree, guaranteed salary, yearly raises, summers off, twenty-plus paid holidays, personal days, a pension, health care—and, most importantly, the chance to change lives? Count me in!

The icing on the cake is that I can continue working my airport gig. Thanks to my high seniority, I have the flexibility to choose shifts that align perfectly with my teaching schedule. While I may not be able to travel as extensively as before, I can still use my summers and holidays to explore new places. It's the best of both worlds: I get to make an impact while continuing my quest to see every country on Earth.

All the stars are aligned. The heavens spoke through Mr. Oglesby. It's funny to think that I almost rushed out of the office, unknowingly sidestepping a potential blessing. It serves as a reminder to slow down and be more present. Confident that the Teacher Residency aligns with my deepest aspirations, I immediately begin looking into the application process.

Surprisingly, the deadline looms just two weeks away. Panic sets in. Do I have to wait until next year? I could be in Timbuktu by then. Well, there's only one way to find out. I call the recruitment office at the School District of Philadelphia to get some answers.

Chapter 2

From Student to Teacher

—

"Hello. Thank you for calling the School District of Philadelphia. Keisha Jenkins speaking."

"Hello, Ms. Jenkins. My name is Tarique Connelly, and I'm interested in the Teacher Residency Program."

"Great. Thanks for your interest, but unfortunately, we've already finished recruiting for this year."

"Ah, that's a bummer."

"But I can give you the details for next year if you're interested."

"No worries. I'll check in with you then."

"Okay. Take care."

"You as well."

Just like that, my teaching dream crumbles, leaving me with the bitter taste of unfulfilled aspirations. But hey, as my mom always says, God's delays aren't God's denials. I just have to be patient. Next year will be here before you know it. In the meantime, I will continue subbing, speaking, and traveling, but my determination remains unwavering. I will join the Teacher Residency and earn my credentials.

A few days later, my phone rings.

"Hello, Tarique! It's Keisha from the district. Do you have a second?"

"Sure."

"I have some great news for you. There's a chance you can join Temple's program this year."

My heart skips a beat. "Really? But I thought you were finished recruiting."

"Recruitment is complete, but two candidates still haven't passed the Praxis after multiple attempts. Temple will give them one more chance, but I think they are ready to move on. I told the recruiter about you, and she wants you to apply; the only caveat is that you have to pass the Praxis in a month."

"A month?! How am I supposed to pass in a month? If these guys have failed so many times, what makes you think I can succeed in such a short time frame?"

"Don't worry. I have a good feeling about you. Just choose a subject you know well. What was your major in college?"

"I studied music business."

"Okay. Well, that won't fly because the school district is only footing the bill for math, English, or science. So, you'll have to pick one of those."

"Right now?"

"Sure, if you are up to it."

I consider my options.

The English Praxis assumes familiarity with all the classics and an abundance of grammar rules, making it an easy option to rule out. That leaves math and science. My highest math class in high school was Algebra II, but it felt more like Algebra I. A math Praxis could cover anything from arithmetic to calculus. *Yeah, right!* So, that leaves me with science, a subject I'm not head over heels about. *What are the chances I can successfully pass a science Praxis?* I remember zilch from high school. However, science has to be the easiest option of the three.

"All right, Keisha, I'll give science a shot," I say tentatively.

"Okay, you have three options: physics, chemistry, and biology. What's your pick?"

I pause again. Physics and chemistry both have a math component, and I want no part of that. Biology, on the other hand, is more straight-forward—mostly theoretical, which makes it easier by comparison. So, through the process of elimination, I make my decision.

"Biology," I say. "I'll become a biology teacher."

"Great! Now start studying for that test."

"I'm on it."

Immediately, I visit the Praxis website for more information. The exam is 150 multiple-choice questions with a two-and-a-half-hour time limit. I've got one shot—fail, and the twenty-eight-day wait to retake it kills my chance at the June first deadline. *Yikes.* My palms grow clammy, and my heart quickens as the gravity of the situation sets in.

Maybe I'm rushing things. I wish I didn't know those two guys had failed so many times. The last standardized test I took was the GMAT, which I totally bombed. In my naïveté, I thought a two-week Kaplan course could magically fill all the gaps from high school. What was I smoking? Now I've got a month to master biology?

I know the odds are against me, but I can only give it my best shot. It's time to buckle down, strategize, and craft a game plan for success. On the Praxis website, they have a short practice exam. I take the plunge to assess my current standing—as if I don't already know. The words on the test look Greek, and there are some that I can barely pronounce.

The first question from the official Praxis® free online sample test reads:

In gel electrophoresis, loading buffer is used to:

a. Visualize DNA

b. Add color and density to DNA samples

c. Separate DNA based on size

d. Carry the electric current through the sample

Geez Louise! I guess "Visualize DNA," but when I check the answer, it's B. Of course, I'm wrong. I push through the rest of the test anyway. I answer two out of fifteen questions correctly. Clearly, "Eeny meeny miny moe" isn't the optimal strategy. I have a ton of work to do. I order several books online: a high school biology textbook, an AP Biology textbook, a biology Praxis study guide, and two complete practice exams from the Praxis website. I will also use the Khan Academy, CK-12, and Crash Course websites.

The test is divided into six categories: Nature of Science; Molecular and Cellular Biology; Genetics and Evolution; Diversity of Life and Organismal Biology; Ecology; and Science-Technology and Social Behavior. Within these categories are subcategories that I'll be tackling one by one. For example, the Nature of Science section includes Scientific Inquiry, Methodology, Techniques, and History. My biggest weakness is my lack of laboratory experience, but I'm going to focus on what's within my control.

I wake up at six, like I do most mornings, to feed my cat, Creamy. Instead of returning to bed, I prepare a turkey bacon, egg, and cheese croissant, and a hash brown. I finish my meal, let it settle for a few minutes, and then dive right into studying. I begin with the first topic: "Characteristics of Living Things." I start by reading the high school biology textbook. Then I move on to the AP Biology book. Finally, I watch the Crash Course biology video.

After completing the chapter, I move on to the test questions. Whenever I get a question wrong, I read the explanation and revisit the book's content. Then, I retake the test, pushing myself to choose the correct answers and understand why the other options are incorrect. It's a laborious process, but surprisingly, I'm loving the ride. Studying biology feels spiritual. It unveils the intricate web connecting all living organisms to each other and to the world around us, which fills me with a profound sense of reverence and awe.

Consider this: all humans share 99.9 percent of the same genetic code, with just 0.1 percent accounting for all the differences we see. We even share about 85 percent of our genes with mice. That's astonishing. Amazingly, I can't recall learning any of this in high school. Granted, I was only there half of the time.

Days later, I receive a call from Keisha.

"Hi, Tarique. I want to give you an update. One of the two candidates still hasn't passed the Praxis, so you're guaranteed a spot in the residency as long as you can pass. Also, would you be open to coming in for an interview and a demo lesson?"

"Sure."

"Would this Thursday work?"

"Perfect."

"By the way, how's the studying going?"

"It's going well. I'm eating the elephant one bite at a time."

"Okay. Well, I'll let you go, and I look forward to seeing you on Thursday."

"Take care."

Goodness gracious. In addition to hitting the books, I've got to whip up a mock lesson and prepare for an interview. Man, it's getting real. In a panic, I start a web search for lesson ideas, feeling like a fish out of water. The web is a treasure trove of resources, but it's like trying to take a sip from a fire hose. After hours of digging, I finally stumble upon a gem: a worksheet named Cell City, cleverly using a city analogy to teach about cell parts. Bingo!

The day of the event creeps up quickly. I arrive at the School District of Philadelphia headquarters ten minutes before my interview. The cool air inside the building provides a much-needed respite from the heat outside. The interior is hollow, with Plexiglas® windows everywhere. It feels sterile. I greet the two school police officers and let them know I'm here for my interview. They sign me in and then guide me to the fourth floor. When I exit the elevator, I notice a small group of people standing on the opposite side of the hallway. I walk over to join them.

They are all teaching candidates. There are about eleven of us, with only one other guy in the group, which doesn't surprise me. We're primarily millennials, with a couple of baby boomers sprinkled in. Keisha emerges to welcome us, her neat locks harmonizing with her grounded presence. Gesturing for us to follow, she guides us down the corridor and into a conference room.

Keisha begins, "Thank you all for coming. We will start with introductions. Please state your name, why you decided to become a teacher, and your ideal vacation spot. Following that, we will begin our demo lessons. Sound good?"

As we take turns speaking, I'm struggling to pay attention to the other candidates. All I can think about is my lesson. I want to sneak a peek at the worksheet to jog my memory, but then they'll know my mind is elsewhere.

After the introductions, Keisha asks if anyone would like to volunteer to present their lesson first—but no one volunteers. Finally, I break the silence and take the plunge. I distribute the worksheets and head over to the dry-erase board. With confident strokes, I sketch out three columns and title each: "City Part," "Function," and "Cell Part." Then, I launch into my spiel.

"A cell is the smallest unit of life, like a tiny building block. Inside, there are tiny parts called organelles, each with a specific job to keep the cell alive. In the next ten minutes, you'll learn all the major organelles by comparing them to different parts of a city."

I write the word *organelle* on the board.

"Can anyone identify a familiar word within the term *organelle*?"

I call on the other dude in the crew.

"Organ," he says.

"Precisely. Organelles are essentially the organs of the cell. Just like organs have specific functions to sustain the organism, a cell's organelles have distinct roles in aiding the cell's survival.

Similarly, a city's institutions are also designed to perform certain functions. For example, who can tell me what the job of the trash department is?"

"To dispose of waste," responds one of the applicants.

"Exactly! In cells, lysosomes act as the trash department, handling the job of removing waste."

I write the information on the board and ask the group to do the same on their worksheets. We repeat this process until we fill out the entire sheet. We discuss the endoplasmic reticulum (road system), nucleus (city hall), ribosomes (construction company), mitochondria (power company), and so forth.

I conclude my presentation just shy of the ten-minute mark. The room erupts in applause, and I feel a surge of pride. However, the biggest challenge still awaits me—passing this frigging exam. The next day, I dive back into studying, keenly aware that the test is just one week away.

When I tackle the first of two practice exams, the score comes in at 70 percent, falling short of my target of 90, a necessary buffer in case I bomb the laboratory questions. Determined to improve, I meticulously review the explanations for the incorrect answers, feeling the pressure of time slipping away. I retake the test. This time, I score 68 percent. *Fudge.* How did I do worse? My head is about to explode, but I can't walk away. I have to make the most of the minimal time I have left.

I give the practice exams another shot the night before the big test. Remarkably, I crush it, scoring 100 percent on both. Watch out! Yeah, right. I've simply memorized the answers at this point. The following morning, I wake up feeling the temptation to squeeze in some last-minute studying. However, I make the wise choice to dial down the intensity, realizing that overloading my brain at this point might lead to a mental lockup. It's time to let the chips fall where they may.

I arrive on Temple's campus with thirty minutes to spare. I meditate in my car to mentally prepare myself for the impending challenge. Fifteen minutes later, "Pie Jesu" blares from my cell phone, signaling it's time for battle. I silence the alarm, gather my belongings, and make my way to the front line.

As I stride across Temple's campus, a vibrant energy surrounds me. I pass scholars engaged in animated conversations, as the scent of freshly cut grass lingers in the air. With each step, I soak in the ambience, envisioning myself as a part of this dynamic community. When I sign in, the proctor tells me to secure all my belongings in a locker, as I'm allowed just a writing utensil inside the testing room. Afterward, he directs me to follow him.

My heart pounds as he guides me to the computer, entering a code that unlocks the obstacle. "You can begin when you're ready," he says. The testing room, with its rows of flickering desktops and scattered test takers, feels oddly similar to the telemarketing companies I worked for in the late nineties—a reminder of the relentless pressure to perform under constant scrutiny.

As my fingers hover over the keyboard, a swirl of anticipation tightens my chest; from this point, each keystroke is poised to unlock the gateway to success or setback. I say a quick prayer and then get down to business.

As I tackle the test, a wave of complexity unfolds before me. Fortunately, the shock I felt during the sample test has faded. I'm still making a few educated guesses, but overall I feel pretty good. There are only thirty questions I need to revisit if time allows; for the rest, I'm fully confident.

With the clock ticking down to my final fifteen minutes, I dig in, determined to make the most of every second. Finally, I hover over the submit button with my heart pounding. Then, with a deep breath, I click it. Closing my eyes, I wait for the computer to deliver my unofficial score. I need only a 73 percent to pass.

I open my eyes, and Good golly, Miss Molly, the screen shows 81 percent.

I did it!

I do a happy dance in my seat. I'd wanted to score 85 percent to achieve elite status, but unsurprisingly, I missed most of the laboratory questions.

I leave the testing center and immediately call Keisha.

"Hey, Keisha! I have some fantastic news. I passed the Praxis!"

"Great, Tarique! Congratulations! I knew you would do it. Okay, so I'm still waiting for the Temple recruiter's reply. As soon as I hear from them, I'll be in touch. Once again, congratulations!"

"Thanks."

A week passes without a word. Then one afternoon, my phone rings. It's Keisha.

"Hey, Tarique." Her voice is hesitant, a little shaky—enough to set off something inside me. My stomach tightens.

"Well, I have some good news and some bad news. Which one do you want first?"

"The bad news."

"Okay, unfortunately, Temple decided to stick with the other candidate."

"Oh, so he finally passed the Praxis?"

"No. They figured his score was close enough, so they just gave him a pass."

"Huh. Okay. So, no Temple?"

"No Temple."

I sigh.

"But your Praxis results are valid for a year."

"Okay. So what's the good news?"

"Tarique, you're an excellent candidate, and I don't want to lose you. I know you would be perfect for our students, so I'm making you an offer.

"I found a position for you, working as a supplemental science teacher. You'll spend the year assisting another teacher while still receiving your full salary."

"Okay, like the Teacher Residency."

"Exactly."

"What school?"

"Okay, that's the kicker. Have you ever heard of Columbia Middle School?"

"I haven't, but I wanted to work in a high school. I'm not cut out for middle school. I don't have the patience."

"Tarique, I understand how you feel. And it's completely up to you. However, you'll only be assisting, so it's not like you'll be alone. It's an excellent opportunity to gain some on-the-job experience while waiting for the residency to start next year."

"Can I think about it?"

"Sure, you don't have to decide now. Can you let me know by Monday?"

"Okay."

The call ends. Silence fills the room. Frustration creeps in as I stare at the ceiling, weighing my options. It feels like all that time I spent studying was in vain. I worked tirelessly to reach the bar, only for them to lower it for someone else. That's unfair, and it robs both the students and me. Lowering the bar doesn't advance equity; it undermines excellence and shortchanges the very kids we claim to care about.

And now they're asking me to work in a frigging middle school. After my last disastrous run there, I swore I'd never return.

Guess the universe didn't get the memo.

But maybe what I'm resisting is exactly what I need to face if I want to unlock my full potential.

Reluctantly, I drag myself over to the computer desk and start researching the school, clicking on their GreatSchools profile. The results? Shocking.

The school has an overall rating of 1 out of 10. Only 18 percent of students are proficient in reading and 6 percent in math. Undoubtedly, the school needs help. I'm just not sure I'm the right person for the job. But if it's not me, then who?

I doubt there's anyone else waiting in the wings. How challenging can it be? It's just a year, and I'll be working with an experienced teacher. Surely, two adults can handle a classroom, right?

Chapter 3

The Shock That Changed Everything

—

I'M SITTING IN MY CAR IN THE TEACHERS' PARKING LOT, meditating, with my favorite classical station, WRTI, playing softly in the background. I'm hoping this calm start will set the tone for a peaceful journey ahead. Fortunately, the first week of school is just for teachers. But the students will be here before we know it, and we only have two days left to prepare. I bet some of my colleagues are already freaking out. Lucky me, I'm only an assistant, so my responsibilities are minimal. Besides, my new partner, Lisa McCaffrey, is a rock star.

"Pie Jesu" resounds sweetly from my phone, signaling it's time to shake, rattle, and roll. I gather my things, take a deep breath, and trek from the parking lot to the school's front entrance. I can only imagine the vibe in a few days when the students arrive, but for now, it's better to stay in the moment and enjoy the serenity while I have it.

I make my way to the classroom, where Lisa is waiting. She's a married mother of two with beautiful emerald eyes and an easygoing personality. Working with her will be a breeze—to think I was nervous I'd get stuck with someone annoying.

Lisa came to Columbia last year after the Catholic school she'd taught at for over two decades closed down. There's a lot I can learn from her, starting with how to impeccably decorate a classroom. From the moment you step inside, you can't help but feel inspired by walls bursting with colorful posters, intricate diagrams, and dense biology jargon. This space speaks volumes about Lisa. Her care is evident, her passion contagious, and her kindness instantly inviting.

"Are you sure I can't give you a hand with anything?" I ask.

"No worries. When you've been doing this as long as I have, you can do it with your eyes closed."

"Cool beans."

Thirty minutes before school ends, there's an announcement over the loudspeakers: "The schedule is ready. The schedule is ready."

I offer to pick them up. The hallway is eerily quiet. No shrieking tweens. No bantering teachers. Just my footsteps echoing off the linoleum.

At the main office, I grab one of the schedules from the pile on the desk. McCaffrey's name jumps out first—four classes. Nothing unusual. Then I spot my name, just a few lines down, separated from hers. At first, it looks routine enough. But as I trace my line, something seems off.

I compare my schedule to McCaffrey's, expecting them to match. The first half aligns perfectly. Then mine takes a sharp turn.

Why are there two classes listed under my name alone? That can't be right.

Dread pools in my stomach and my heart pounds.

I fold the schedule and walk straight to the principal's office.

"Hey, Principal Johnson. Can I chat with you, please?"

"Sure. Let me close the door. Is everything okay?"

"There seems to be a mistake in the schedule. It looks like I'm teaching two classes alone."

"No, Mr. Connelly, that's not a mistake. We're missing a few teachers and need you to fill in the gaps. That's the role of a supplemental teacher."

"How? I've never taught a day in my life, and I've had zero training. Now you expect me to teach two classes on Monday? That's ridiculous."

"Don't worry, Mr. Connelly. You'll have support. Mrs. Mayfield, the science lead, and Mrs. McCaffrey are both excellent resources."

"But I've had no training! I have no idea what I'm doing!"

"Don't worry. You'll learn the ropes."

"A part of me is considering whether I even want to."

"Well, that's a decision only you can make."

An awkward silence hangs in the air. I'm at a loss for words. And that's a rarity.

I break the silence by saying, "I just—I just don't get it. How is this even legal? Then you wait until the absolute last minute to tell me. I have no time to prepare. You're setting me up for failure."

"I'm sorry you feel that way, Mr. Connelly, but you're not alone. You have support. Just take it easy. It's only two classes."

"Oh, that's easy for you to say."

"Well, Mr. Connelly, I don't know what else to say. It was never our intention to have you teach your own classes."

That's some bull schnitzel.

"We've been trying to assemble this schedule all week. Our goal is that every student will have a teacher on Monday morning."

"I hear you, but 'a' teacher is not good enough. How about someone qualified to do the job?"

"Unfortunately, I have to cut this short. Ultimately, the choice is yours. Is there anything else, Mr. Connelly?"

I shake my head and leave the office. I call Keisha immediately.

"Hey Keisha. It's Tarique. I just learned that I'm teaching two classes by myself on Monday. Can they do that?"

"Technically, they can. You have an emergency certification and passed the Praxis, so you are eligible to teach."

"Oh, so passing the Praxis qualifies me to teach an entire class?"

"In the city of Philadelphia, it does."

"What happened to me just being an assistant?"

"Well, that was the plan, but unfortunately, plans change."

"This was probably the plan all along."

"Well, you're entitled to your opinion, but that was not my understanding."

"How do they expect me to teach middle-school science when I only passed the Biology Praxis?"

"A high school science certification covers middle-school science as well."

"But how is this even legal? I have no classroom-management or lesson-planning skills. I swear this isn't fair to me or the students."

"I didn't say it was fair, but sadly, it's the nature of the beast."

There's an awkward silence.

"Tarique, just take a deep breath. I know it's a lot to process, but I also know you've got what it takes to succeed. If you could pass the Praxis in a month, when some biology majors fail to pass it at all, I know you can handle this."

I want to tell her to take her toxic positivity and shove it. Instead, I say, "We'll see." The call ends.

I can't believe this is happening. I feel completely deceived. First, they make me jump through hoops to get into the Teacher Residency, only to lower the standards for someone else. Now, they hire me under false pretenses and set me up for failure. This is insane. It's only been four days, and I'm already considering quitting. Teaching isn't like passing the Praxis, where I could just study, regurgitate answers, and pass. These students will present a daily test I don't have the skills to pass. And I hate failing!

I'm so pissed I could punch a wall. I return to McCaffrey's class. She glances at me and immediately sees the vexation etched across my face.

"Are you okay, Connelly?"

"No! I just learned that I'm teaching two classes by myself."

"Shut up! Are you serious?"

"Yes, they played me." I give her a copy of the schedule. "I'm ready to quit because this is absurd. Then they wait until now to tell me. They couldn't tell me on Monday? What am I supposed to do right now? It's Thursday. The week is almost over!"

"That sucks. I would be livid too. So, what do you do?"

"I don't know." I take a deep breath and pause to gather my thoughts. Then the bell rings, signaling it's time to go home.

"Will I see you tomorrow?" she says.

"We'll see."

I drive home in silence, completely flustered. My mind is racing like a roller coaster. I get to the crib and hop straight into bed. Of course, I can't sleep. I'm still too riled up. I can't shake the feeling of being used and thrown to the wolves like a sacrificial lamb. I knew 50 percent of teachers were gone within the first five years. Now I can see why. You can't exploit people, treat them like crap, and then expect them to stick around.

Maybe I should just quit and go back to substituting. But if I quit, I'm essentially saying "sayonara" to my teaching career. There's no way I can resign from this position and expect the district to rehire me next year as a teacher resident.

Suddenly, I remember the principal mentioning that some students haven't had a science teacher since starting middle school. I imagine myself in their shoes, like acorns thrown on stony ground with no opportunity to actualize their fullest potential. They don't deserve that. But they also deserve more than what I can currently offer them. I guess having a teacher with virtually no experience is better than none at all, but either way, it's a profound disservice.

I've already invested so much time and energy into this process that it would be ridiculous to quit now. All I can do is try to make the most of the situation. I genuinely believe that whatever God brings me to, He'll bring me through. He knows how much I can bear, even if the problem seems unbearable now.

I have to fight to stay positive, which isn't easy because I already feel like I'm descending into a black hole. This pity pot is very comfy, but I can't stay here forever. All I can do is take it one day at a time.

I return to Columbia the next day. I walk into the main office to sign in. The principal walks out.

"Good morning, Mr. Connelly."

"Good morning, Principal Johnson."

"Before you leave, I have something for you." She hands me an envelope with the number 308 written on it and keys inside. "These are your room keys."

"Thanks."

"Let me know if you need anything. Have a good day, Mr. Connelly."

"You too."

I go to check out my new digs. The room is rectangular with hardwood floors. The floors have seen better days; they're groaning with every step I take. Some parts by the radiator are flat-out missing, and some sections have been replaced with wooden planks that are two tones too light.

However, I love all the natural light flooding into the room. There are windows lining the entire length of one side, which faces a field. There's a chalkboard, dry-erase board, and smartboard. They don't make up for textbooks, but at least I have something to work with.

Good thing we have the whole day to prepare. I'm going to need it. There's dust and mouse droppings everywhere. I start by sweeping. Then I mop the floor with the Pine-Sol I grabbed from the custodian. Afterward, I go to the teachers' lounge and get some rolls of colored paper to cover the walls. I go for a blue-and-orange color scheme. Now, I just need something to put on them.

I make a Staples run to pick up some posters, Lysol, Air Wick, a hand stapler, Swiffer, tissues, hand sanitizer, and other knick-knacks. I return to school within an hour. I pour all my anxiety and frustration into decorating my classroom. There's something about organizing the external world that brings a sense of order to my inner world. After a couple of hours, my room is starting to look legit. It still doesn't compare to Lisa's class, so I order more posters online. Then, I arrange the tables into eight groups of four.

Suddenly, I feel a twinge of pride. It's not perfect, but it's getting there. Now, it's time to figure out what I'll do with them next week. I'm nervous because one of my classes is ninety minutes long. I would've gone bananas in a class that length in middle school. I'm so lost in the sauce it's not even funny, so I visit Lisa to see what she has planned.

"Lisa, I'm freaking out."

"What's up?"

"What am I supposed to do with them on Monday?"

"Well, typically, you just review the rules, expectations, semester timeline, and supplies they'll need. I can give you some of my material if you like."

"That would be amazing."

"No problem. Don't worry about the first few days of school. Honestly, no one really teaches the first few weeks. The students need time to settle back in."

"Okay. I still can't fathom how to fill a ninety-minute class, but it is what it is."

"Have you spoken with Mrs. Mayfield?"

"No, I'll go check her out now."

"I think you should. I mean, she is the science lead."

I walk to Mrs. Mayfield's office on the second floor. She's a sweet Southern gal with a big personality. I love her accent. It reminds me of my family in South Carolina. I find her in her office.

"Hey, Mrs. Mayfield. Do you have a second?"

"Sure, baby. How can I help?"

"Principal Johnson told me you could assist me with some science materials."

"No problem. Right this way. Now, we don't have textbooks, but I'll show you what we do have."

We arrive at a room in shambles with stuff strewn everywhere. She begins digging through boxes like it's some kind of scavenger hunt, looking for Lord knows what. Finally, she says, "Here they are." She dusts off the plastic wrap surrounding the material and then opens the packaging. "Perfect! This is exactly what I was looking for." She hands me a stack of *Science World* magazines. All the dust they kick up makes me sneeze.

"Bless you, baby."

"Thank you."

"What am I supposed to do with these? They're not even from this year."

"Look now, you have to work with what we've got. I am not a miracle worker."

"Oh, but you expect me to be one come Monday."

"Don't worry, Mr. Connelly, you'll be fine. We've all been there before."

"All right, so what else do you have?"

"Did I not just hand you a stack of magazines! Boy, you better stop playing with me."

"Are you kidding me? This is it?"

"Well, this is all they used last year. You'll receive the new editions when they arrive. Just have the kids read an article and then write about it. That'll keep them busy."

"Yeah, right. After an hour, they're going to be bouncing off the walls."

"Mr. Connelly, you gotta calm down. The first few weeks are a piece of cake, trust me. Just take it easy and get to know the students. All right?"

"We'll see," I reply, worry still etched across my face.

"Goodbye, sir, because now you're stressing me out."

"Okay, thanks." I want to say *thanks for nothing*, but I just keep it moving.

Back in my classroom, I look at the dusty magazines and laugh to myself. Do they even expect me to teach? I swear I'm just a glorified babysitter. Regardless, the students have nothing to do with the administration's incompetence. They're innocent and deserve better. The only question is: How can I offer that under these impossible circumstances?

I guess I will have to figure it out on my own.

At least I can smile that my room is finally coming together. I have to celebrate the small victories. The bell rings, echoing down the empty halls. It's time to go home and spend my weekend figuring out what I'll do come Monday. I know my colleagues told me not to worry, but inside, I'm losing it. Regardless—ready or not, here they come.

Lord, have mercy on my soul.

Chapter 4

The Classroom Crucible

——

THE CEILING BLURS ABOVE ME. I'VE BEEN STARING at it for hours, tangled in sheets, thoughts bouncing between excitement and dread for the first day of school. When I roll over to check the clock, it glows 4 a.m. . . . and Creamy hears me.

Her wail starts low—a single note of protest—then climbs into a full-throated feline aria in the key of "Feed Me". She knows it's not breakfast time but belts anyway, her upper octave shattering the stillness of the night. There's no winning.

I throw off the covers, silence my furry alarm clock, and head to the kitchen. Within minutes, the house fills with the scent of turkey bacon sizzling, eggs hissing softly in the pan, and a croissant warming beside a crisp, golden hash brown. I pause, wrapped in the quiet hush of early morning, watching the first light spill over rooftops as the horizon blushes.

This is my favorite part of the day—a time for reflection, setting intentions, and savoring a peaceful cup of coffee while birdsong spills softly into the room. It's a fleeting interlude I must savor before the next fourteen hours sweep me into nonstop motion.

Today, I'm at school from eight to three, then cleaning planes from five to ten. It's a brutal schedule, right? But it's a small price to pay to do the two things I love most: traveling and serving humanity . . . though if teachers were paid what we're truly worth, I wouldn't have to work so hard. So, I hustle like a madman, though I largely have my father to thank—or blame—for that.

But first, I let the warm water massage my back, jolting my senses as I close my eyes and zone out, savoring one of life's simplest pleasures. The gentle cascade leaves me a little wobbly, so I shake it off and fast-forward through my morning rinse ritual, stepping out refreshed and ready to take on the world.

My outfit is already set in stone. All teachers will be wearing their Columbia T-shirts. To complete my fit, I wear black jeans, a black Phillies hat, and my red and black Jordan XI sneakers. As I leave the crib, I can already feel the humidity in the air. It's going to be a scorcher.

I arrive at school an hour early despite the traffic on I-95. The parking lot is half full, and kids are already moseying around the building. After parking, I gather my supplies and make my way to the main office to punch in, passing a couple of students along the way.

"Good morning, students!"

"Good morning."

"Welcome back to school!"

"Thank you!"

The office hums with early-morning activity: parents linger at the front desk, students shuffle in with backpacks and forms, and the faint aroma of coffee drifts through the air. At the center of it all is the secretary, Ms. Maritza Garcia—a vibrant soul, her colorful makeup and booming voice impossible to miss.

"Buenos días, Señora Garcia."

"Buenos días, Señor C. ¿Cómo estás?"

"Muy bien. ¿Y tú?"

"Todo bien, gracias."

She's the lynchpin, the facilitator, the glue that holds this office together. I'm excited she's willing to practice Spanish with me. Learning

Spanish is one of my favorite pastimes. Finding chances to speak is tough, so I have to grab them whenever I can. Maybe one day, I can share this passion with my students, but baby steps. First, we just have to get through day one.

"Adiós."

"Hasta luego, amigo." ("See you later, friend.")

I head to my classroom to finish setting up. I have less than an hour to take care of everything.

The second I walk inside, the smell of the Air Wick I left running on high all weekend punches me in the nose. Holy moly! Somebody is going to have an asthma attack. I unplug it and immediately open all the windows, which provides some relief. I can feel a faint breeze wafting in. It works for now, but with a 95-degree temperature and thirty students, we might have a problem. I hang up a few posters, write the date and agenda on the board, and finish arranging the desk.

The hour flies by in the blink of an eye. Then the bell rings, and an announcement comes over the loudspeaker: "All teachers should be outside welcoming students. All teachers should be outside welcoming students." I rush to join the festivities. The scene is lively, with kids scattered everywhere. Some run, others stare into space, while the majority inch toward the scanners. The metal detectors make the school feel more like a prison, but I feel safer having them. Still, you can't help but feel how they criminalize the environment.

The flow of kids clashes with the scanners. The lack of organization surprises me. I imagined the principal with her bullhorn, welcoming students back in a pep-rally style, with all the teachers cheering as they entered the building. Yeah right! It's a hot mess. It's time to escape this bedlam and return to my room. Luckily, I don't have an advisory. That gives me a few minutes to gather myself. I reach my class, close the door, and meditate.

Moments later, my bliss is interrupted by screaming tweens jetting down the hallway like they're running in the Penn Relays. I think about intervening for a millisecond but decide to chill out instead. I need to pick my battles, and the hallway isn't one of them.

Now the halls are swarming with students. I glance through the door window, watching them sprint back and forth repeatedly. *Should I say something? Nah. I'm already doing enough.* Besides, they pay me to teach science, not to police the hallways. I would have more room to care if I were assisting as planned. However, I'm already going above and beyond what I signed up for, so I refuse to give an inch more. *Hear no evil, see no evil, speak no evil.* My only concern is what goes on in this classroom.

An announcement comes over the loudspeaker: "All students should be in advisory. We will be transitioning to our first-period classes in five minutes." That means I'll have to leave my sanctuary, brave the hallways, and assist Lisa with her first-period class. It's a ninety-minute eighth-grade science course. I'm dying to see how she fills the time. When the first-period bell rings, I grab my bag and make my way to her room.

Kids are posted everywhere, like it's a nightclub. After someone nearly knocks me over, I snap, "Slow down! Stop running." *Where are the hall monitors?* From the look of things, the kids are definitely running the show. I make it to Lisa's room as the late bell rings. There are only seven kids in the class. The rest seem to be having too much fun catching up with their friends. Lisa gives the stragglers a few minutes and says we will start shortly. *We'll be waiting till the cows come home.*

I'm physically here, but my mind is on the first class I'll teach in an hour. It's a forty-five-minute sixth-grade science enrichment course. Since there's no set curriculum, I'm still deciding what to cover. Right now, my only goal is to make it through the day. My thought process is interrupted when Lisa asks me to introduce myself to the students. After that, the rest of the period goes by smoothly. Lisa clearly knows what she's doing.

As the clock winds down, I say to her, "I'm heading out in fifteen minutes to get ready for class."

She replies, "No problem. You can go now if you want."

"Are you sure?"

"I insist; I'll see you tomorrow."

"Great. Peace, Mrs. McCaffrey. Peace, students. I'll catch y'all later."

As I leave the classroom, the hallway still swarms with students. I'm annoyed, but I keep moving, heading straight to my room. I leave the door open, ready to greet my students. My heart hammers; I take a deep breath. The bell rings. Game time.

As I walk to the door to welcome them, I see a blonde, blue-eyed teacher clutching her notebook with students in tow. She smiles as they approach; I'm guessing these are my guys. The students are orderly as they walk against the wall through the hallway's chaos. That's impressive.

"Good morning, Mrs. Winokur."

"Good morning, Mr. Connelly."

"Good morning, students."

Only a few bother to respond. I'm guessing the rest are shy or too overwhelmed by all the seventh- and eighth-graders in the hallway.

"Thanks, Mrs. Winokur. I can take it from here."

She leaves and tells the kids she will see them in a bit. The students begin talking and getting out of line the second she walks off. "Can we go inside now, Mister?"

"Hold up. I'll know we are ready to go inside when everybody is quiet and in line." Surprisingly, they listen. I wait for an extra beat, then tell them they can enter.

"Where my seat, Mister . . . ?"

"It's Mr. Connelly."

"Okay, where my seat, Mr. Connery?"

Rats. It didn't even dawn on me to do a seating chart. I wish someone had told me. I improvise on the spot. "You can sit anywhere you like for now, but I will make some adjustments if necessary."

What a rookie mistake.

I may look unprepared, but by the same token, I'm okay with students having the freedom to sit wherever they like. I don't want to control their every move; that requires too much energy. I would rather give them the boundaries and tools to regulate their own behavior. Once the class settles, it's funny to see how they've self-segregated by gender. The boys and girls are still anathema to each other at this age. I hit the screensaver on my laptop to show the presentation on the smartboard. Before I begin my spiel, a hand goes up.

"I gotta use da bafrum."

"Ohh, I gotta go, too. Can I go with her, please?"

"No. Let me explain how the bathroom works. There's one person allowed at a time. The next person will be able to go once the first person returns. If you abuse your bathroom privileges, you will lose those privileges."

"Whaaatt?" a student mumbles under her breath. "Ain't nobody stopping me from going to the bafrum. If I gotta go to the bafrum, I'm going to the bafrum."

"Excuse me, young lady. What did you say?"

"I ain't say nothing."

She clearly did and, like a chump, I let it slide. I should've asked her to step outside into the hallway and nip the disrespect in the bud, but I want to avoid the hallway like the plague. Again, I'm picking my battles, but I have to be careful because control can take days to establish but only seconds to lose. The students push a little here, then a little there, and before you know it, it's a full-on insurrection.

Actually, she's right. I can't stop anyone from leaving my classroom. These kids are savvy and probably know that already.

"What's your name?"

"Anisha."

"And yours?"

"Ava."

"All right, ladies, who's going first?"

"Ava can go first. I can wait."

"Hurry back because we're reviewing the semester's rules and expectations."

The students have given me my first test, and I failed. I should've allowed the students to settle in, begun the lesson, and allowed Ava to use the bathroom afterward, but you don't know what you don't know. I pull up my Google Slides presentation on the smartboard. The first picture is me skydiving on the North Shore of Oahu. I hear the oohs and aahs of the students.

"That's you, Mister . . . ? What's your name?"

"Feel free to call me Mr. Connelly or Mr. C."

Ten minutes later, Ava comes back looking out of breath.

"Sorry I took so long, but the hallway was popping." I'd forgotten she'd left.

"Relax. Have a seat."

"Now, it's my turn," Anisha announces.

One of the boys chimes in, "I'm going next." They are all copycats, but technically I'm in no position to say no, so I let them go.

The class is flying by. One final task remains before dismissal. I distribute construction paper, asking the students to fold it and write their names in big letters. I have to remember them all—respect and connection start with simply knowing who each student is. I'll have my work cut out, but I'm committed to the challenge. We have fifteen minutes left. I tell the students they can relax for the rest of the class, and we'll pick things up tomorrow.

I retreat to my desk. It creates a physical barrier between the students and me. I'm nervous that the more I engage with them, the more they'll realize that I don't know what I'm doing, so I leave them to their own devices. The bell rings.

"Remember to bring your notebooks next time and have your parents complete the contact form. That will be your first graded assignment. Line up."

Mrs. Winokur is at the door waiting for them. She is so sweet, I can't even imagine her getting angry.

"All right, students, remember the procedure. Take care, Mr. Connelly."

"Later, Mrs. Winokur."

My first class went okay. I felt somewhat in control. The students were chatty, but that's their nature. Now, it's time for my forty-five-minute lunch. I have to get out of this school. With all the ruckus in the hallway, I couldn't relax if I tried. I'm still stunned by how many students are constantly in the hallway. Where are the hall monitors? It doesn't make sense to me. Are there any consequences? I remind myself to pick my battles.

It's hard enough trying to manage my classroom independently; I can't control the hallways too. Shucks, I still have no idea how I'll make it through my last class. If I struggled to fill forty-five minutes, ninety feels impossible. Anyway, time to steal a few minutes for a brain break before the fun begins.

I slide into my car seat, set the alarm, and close my eyes. The second I drift off, it rings. OMG—I am not ready. I bolt upstairs to beat my eighth-grade science students to class. As I turn the hallway corner, I notice the door is wide open. I rush inside. About five kids are in the back, just chilling like they own the place.

"What's up, mister? You the substitute?"

"No, I'm the full-time teacher. But more importantly, how did you all get in here?"

"The door was already open," responds one of the young ladies. I thought I had locked it, but in my haste to sequester myself in my car, I guess I could've forgotten. The late bell rings.

Suddenly, there's an announcement over the loudspeaker: "Mr. Connelly, please come to the lunchroom to pick up your class. Mr. Connelly, please come to the lunchroom to pick up your class."

It would've been nice if someone had told me that that's the protocol. I figured someone would bring them to class, the same way Mrs. Winokur did with the sixth graders. Why do eighth graders have to be escorted like elementary-school kids anyway?

I tell the students to chill until I return, then make my way to the lunchroom. Only a few students are waiting. I don't make them line up; I simply tell them to follow me. God only knows where the rest of them are. I hustle up the three flights of stairs to get to class. As I round the corner, I spot a bunch of students standing outside the door.

My jaw clenches. I want to spaz, but technically it's my fault that I didn't pick up the class.

In my calmest voice, I say, "If you belong in this class, please come inside." All the students file in. Now the classroom is packed with over thirty students, but there's no way they should all be here. I take a slow breath, trying to keep my voice steady.

"Listen, if you don't belong here, please go where you belong." Three students stand up and leave the room. Nobody else moves, and the rest continue talking. I raise my voice. "Let me repeat myself: If you don't belong here, go where you belong!"

One student asks me, "Mister, you a substitute or a real teacher?"

I want to say I'm a substitute masquerading as a real teacher, but instead I say, "Yes, I'm a real teacher. Why do you ask?"

"Because you don't seem like a teacher."

Another student chimes in, "Why don't you just take the roll?" That makes me realize I didn't finish the roll in the first class either. The bathroom hijinks threw me for a loop.

I complete the roll. A couple of names need adding, but for the most part, it looks like everyone is here. I walk to the board, ready to start my presentation.

Just as I begin, two students walk toward the door. I sprint after them. "Wait!! Don't leave . . ."

"Bro, we not even in this class," they respond, laughing like I'm the punchline. I feel a tight knot in my chest and my patience begins to unravel. I take a deep breath, trying to hold it together.

"Okay, then for the third time, if you don't belong here, please leave."

Another one bites the dust.

Suddenly, a student gripes, "Mister, what's up with the AC? It's hot as balls in here."

"Watch your language!"

"My bad," he says.

"We're all suffering together."

"Well, I'm about to dip—it's hot as shit in this class," says a young lady.

"Look, watch your mouth!"

"What! You don't hear all these other kids cursing? Why you worried about me?"

"Because you're the only one I hear right now."

She stands up, grabs her bags, and says, "Man, fuck this! I'm out. It's too hot for this shit."

I want to stop her but secretly envy her escape from this sauna, so I just let her go.

"Listen, I know it's hot in here, but there's not much I can do about it."

I turn off the lights, hoping that that will help some. It doesn't, but the natural lighting helps chill me out. I look at the clock. Half of the class is already over, and I still need to review the same rules and expectations the students have heard four times in their other classes.

"All right, let me get everybody's attention." I must be talking in Mandarin because no one pays me any mind. Some students give me the stink eye. It's like they're thinking, *Here we go again with another teacher who can't control the class.*

I raise my voice a little louder. "I need everyone to be quiet in five, four, THREE, TWWWWOOOOOO, and one."

"Mister, it's hot in here."

I wish I could say, "No shit, Sherlock," but instead, I say, "I feel you, man; I'm hot, too. I'm right here with y'all."

The students begin talking again.

"Look, all I'm asking for is fifteen minutes of your time. I know everybody is excited about the first day of school."

"No, we're just hot," a student grumbles.

"All right, I understand everybody is hot, but you will be surprised if you sit still how much that'll bring your temperature down."

While I'm talking, a student runs into the classroom. He's one of the students who had left, saying he belonged elsewhere.

"Leave immediately!"

"No, seriously, I'm in this class."

"Listen, stop playing with me! Are you in here or not?" Of course, all I have to do is check the roll, but that idea gets lost in the sauce somewhere.

He replies, "Yo, who are you talking to?"

"I'm talking to you!"

"Shit, you got me fucked up. Let me get out of here before I knock bull the fuck out."

"Ha ha ha! You got jokes."

Now, I would never initiate contact with a child, but I will defend myself if I have to. But this kid isn't stupid. I'm built like a mini Terry Crews.

His friend says, "Come on man, we out," and drags him out of the classroom. The class is dead silent for once. I finally have their undivided attention; unfortunately, it's at the worst moment.

By arguing with a child, I came way down to his level instead of demonstrating how to rise to mine. No one has taught me an important rule: that you never reprimand a student, especially a middle-schooler, in front of their peers. The teacher may win the power struggle, but it's a Pyrrhic victory—one that weakens their authority and sacrifices students' respect.

But you don't know what you don't know.

"Listen. I'm only asking y'all to be quiet for fifteen minutes. That's all! I shouldn't have to beg y'all to just do my job."

A student asks, "Why you talking to us like that? We ain't do nothing to you."

I want to reply, *Because I'm hot, triggered, frustrated, out of my league, and seriously considering whether you can even shut up for two seconds.* I apologize instead and say, "I'm not mad at y'all. I just want to get through this presentation."

But I am furious, and the person I'm furious with is myself. How did I get emotionally hijacked by a kid? Why did I let myself come all the way down to his level?

How you start something influences how you finish, and this start is disastrous. Getting their attention feels like a losing battle. I begin my spiel for the fifth time. The students are silent for a second, then start talking again.

Finally, I throw in the towel.

"Look, y'all got it. I give up. I'm a let y'all do y'all, and I'm a fallback."

I return to my desk, stare out the window, and act like they aren't even there.

The entire time, I'm thinking, *What the heck have I gotten myself into?*

Chapter 5

Surprise: I'm Your Teacher Coach

———

I ARRIVE AT SCHOOL WITH FIVE MINUTES TO SPARE. THE parking lot looks leaner than usual. We're returning from a three-day weekend in celebration of Yom Kippur. I should be excited and energized, but instead, I'm filled with dread. The students were in rare form last week after returning from Labor Day. They were hell-bent on packing five days of foolishness into four. Hopefully, today will be different. I rush to the office with a minute to sign in.

"*Buenos días, Señora Garcia.*"

"*Buenos días, Señor C.* I have a present for you."

"Oh, I like gifts."

She hands me an orange slip that says "Coverage" on it.

Fudge!

"We need you to cover this advisory," she says.

"That's right now."

"Sorry, we have a few call-outs and teachers running behind."

"Okay."

"Gracias."

Just when I thought my substitute days were over, I'm back at it again. I'd understand if it were June, but we're only three weeks into the school year. I can already tell it's going to be a long day. The bell rings. I'm already late, so I take my time.

Students flood the halls, their enthusiasm lighting up the space after the long weekend. Their excitement will go into overdrive once they learn how many teachers are out. I'm not that surprised that my colleagues are already tapping out. The stifling heat inside the building has turned it into a powder keg, always on the verge of exploding.

Fights are starting to break out—and it's barely September. I just pray it never happens in my class. Everyone, students and teachers alike, seems triggered and on edge. Maybe it's the heat. Maybe it's the culture. Go figure. One thing's for sure: starting the school year with three short weeks makes it incredibly difficult to get students out of summer mode. Every day, I feel like I'm taking two steps forward but five steps backward.

Regardless of how well-intentioned the district is with its holiday policy, the inconsistency of the schedule impedes learning. The first weeks of school end up mostly wasted as students struggle to get back in the groove. Many start the year a step behind, thanks to the infamous "summer slide"—the skill loss that happens when students stop practicing what they learned the year before. This regression is made worse by all the time students lose—not just at the start, but at the end of the school year too.

Maybe things would be different if my classroom management and teaching skills were up to par. I know that kids benefit from routine and structure. I just don't know how to give them that yet, but I'm committed to learning. I might be the only full-time teacher they have this year, so I have to ensure that I'm not contributing to the school-to-prison pipeline and mentally handicapping them by wasting their time and not teaching them anything.

On the bright side, I'll finally meet my first-year teaching coach today. It would've been nice to meet her before the school year started so I could've come up with a bona fide game plan, but beggars can't be choosers. She's coming during my class with the sixth graders, so I put together a nice lesson to make myself look good. I've already told the students they better not embarrass me.

I arrive at the advisory class that I have to babysit. I notice all of my eighth-grade science students in the hallway.

"What's up, Mr. C.!"

"What's up, y'all!"

"Are you watching us for advisory?"

"I'm the man." At least I'm covering my students. I'm happy it's them. I would be even happier if the door were unlocked. I ask one of the students to get the key from Mr. Jefferson, the seventh-grade lead.

He's a tall fella with a box haircut and glasses who gives off preacher vibes. He always looks super slick in his three-piece suits, looking more ready for Sunday service than school. Within seconds, he comes to the class to open the door.

"Good morning, brother!" he says.

"Good morning, sir."

"Let me get that door for you."

"I appreciate you, brother. Lest we add to the madness that is the hallway."

"Yeah, man, it's unbelievable. These call-outs are killing us."

"What's going on?" I ask.

"We're still missing a few teachers, so we have to rely on substitutes to fill in the gap. You remember what it was like back in the day when the teacher was absent."

"Facts."

I loved having substitutes. I also remember being the chill substitute who ignored the additional five kids in the classroom as long as they weren't tripping.

But I never remember starting a school year where half my teachers were long-term substitutes with no teacher training. Technically, I'm just a substitute myself. It's no wonder the kids go apeshit. Coupling the most inexperienced teachers with the highest-needs students robs generations of kids of a chance to realize their potential. It's not that they can't read or excel in math; in many cases, they simply aren't given the opportunity because their teachers don't have the skills to teach them effectively.

Mr. Jefferson continues, "Also, the students remain inside the building all day; that's why they're always tripping by the end of the day."

"Wait. The students don't go outside for recess at all?"

"No sir. The students don't go outside for recess."

I'm blown away. Now the conditions inside the school make a lot more sense. The kids aren't allowed to go outside to play, so they've effectively turned the entire school into their indoor playground.

"We attempted recess last year, but too many kids were escaping, so we got rid of it."

Seriously? They cut recess because the staff couldn't keep the kids in check? That's outrageous.

Kids need to run, play, and interact with their peers. The social side of school matters just as much as academics. If I were indoors all day, I'd be bouncing off the walls by the end too. Children naturally want to move, explore, and have fun. When you curb this instinct, that energy doesn't disappear—it just finds other outlets.

"Okay, that's unfortunate. So, what are we doing about it?" I reply.

"Well, that's what we'll discuss in our next professional development meeting this afternoon."

So, not only am I losing my fifteen-minute chill-out session covering this advisory, but I'll also miss my prep for a professional development meeting later. Great! During the meeting, the principal introduces our new restorative justice program.

Essentially, instead of suspending students and keeping them out of school, they'll serve an in-school suspension. But first, they'll have to face a jury of their peers. All this talk of juries, justice, and in-school detainment sounds like we're grooming kids for the school-to-prison pipeline. Regardless, I don't know the answer, but competing with the daily lure of the hallways is nearly impossible, so I'm willing to try anything.

After the meeting, I arrive at my class and find my teaching coach standing outside my door waiting for me.

"Good morning!" I say. "You must be Mrs. Montgomery."

"Yes, I am. Good morning, Mr. Connelly. It's nice to finally meet you in person."

It would've been better weeks ago, but I reply, "Likewise."

I hold the door open, letting her go in first.

"Thank you, Mr. Connelly. You're such a gentleman."

"I try my best."

She says, "I'll only be here for ten minutes, then I'll come back at the end of the day to go over my observations."

"Sounds great!"

I've randomly chosen an article about dinosaurs with a few questions at the end to keep the students busy. I'm still figuring out what I'm supposed to be teaching. I greet the students at the door and welcome them inside. Mrs. Winokur gets out of Dodge in a flash. As she leaves, her face says, *Take these kids before I lose my mind.*

The students come in and play musical chairs as usual. I still haven't bothered making a seating chart. I remind them that we're working on an article today and will go over everything once everybody is finished. After explaining the instructions and handing out the papers, I return to my desk and sit down. Mrs. Montgomery is there waiting for me.

She's taking notes on her laptop. I already feel like I'm doing something wrong, but I'm just happy the class is quiet for once. The students are faking the funk for me. Maybe they like me after all. They're definitely on their best behavior. It feels like I'm in a different class. Typically, students are walking, okay, running around the classroom; not today.

In any case, now that I know they don't have recess, I'm okay with some noise and activity. A quiet class is a boring class that no one fancies. Telling students to remain seated all period is futile. Some have jumping beans in their pockets and need to move every fifteen minutes, and I understand because I was one of those kids.

No one has even asked to use the bathroom. By this time, I usually would've had at least five requests of one sort or another. I miss the chaos. I'm torn between whether I like the calm or chaotic class more. Mrs. Montgomery asks me, "How do you know if everyone's on task?"

I want to say, *I don't give a schnitzel as long as they're quiet.* Instead, I say, "I'm not sure."

"It would help if you checked in with them."

What, and leave my desk sanctuary? I don't want to rock the boat too much, but her suggestion feels more like a demand, so I oblige. She says, "You should aim to check in with each student three times daily." *Oh, so my job isn't to bark orders, vomit a bunch of information, and hide behind my desk for the remainder of the period? That's good to know.*

Ten minutes later, she says, "I've seen everything I need to see and will come back to do a debrief at the end of the day."

"Great. Take care."

"Bye, Mr. Connelly. Bye, students."

I breathe a sigh of relief. I hate feeling like I'm being put under a microscope, but I think things went relatively well.

The second she leaves, I notice my students relax a bit too.

"Who was that, Mr. C.?" one of them asks.

"I told you all yesterday, that's my teaching coach. She'll be with us all year, so you might as well get used to her. Did anybody finish the questions?" Two students raise their hands. They're my little overachievers. I never have to worry about them. If only all of them were this studious; but hey, you gotta love them all. From the back of the room, another student calls out.

"Mr. C., can I go to the bathroom now?"

"Sure, once you finish your worksheet."

"Can I finish it for homework, please?"

"We have fifteen minutes left in class, so you can complete it now."

She slams her pencil down in protest and crosses her arms. "I don't feel like doing this corny worksheet." Clearly, she has more pressing things to attend to in the hallway.

Ultimately, I can't make her do the work; but as long as she's quiet, I can ignore her intransigence.

Minutes later, she stands up and bolts out of the classroom. "I don't care. I'm out; I have to use the bathroom."

"If you leave this classroom, go to the office afterward because you're not coming back."

"I don't care!"

She thinks I'm stupid. There are only ten minutes left in class, which coincides with the most happening time in the hallway. During this time, the seventh graders abandon the lunchroom and parade around the school. I call the office to inform them that I have a deserter.

"Hello, this is Ms. Carmine speaking."

"Good afternoon, Mrs. Carmine. It's Mr. C. from room 308."

"Hey, Mr. C. How can I help?"

"One of my students left the classroom without permission, and I want to report her."

"Okay." There's an awkward silence. "So, why are you calling the office?"

The response surprises me. "Uhm . . . I guess to cover my butt or for reinforcement."

There's another awkward silence. I hear her exhale as if to say, *Why are you wasting my time?* She says, "Okay, so what are your consequences?"

"Well, there's nothing I can do to make her stay inside the classroom."

"Yes, there is. Have you tried calling her parents or issuing a lunch or afternoon detention?"

Yeah, right. The last thing I want to do is spend my lunch or after-school time watching kids. I'm already giving enough of my time and energy. The fact is, I'm just as guilty of having no consequences inside the classroom as the administrators are for having none outside it. Most punishments would demand more energy and effort from me, and given how jaded I am, that's not happening. I thank her and hang up.

Now the students are giving me the stink eye.

The look on their faces says, *Damn, Mr. C., you're snitching on us now.*

It may be time for me to enlist the help of some parents. I haven't called any since I started. Maybe that's because a part of me thinks the parents are the problem. Aren't they responsible for teaching their children to value education and respect their elders? Then again, just because you bring a horse to water, it doesn't mean it will drink.

Anyway, I work after school, so I don't have much time to contact parents, and my lunch is off-limits. I remind myself to pick my battles and sweep our little infraction under the rug. When the bell rings, I can feel the flood of dopamine coursing through my veins. It's time for lunch, and the only thing I want to do is get out of here.

"Take care, students."

"Bye, Mr. C."

As I settle into my car seat, I hear my conscience say, *Call her parents.* I dismiss the idea and try to rest. However, I can't, because thoughts of being a lazy and inept teacher keep circling in my mind. My ignorance isn't the problem, but my unwillingness to learn is. Ultimately, my job is to help students become lifelong learners. That's a tricky prospect when I can't even learn, adapt, and rise to the challenge myself.

I just feel so victimized by this wretched system. Why should I care and go out of my way when the students, parents, and administrators give zero fudges about me? I hear my conscience say, *Because it's not about you, but what God can do through you.*

Whatever.

As usual, my lunch feels like it's over before it begins. I feel my anxiety rising. My last period is the one I dread the most. My class feels like the recess that they're deprived of. Nevertheless, it's game time, so I rush to the lunchroom to pick them up.

I'm expected to go inside, gather my students, line them up, and take them upstairs to the classroom. As I step into the cafeteria, I'm immediately overwhelmed by the noise and chaos, which hits me like a tsunami. I retreat to the hallway, where the other teachers are already waiting with their faces mirroring my own desperate plea: "Please, Lord, let this day be over soon."

Opening the lunchroom door feels like opening Pandora's Box. You never know what will come out. The eighth graders have the last lunch of the day from one o'clock to one thirty, which means they have to wait five hours before they get a break. After lunch, most of my students won't even lift a pencil, let alone complete an assignment. And it drives me up the wall.

I could accept being a glorified babysitter when I was a substitute, but it sucks now. Every day, I wrestle with a sense of futility. I became a teacher to educate, liberate, and inspire. Now I feel lucky just to make it to the end of the day. The students have zero motivation after lunch. I gather it's because they're digesting their food and the blood goes from their brains to their stomachs, or maybe I just haven't cracked the code yet.

The bell rings, and the students come pouring out of the lunchroom. A few of them spot me and wave; I tell them to meet me upstairs. As they file into the classroom, the usual mix of energy and chaos fills the room. On the bright side, their behavior has improved, though they're still as lazy as ever.

Of course, some continue to curse like sailors, but most of us live what we learn, so I can't entirely blame them. Looking back, I wish I had set a better tone early on, with a solid plan and clear expectations. I regret listening to my colleagues who said not to worry about the first few weeks. That was a big mistake.

The students came in with a plan to do nothing. Sadly, I gave them the okay with a weak alternative. I know they're in a rut that's been years in the making, but somehow, I have to figure out how to get them out of it. That starts with climbing out of my own black hole.

The problem is that I lack fundamental teaching skills. Many people would love getting paid to do nothing, but it's robbing me of my joy. I can't shake the feeling that I'm facilitating the mental handicapping of hundreds of students. I knew the system was rotten and unfair when I was a kid, but now I feel like a willing accomplice.

Was I a fool to think I could come into this environment and make a real difference when the cards are stacked to the stratosphere against me? Am I setting students up for the school-to-prison pipeline by not expecting more from them and not helping them think critically about their lives?

Still, I know the students like me even if they don't respect me. They tell me I'm the best teacher in the building, but that's not enough to make them listen. It's my fault for not demanding more from them. Students will either rise or fall to meet your expectations.

For example, of thirty students in the class, only a few do the assignment, but I don't press the issue. I focus on my faithful five and tune out the rest.

I tell my overachievers they can chill once they finish their work, and we go over it together. The review is my way of checking for understanding and getting the work before someone else can copy it. Afterward, they ask if they can draw on the smartboard. "Sure. Why not?" I love seeing kids have fun. Besides, I'm still pissed they don't have recess. Not having a science teacher for two years is bad enough, but no recess?

The class looks a little chaotic, with students out of their seats; some are creating TikTok videos, some are roughhousing, and some are asleep. Others are playing games or engaging in Lord knows what on their smartphones. There are only ten minutes left until we're out of here. It can't come soon enough. I stare at the clock, letting the students do their thing, when suddenly, my teaching coach walks into the classroom.

Fudge!

I thought when she said she was coming at the end of the day, she meant after the students were gone.

The look on her face says it all, and the embarrassment on mine speaks volumes too. It's like doing a downward-facing dog in yoga class, letting one slip, and catching the disgusted looks from your fellow yogis.

"What's going on here, Mr. Connelly?"

"We're just wrapping things up for the day. I decided to let the students relax after completing their classwork."

"What are they supposed to be working on?"

I don't know, their digestion? Snapchat? A battle royale on Fortnite?

I show her the worksheet that I had assigned.

"Okay, did you review it?"

"Yes, with the five students who completed it."

"And the others?"

"They're a work in progress."

"And what are the consequences if they don't finish the assignment?"

"Unfortunately, I have yet to think that through."

She takes a deep breath and says, "We have a lot of work to do. Let me take the floor."

"Please do."

"Listen up! I need everybody in a seat now!" Her voice is so loud it makes me jump in my seat. I can tell she's done this a time or two. She's giving off tough, demanding, you-better-not-try-me Mama vibes. Most students comply, but as usual, there's always that one student who has to be complicated.

"Did you not hear me, sir? Take a seat."

"Look, Miss, I ain't bothering nobody. Mr. C. is okay with us standing up. Why you trippin'?"

Jumpin' Jehoshaphat, that little booger threw me under the bus!

"I'm not asking you; I'm telling you to have a seat or step outside in the hallway."

The students and I are enjoying the spectacle and dying to see the resolution. The only thing I'm missing is some popcorn. The student opts for the hallway. He leaves the class, and Mrs. Montgomery follows right behind him.

The class and I are dead silent, listening as everything transpires. Mrs. Montgomery talks loud enough to ensure we all hear her.

"Dial your parents' number right now!"

"I don't know my mom's number."

"Listen, if I have to go to the office and get the number, you will not return to this school unless you bring a parent. So, how do you want to do this?"

The kid takes the smartphone and starts dialing. Wow, she's contacted more parents in thirty seconds than I've managed in three weeks.

Within minutes, the student is back in class mean mugging but seated. As my mentor teacher starts scolding the students about being off-task and wasting time, I can't help but feel like she's talking to me too. The students are huffing and puffing but quieter than a doornail. I admire my coach's ability to get the students to shut up and sit down.

However, all her antics only result in three students putting their names on the paper and two starting the assignment. The rest just act like they're doing work. When the final bell rings, the students bolt out of the classroom, leaving their pencils and papers behind. I feel like doing the same thing, but I'm forced to stay back to be reprimanded.

"Mr. Connelly. Mr. Connelly. Mr. Connelly. We have some work to do."

"I'm all ears. Unfortunately, I only learned four days before school started that I was teaching full-time. I didn't have the time to think through my approach thoroughly."

"Okay. What's done is done. The question is, what will you do now? Because what I just witnessed? That ain't it. So, first things first, where are the rules and regulations in the class?"

"I shake my head to acknowledge that there aren't any."

"How can you expect students to follow the rules if they're not posted? Secondly, what are the consequences for noncompliance?"

I look at her like a deer in headlights again.

"Okay, we need to have that posted too. How many parents have you called?"

I lie and say, "I've contacted a few."

"Are you logging these calls in SIS?"

"Nope. I didn't know I had to."

"All right, Mr. Connelly, you have some work to do before I see you next time. I need you to focus more on tightening up your classroom procedures, posting your rules and expectations, and coming up with consequences for noncompliance. I also need to see a plan for the entire ninety-minute period. The expectation is that students are working the entire class."

Yeah, right. That's balderdash.

"How would you structure a ninety-minute class, Mrs. Montgomery?"

"The first fifteen minutes for a Do Now to get the students settled, thirty minutes for lecturing, thirty minutes on independent work, and fifteen minutes for review and wrap-up."

It sounds good. Now, show me where I can find all the content to fill in that time.

"Mr. Connelly, as your coach, I will have to evaluate you at the end of the year and give a yay or nay about retaining you for the next school year."

Like you have a million candidates kicking down the door. But I'm trying not to let the cynicism show on my face.

"If you are serious about being here next year, I need you to shape up. Do you have any questions for me?"

"Many students aren't engaged because the quality of the assignments is not the best. Can you please help me find some engaging lessons? I have no textbooks, computers, lab equipment, nothing. I'm winging it and downloading what I can from the internet."

"Have you checked the School District of Philadelphia's teacher portal?" she says.

"Yes, I have. There's a ton of what to teach there, but no info translating that into a daily, weekly, or quarterly lesson plan."

"Okay, let me reach out to my contacts and see what I can put together for you. Meanwhile, I expect you to have rules and regulations posted next time, and to establish firm procedures."

"Okay. I'll hop on it."

As Mrs. Montgomery gets ready to leave, she sees the frustration on my face. I'm overwhelmed by her unrealistic expectations.

"Don't worry, Mr. Connelly, things get better. The better you are as a teacher, the better the kids will be as well."

Herein lies the problem: I'm not a teacher but an imposter. One day, I may be what I'm pretending to be, but that'll require time, patience, and a lot of practice. At this point, I'm surviving on a wing and a prayer. I know I should cut myself some slack, but the voice inside my head won't let me. There's always this sense that I could do so much more, but I'm already beyond overwhelmed. And everybody is telling me what to do but not showing me how to do it. It's nearly impossible to learn the job while doing it. My only frame of reference was substituting, and, in many ways, I'm still unconsciously reading from that script.

I say, "I envy teachers with years of experience who have lessons they could teach with their eyes closed."

"Mr. Connelly, you would be surprised. You might have one teacher who teaches for thirty years and does the same thing year in and year out. Then you have another teacher who improves each year, incrementally. You have to decide which teacher you want to be. I have to check in with Mr. D'Antoni next door, but I'll send you a recap of our meeting in an email. Bye, Mr. Connelly."

"Take care, Mrs. Montgomery."

The biggest problem is still unresolved. How do you motivate and engage students with minimal training and resources? Expecting every student to be over the moon about every lesson is unrealistic. Each student is different. Some will like science, and some will not. Some will excel at reading, and some will detest it.

Regardless, it's my job to try to engage every student. I can't separate the students' lack of motivation from the crappy assignments I give them. I wish I could mirror Mrs. McCaffrey, but she has the computers, textbooks, and supplies I only wish I had. In this building, resource distribution is uneven—some teachers get what they want; others just get by. Most of the time, students are fooling around on the computers anyway.

I'm just salty because I don't have any.

I know I should stay behind and start working on a better game plan, but it's time for part two of my working day, so off to the airport I go. The millions of things I have to do can wait until tomorrow. But I know it's past time to start working on a better game plan. As Benjamin Franklin said, "If you fail to plan, you plan to fail," and frankly, I'm tired of failing.

Chapter 6

Breaking Point #1: Chaos in the Classroom

———

IT'S JUST ANOTHER MANIC MONDAY. I'M EXCITED because it's our first full week of school after three choppy ones, and I have a new game plan. I spent all weekend designing a lesson for my eighth graders, inspired by my teaching coach's advice. My sixth graders are still a work in progress. Today's plan is simple: fifteen minutes for a Do Now, thirty minutes for lecturing, thirty minutes for independent work, and fifteen minutes for an exit ticket. I stay inside for lunch to make sure that everything is in order. First, I write the question on the dry-erase board:

What do all living things have in common?

Usually, I say just enough to introduce the day's assignment before retreating to the sanctuary of my desk. But today, I'm committed to turning over a new leaf. Like Maya Angelou said, when you know better, you do better. Also, time is the most precious resource we have, and I no longer want to waste theirs or mine. Over the weekend, I bought a ton of notebooks that were on sale for ten cents at Walmart. At that price, I decided to buy one for each student, lest I be accused of picking favorites. I also bought four three-tiered plastic containers to keep the books organized. The bins definitely take my classroom aesthetics up a notch.

I made it rain at the dollar store too. I bought pencils, sharpeners, hand sanitizer, crayons, colored pencils, tissues, air fresheners, erasers, calendars, thumbtacks, and other supplies. So, my students who show up with just the clothes on their backs—and let's not forget their $1,000 cell phones—but without a pencil or piece of paper to save their lives will have no excuses today.

Sometimes, I resent spending dough on supplies that parents and schools should provide, but if this is the price I have to pay to ensure students learn something, then so be it. Besides, I could never repay the impactful educators like my beloved eighth-grade math teacher, Mrs. Rachel Cohen, and my high school guidance counselor, Mrs. Lorraine Battle, who completely changed my life. These ladies showed me love and compassion when I needed it the most, and I'm forever grateful that God brought them into my life. So, I'm humbled to pay it forward in their honor.

It's five minutes till showtime. I head down to the lunchroom to pick up my class. My colleagues and I don't even bother going inside anymore. Typically, we stay in the hallway and commiserate. It's like our daily group therapy session. It's cathartic even though the conversations are becoming monotonous. But today, I'm filled with hope because I have a tremendous opportunity ahead of me. The lunch bell rings, and the students burst out like it's the first day of summer. I give them the signal to meet me upstairs. "No lollygagging, because we have work to do today!"

I find two of my overachievers already stationed at the door when I arrive. They avoid the lunchroom like the plague as well.

"Hey, Ladasia! Hey, Ciani!"

"Hey, Mr. C.!"

"Let me open this door for you ladies. We have a fun class today. You can grab one of the notebooks on the desk. From now on, we'll use these to write our Do Nows."

I give the other students the spiel as they arrive.

"Let me know if anybody needs a pencil."

I can only imagine where my stragglers are. Maybe they got word that I'm actually teaching today and decided to go home instead.

"Let's get started."

"Where do we find the answers?"

"You can use your phones."

Choruses of "I don't have any data" and "I don't have a phone" fill the room. I could really use some laptops. It was presumptuous of me to assume that everyone had a cell phone.

"Okay! If you don't have a phone, I want you to buddy up with someone who does. I have two textbooks that you can borrow as well."

A few more students walk into the room.

"What's up, Mr. C.?"

"What's good?"

"We cooling."

"Y'all are also late. Take a notebook. If you need a pencil, let me know. Get started on the Do Now."

Not a single kid has thanked me for the books or even noticed the new bins—not that they asked for them.

"Where do we find the answers?"

"You can use Google, or I also have a textbook you can borrow."

"I got you, Mr. C."

This would have been a perfect time to talk about using Google responsibly and how to vet resources, but we'll get to that later.

"Let me get everybody's attention. I want to go over a few norms for the Do Now. Always write the date, question, and answer in at least three complete sentences. When you are finished, let me know so I can check the answer. Any questions? Cool beans. Let's get started."

The class is relatively quiet. Most students seem on task, though I'm not too eager to test that hypothesis.

"Mr. C., we're finished."

"Good job, ladies."

I hop over to check their work. They've written: "Made of one or more cells, Growth and Development, Reproduction, Homeostasis, Sensitivity, and Nutrition." The answers are correct. Some versions might also include adaptation or evolution, but it's all good. I ask the girls if they know what any of these terms mean. They shake their heads.

"But you know what nutrition means?"

"Like food?" one of them responds.

"Exactly. All living things require energy to carry out life's processes. We'll go over the other ones in a second. Next time, make sure you answer in at least three complete sentences. Overall, good job, ladies."

I'm learning that it also helps to provide an exemplar at the end—something students can reference to see what a model answer looks like and use to improve their own responses.

Most students will copy what they see on the internet verbatim, so it's always good to encourage them to put things in their own words as much as possible. But Rome wasn't built overnight.

"Okay, thanks, Mr. C. What do you want us to do now?"

"Just chill for a few minutes."

I have to do something about these latecomers. Only a third of the class is here, and the noise level rises with each passing minute. I stretch out the Do Now to give the stragglers time to join us. Waiting for the slowpokes punishes the students who showed up on time, but I really want everyone to participate. I wait for about five minutes, and by then, most of the students have trickled in. I wish I could record my spiel and replay it every time someone graces me with their presence, but then I wouldn't have the chance to work on my patience.

My overachievers look bored and frustrated.

Ladasia asks me, "Mr. C., what's the assignment for the day?"

"Take it easy. I'll give it to you after the lecture."

"Lecture!? Mr. C., you are cutting up!" She chuckles, surprised that I'm daring to teach today.

"Okay, is anyone else finished?" A couple of students raise their hands. Of course, my stragglers don't because they've been talking incessantly from the moment they entered; but once again, I'm picking my battles.

"Let's get started. Let me get everybody's attention." No one pays me any mind except for my overachievers. I walk over to the tables in the back and ask them to be quiet.

"Please open your books and write down the answer. Even if you didn't look it up, I'm reviewing it now, so you can still catch up."

"I ain't got no pencil, Mr. C."

"I don't either."

Irritation surges through me, but I push it down and head to the desk for pencils. Naturally, the class gets even louder.

"Keep it down."

I give them the pencils.

"Let me get everybody's attention in three, two, one. Thanks. Can someone please read the Do Now?"

One of my overachievers raises her hand. She begins but is interrupted by one of her classmates.

"I'm sorry, Ladasia. Wait one second. Kyleem obviously has better things to talk about because he keeps interrupting us. Stop talking."

He replies, "Aight, aight, aight."

She begins again. "What do all living things have in common?"

"Thank you. Okay, the title of this unit is 'The Characteristics of Life.' We will explore what all living things, from bacteria to fungi to humans, have in common. Now, who can raise their hand and give me one of the characteristics of life?"

One of the students shouts out, "Made of cells."

"Exactly. Next time, please raise your hand. Yes, all living organisms are composed of one or more cells. For example, you have unicellular bacteria consisting of one cell. Then you have humans who are multicellular and composed of . . . how many cells do you guys think?"

The three students paying attention stare at me with blank faces. "What do y'all think? Thousands, millions, billions, or trillions?"

Ladasia says, "Millions."

"Scientists estimate that we have about 37.2 trillion cells. That's incredible, right?" I write "cell organization" on the dry-erase board. "Write it down now if you don't have that in your notebook. Kyleem, why aren't you writing anything?"

"Because I don't have a pencil, Mr. C."

"You just saw me get them pencils and heard me say several times, 'If you need a pencil, let me know.'"

"All right, my bad."

"Come on, let's get to work. Stop playin'." I walk over to my desk to grab him a pencil. The classroom's volume increases again.

"Okay, bring it back. Who can give me another characteristic? Ladasia?"

"Growth and development?"

"Good job." I write it on the board. The two tables in the back, filled with my late arrivals, are all off-task.

"Let's keep going."

The students are starting to get restless, so I ask them to shout out the rest of the characteristics. Ladasia reads the remainder of the list. Most of the review has been a dialogue between us anyway. I write all the attributes on the board.

"Make sure you have these seven characteristics written down in your notebooks."

"Mr. C., you want to check my Do Now?"

"Yeah, let me take a look at it."

"Good job, Jazir. Just give me three sentences next time."

"I got you. I get a grade for this?"

"Of course."

"Say no more."

I should grade them daily. That would be an excellent way to hold students accountable and incentivize them to show up on time. However, this is on-the-job training, and I'm a work in progress. I'm learning to give myself more grace in spite of my desire to do better.

For example, at this point, I should've been fifteen minutes into my lecture, but things don't always go according to plan. I think about chalking it and giving the students their independent work. I can tell they're tapping out. But I've already invested so much time and effort preparing, so I'm not abandoning the mission.

"Take a two-minute break while I set up the Google Docs presentation." Inevitably, the class gets noisier.

"Use your inside voice!"

They couldn't wait for me to shut up so they could start yapping their gums. I hurry up and take the roll before I forget. I know everyone by now and don't even bother calling their names anymore.

I fear that I'm losing them. I hurry and stand in front of the smartboard. My laptop screen isn't displaying. I keep pressing the button, but . . . nothing.

I keep fiddling. Finally, voilà. We're in business. "Okay, let me get everybody's attention."

My overachievers are the only ones listening. The other students are practically giving me a subliminal finger with their insubordination.

"I need silence in three . . . two . . . OOOONNNNNNNNNEEEEE-EEEEE. Stop talking, Aniyah!"

"Mr. C., I'm not the only one talking!"

"Worry about yourself. Don't worry about everybody else."

"Kyleem! For the fourth time, STOP TALKING!"

"Yoooo."

"You too, Moniqua."

Here I go again, breaking a cardinal rule by reprimanding students in front of their peers. But I'm triggered and in danger of losing self-control.

"Go holla at them, Mr. C.!"

"No, I'm talking to all of you."

Students start snickering, amused by how frustrated I'm becoming. It's like a game of Whac-A-Mole. Once one student stops, another starts on the other side of the room.

The talking is the students' way of saying, *We can't stand another minute of you lecturing us. We have exhausted our capacity to pay you any mind; give us independent work, and leave us alone.* But I refuse to raise my white flag. I spent all weekend preparing this lesson, and they will let me get through it.

"Just give me fifteen minutes, and then I'll leave y'all alone."

I begin my spiel despite the murmuring I hear percolating in the back. I will never get through this presentation if I stop every time a student talks. Instead, I keep it moving for the sake of the three students who care. I hear myself gradually getting louder to drown out the increasing chatter, which is impossible to ignore. I glance at the ceiling, teetering on the edge of a meltdown. I take a couple of seconds to calm myself. There are two problems.

First, I'm focusing on the negative behavior instead of reinforcing the positive behavior I want to see. Secondly, there are no consequences, and the students know it.

Typically, by this time, I would have retreated to my desk, but I have worked so hard on this lesson. I know they're trying to make me give up, but failure is not an option.

"For the hundredth time, stop talking! There are students who actually want to learn something."

Now they are completely ignoring me. My patience, once a quiet river, now feels like a dam about to burst. I take a deep breath, but it does nothing to quell the storm brewing within me. Finally, with my last shred of composure unraveling, I snap.

"You know what! SHUT UP!" The words hang in the air, shocking both the students and myself.

"Why do I have to keep telling y'all over and over and over again to be quiet?! It's not that hard! You don't want to learn anything? Cool. Just shut up!

"I try to be cool! I try to be Mr. Nice Guy, but that doesn't work! I shouldn't have to scream at the top of my lungs to get your attention! I shouldn't have to beg y'all to do my job!"

I see a young lady in the back snickering, which fuels my frustration even more.

"Oh, you think it's funny. Well, laugh now, cry later. You don't want to listen to me. You don't want to follow the rules. Cool. There are places for people like that. It's called prison. And America loves to incarcerate its citizens. We live in a country that spends more per person on incarceration than on education, so y'all do the math.

"But y'all think it's a game. Do you even understand the price our ancestors paid for you to be here? It wasn't free. They gave their lives so y'all can sit in these chairs—just for y'all to come in here and bullshit every day. But you know what, mark my words, life has a way of humbling all of us.

"So, you better wake up—and you better wake up fast, because before you know it, you'll be adults. You'll see how hard it is out here, and you'll wish you hadn't wasted this time."

I take a second to catch my breath. The class is dead silent now. You could hear a pin drop.

"I want to show all of you something. Pay attention! Because this might be the most important lesson you learn all year.

"I have a question for you. Is it possible to legally be a slave in 2018? Raise your hand if you think it's possible."

Nobody raises their hand.

"Impossible?" Three-quarters of the class raise their hands.

"Well, let me show you something." I go over to the smartboard and search for the 13th Amendment. I read the statement to them.

Section 1

Neither slavery nor involuntary servitude, except as a punishment for crime whereof the party shall have been duly convicted, shall exist within the United States, or any place subject to their jurisdiction.

"So, under what conditions may someone become enslaved in the year 2018?"

Ladasia replies, "If you go to prison."

"Exactly. And prison is big business. And schools like this funnel kids there. God forbid you can't read. God forbid you can't write. Where does that leave you?

"But understand—not all slavery is physical. You can be a slave mentally too. But y'all want to play all day. Cool. Y'all win. I'll fall back because clearly y'all think it's a game. Maybe I need to stop caring and just collect my check like everyone else."

I bow my head and retreat to my desk, defeated, my white flag raised. The class is so silent you can hear my footsteps on the creaky floors. I can see the shock on the students' faces. I completely lost it. It was like an out-of-body experience. Once I went over the edge, I couldn't stop. All the frustration from the last few weeks culminated at that moment.

My heart is still racing like a Lamborghini. There are ten minutes left in class. I wish I could dismiss them early. Instead, I stare out the window and act like they're not there. Funny, it's the quietest it's been all year. Why should it have taken me acting like a madman?

"Mr. C., are you okay?" Ladasia asks.

"Yeah, I'm okay."

"Are you sure?"

"I'm cool."

But I'm not. And she knows it. I'm mad at myself. I have worked hard to shed the person I once was. I spent half my life in fight mode, angry, full of rage, always seconds from spazzing out. I hated living like that, but growing up in the mean streets of Philly left me no choice. Now, just when I thought my spazzing days were over, here I am, right back where I started.

Obviously, I still have some work to do when it comes to regulating my emotions and controlling my mouth. And I'm the first to judge the students when they talk greasy. That's why you can't forget where you came from; all it takes is the right trigger, and you can be right back there. I'm gutted the lesson didn't go as planned, but that's life. I can't control what happens. The only thing I can control is my response.

I thought I could force the students to learn. I pictured them working quietly, taking notes, and asking thought-provoking questions. I hoped they would notice the time, effort, and supplies and acquiesce to my every request out of gratitude. *Yeah, right!* Respect isn't given;

it's earned. One planned lesson and a few supplies won't change the conditioning of my students or my lack of teaching experience. Those are battles we must win one day at a time.

My students have spent years conditioned by expectations that might as well be buried in the Mariana Trench. They didn't develop their bad habits overnight, so it's foolish to expect them to change so suddenly. As my Pop once said, "Habits, once formed, are not easily changed." They say it takes twenty-one days to build a new habit, and this is just day one—but man, I already feel like I'm tapping out.

I know I have to change if I hope to educate my students. I must demand more from myself before I expect more from them because where the head goes, the body follows. It takes time to unlearn bad habits. Just as I strive to offer myself grace while evolving and learning, I must also extend that same grace to my students. Hopefully, I can win them over in time. When the bell rings, the students bolt out of the classroom faster than the Flash. My two overachievers, who were the first there, are now the last ones out.

"Bye, Mr. C."

"Take care, ladies. Good job today."

I wish I could say the same about myself, but once again, I feel like an abject failure.

Chapter 7

Breakdown to Breakthrough

——

IT'S FOUR O'CLOCK IN THE MORNING. I'M LYING IN MY bed wide awake, staring at the ceiling, dreading the day ahead. The thought of having to face my students has kept me up all night. What can I say to make up for the way I acted? What can I do to earn my students' respect? Do I even have the will to keep fighting this daily battle? All the stress is causing me to grind my teeth, which has given me a throbbing headache.

I grew up in the church, where the saints would often say that if your situation isn't changing, it's because God is trying to change you. I need to change. I'm just unsure how. And frankly, adjusting and learning on the fly doesn't give me the time and space to do it. I'm constantly battling the feeling of being thrown into the deep end, flailing with nothing but hope and a prayer to keep me afloat. I can't do it today. I think it's time for my first mental health day.

I've had the urge to call out since the first week of school, but I don't want to let my students down. So many teachers are already missing in action on any given day. I feel guilty adding to the dysfunction, but I'm tapping out. I imagine my students thinking, *Dang, Mr. C. is calling out now, too? None of these teachers care about us.* Maybe I'm projecting my childhood abandonment issues though. Perhaps they'll be excited to get a break from me begging them to be quiet and complete their assignments. I know I always did a happy dance when my teachers were absent. Back in the day, a teacher's absence was the exception; now, it's the rule. What's changed?

Go figure. Maybe it's a sign of the times. I have fifteen minutes to call out before the system prevents me from doing so. I can't make up my mind. I keep going back and forth: *Call out. Don't call out. Call out. Don't call out.* Finally, five minutes before the cutoff, I say, "To hell with it," and pull the trigger. I resolve the dissonance by imagining my students excitedly telling their friends, "There's a party in Mr. C.'s class."

Welp. There goes my perfect attendance streak, a solid month-plus down the drain. It feels like a betrayal of my commitment, but I can't pour from an empty cup. It's time to go into self-preservation mode. It'll be a cold day in hell before an administrator says, *"Mr. C., we see how hard you're working and think you should take a day to regroup,"* so I'll take it upon myself. At first, I looked down on teachers who called out, but now I understand. Sometimes, you need an extra day to hit the reset button.

Teaching demands countless hours of effort that often go unnoticed and unpaid. We celebrate educators who pour their souls into their students, but what good is lighting a fire if it leaves you burned out? If I grow jaded and resentful, it limits what I can offer my students. To give them my best, I must prioritize my own well-being, tending to my flame before it flickers out. As they say on airplanes, *Put on your own oxygen mask before assisting others.*

I know my students will feel my absence. I may be the most consistent male role model some of them have. When I became a teacher, I never imagined I would also become a surrogate father. Yet, I find myself spending more time engaging with students than many of their parents. It's a labor of love but incredibly exhausting for an introvert like me. I don't see how my colleagues with kids and spouses do it. So, after giving so much of my time and energy, it's my turn to take a little back.

Besides, it'll be good to give my students a chance to miss me. In the School District of Philadelphia, we are entitled to three personal days. That's three days you can call out with no questions asked. Fortunately, I'm off from my airport gig as well. I go back to sleep shortly after calling out. I wake up around nine and prepare my go-to breakfast: a turkey bacon, egg, and cheese croissant with a hash brown, and then get right back into bed.

Given that I have the whole day free, I want to hit the gym, get a haircut, pick up groceries, go to acupuncture, and grab a drink at happy hour. *Yeah, right!* Twelve hours later, I'm still in bed. I have spent the entire day snuggled in my comforter, drifting in and out of sleep. My body is saying, *Sit your gallivanting derrière down and rest.* Why rip and run if you don't have to? It's like returning from vacation more tired than when you left because you had an endless checklist of things to see. In the US, we have a work-obsessed mentality, always feeling compelled to stay busy, and I'm guilty as charged.

It's such a treat to chillax and do nothing. I have to listen to my body's whispers lest I hear the screams again. While resting, I keep thinking about the millions of things I could be doing for my class. However, today I'm giving myself permission to be selfish—to think of nothing and no one but myself.

The only problem with sleeping all day is that it's impossible to sleep at night. Thus, I stare at the ceiling, feeling like I'm starring in *Groundhog Day. Should I take another day off?* I can't stand the thought of my students going two days without learning anything. But let's be honest—most of the time when I'm there, they're not learning schnitzel anyway. So what does it matter? In the silence, I hear my conscience say, *"Your presence matters. Never underestimate the power of your presence."*

My presence? *What'choo talkin' 'bout, Willis?* I thought my most significant contribution was the knowledge I had to share. Suddenly, I'm reminded of a poster in the teachers' lounge that reads: KIDS DON'T CARE HOW MUCH YOU KNOW UNTIL THEY KNOW HOW MUCH YOU CARE. And the best way to show students I care is by showing up.

IN THE MORNING, I ARRIVE AT MY CLASSROOM fifteen minutes before school starts. The floors are clean, but the broken bins, ripped posters, and expletives on the board give me some insight into how the students behaved. While surveying the damage, Ladasia runs in. "Hey, Mr. C.!"

"What's up, Ladasia?"

"OMG. Where were you at?"

"I needed to woosah."

"Mr. C., you are cutting me up."

"I'm just taking a page out of your book." Another student, Steve, runs into the class.

"Yo, Mr. C.! You back, man."

"Yeah, I'm back."

"Are you chillin' now? I heard you cussed the class out."

"Yeah, I'm good."

"I'm so mad I missed that."

"You got jokes. Sorry for spazzing on y'all, Ladasia."

"You don't have to apologize, Mr. C. These kids are too disrespectful."

"True, but that doesn't give me the right to scream at y'all. Anyway, I'm human and make mistakes. When I drop the ball, I'll be man enough to admit it, but you can be confident it'll never happen again. Shouldn't y'all be in advisory?"

"Yeah, but we got a substitute. Can we stay here with you?"

"No, y'all should go to advisory and get marked present."

"We did!"

"Well, get a note saying it's okay to stay here, and then come back."

"All right, Mr. C. We'll be right back!"

They like me. They really like me. Getting them to respect me is another story, but baby steps. It feels good knowing that within minutes of entering school, their first thought is to run and see if I'm here. These moments, however small, reassure me I am making a difference. After spending a day in virtual silence, I welcome the screams and laughter echoing from the hallway.

It's incredible how the madness becomes a part of you after a while. The beauty of the human spirit is that we can adapt to the most challenging circumstances. The students return to the class with a note. A few more follow, asking if they can stay too. "Sure."

I thought my outburst would drive a wedge between us, but they're carrying on as if nothing happened. I marvel at children's ability to forgive and forget. Kids will knock each other's heads off one second and be friends the next. Adults can learn a lot from them about embracing the present and compartmentalizing experiences. I'm discovering I have as much to learn from my little teachers as they do from me. I just have to be open to the lessons they offer.

There was a rupture, and I'm still responsible for the repair. Having these moments to enjoy each other's company is a part of it, but I still have a lot of work to do—the bell rings. A student enters the class and hands me a piece of paper. It's a coverage slip—my reward for taking yesterday off. Normally, I would be angry, but since I took a day off myself, covering for a colleague isn't so bad. Hey, if you can't beat them, join them, right?

For lunch, I retreat to the sanctuary of my car and turn on WRTI Philly, my favorite station for classical and jazz. I set my alarm for thirty minutes, recline the seat, close my eyes, and drift away to the lush melodies. It's incredible how some of these songs have been around for centuries, but they still have the power to captivate you from the first note.

Composers from Dvořák to Vivaldi can hypnotize you with their virtuosity and help soothe the day's tension. What happened yesterday, today, and what could occur in the future becomes irrelevant. The music demands your attention, for its beauty lies in both the subtleties and the unfolding. No other genre moves me like classical music. Time doesn't fly; it stretches, compresses, and pulses with emotion. In moments like these, I'm reminded that even teachers need a pause, though I can't escape the guilt that comes with it.

After all, I could use this time to bond with students, call parents, host lunch detentions, or do any number of other teacher tasks, but I have to prioritize my well-being. The way I honor and treat myself sets the standard for how others treat me. As an introvert, I have to respect my need for quiet and solitude. They are non-negotiables. "Pie Jesu" plays from my phone, signaling I have five minutes until I have to meet my eighth graders in the lunchroom.

I turn off the alarm clock, slowly emerge from my meditation-induced haze, and gather my belongings. It feels like that moment when you're told your massage is over—you're reluctant to leave the blissful state but know you need to move on. Now I have three minutes to make it to the cafeteria. I hope my last class flies by as quickly as my lunch. I rush inside to meet my students so they won't think I abandoned them again. The way they talk, I'm sure this class has already gotten word that I'm back.

I arrive at the lunchroom just as the bell rings, and within seconds, a few of my students emerge.

"What's up, Mr. C.?"

"What's good, Nyzim!" We dab each other up.

"Where were you yesterday?!"

"I was at home."

"Word! I ain't mad at you."

Another student, Aniyah, leaves the lunchroom.

"No! No! No! You have some explaining to do, Mister! Why weren't you here yesterday?!"

I smile and say, "I needed some woosah time."

"We be getting on your nerves, don't we, Mr. C.?"

"What do you think? How would you feel if you were in my shoes?"

She rolls her eyes and lets out a loud gasp.

"Mr. C., I could not be a teacher. You want me to go to jail?"

I shake my head and chuckle, knowing exactly what she means. The students follow me upstairs. Some are waiting for me outside my classroom.

"Good afternoon!" I say.

"Hey, Mr. C. Where were you yesterday?" *Holy moly, if I get that question one more time.*

I thought I could call out with no questions asked, but now I see I have mini-bosses to answer to. "I just needed a day off," I say.

"I gotchu, Mr. C."

I haven't decided yet what I'll say to my students, but I know it's past time for us to have a heart-to-heart about the conditions in our class.

"Okay, let me get everybody's attention in three, two, one." Most students stop talking, but there's always that one. I refuse to speak until there is complete silence. I'll wait ninety minutes if I have to, but I will not lose my cool.

Finally, Aniyah yells, "Shut up!" to the boys in the back. "I do not want to hear him scream again. I hate this school."

I appreciate the assistance. Students can get each other's attention in ways I can't, so if I have to rely on little peer pressure to get the job done, then so be it. Finally, the class is completely silent.

"I want to have a class discussion instead of a Do Now today. First, I want to apologize for screaming at y'all. I'm human. I make mistakes, but I can also admit when I'm wrong and ask for forgiveness. So, y'all forgive me?" The whole class gestures and says, "We're cool."

Aniyah chimes in as usual. "Mr. C., I don't know why you apologizing. Our parents scream at us all the time."

"So, because your parents do it, does that make it right?"

"No, but it is what it is."

"Yeah, but it doesn't have to be that way. We can choose differently. You don't have to talk disrespectfully to your kids if you decide to have them. And you don't have to beat them into submission either. Most people live what they learn, me included; but we can also learn to make better choices. You know what? Forget life science. Let's just rap. Can I teach y'all about real life today?"

Everybody nods, giving me the go-ahead to continue.

"All right. Dig this. People can treat you in one of three ways. They can treat you like you are above your level, which will help you mature. They can relate to you on your level, which will keep you there. Lastly, you can be treated like you are beneath your maturity level, which can cause you to go backward. What do you all think? Suppose I'm scream-ing, hollering, and trying to control your behavior. Is that above, below, or same-level treatment?"

Most students say, "Below." A few students say, "The same."

"Why do you think 'below,' Ladasia?"

"Well, screaming and hollering is disrespectful."

"Okay. Kyzim, why do you say 'the same'?"

"Because, like Aniyah said earlier, it's how our parents talk; it's the way we talk, so it's all the same for us."

"Okay, think about this for a second. How do you feel when some-body is yelling and screaming at you? Does that make you feel good? Does that make you want to do better?"

Makai says, "Nah, it just makes me mad, and I want to snap back."

"I feel you. It comes down to respect. If you want respect, you have to give respect. You have to treat people how you want to be treated. I treat y'all like you're more mature than you are because I'm trying to help y'all level up. I will never make y'all line up outside the lunchroom and walk upstairs in a single-file line. What level is that school policy on: above, below, or the same?"

Most kids say, "Below."

"Precisely. We walked to classes by ourselves in middle school, which helped me manage my time better. Unfortunately, we're robbing y'all of the opportunity to build those skills. That's why y'all rebel and don't do it anyway. Also, do y'all think it's normal not to have recess?"

Most of them shake their heads.

"How do you feel about that?"

Emmanuel jumps in. "That shit is ass, man."

I give him the look.

"My bad, Mr. C."

"Recess is just as important as academics in my book. That's where you learn how to deal with folks. Yet again, we rob y'all of that oppor-tunity by keeping everyone locked indoors all day like prisoners. Sure, the situation is easier to manage, but it limits your ability to develop the social skills you need to be successful. Now, I have a confession to make. I want to be honest and fully transparent with all of you. This is my first year teaching, and I only learned I would teach this class four days before school started."

"For real, Mr. C.?"

"Real talk. I was only supposed to be an assistant, so I came in the door with virtually no teaching experience. Granted, I have a lot of life experience, but I have yet to learn how to manage a classroom and teach correctly. So, I admit I'm still figuring it out. But I'm committed to getting it right because every day my heart breaks when I see how little learning goes on in this school. For example, raise your hand if you had a substitute today."

Three-quarters of the class raise their hands.

"Two substitutes?"

Again, three-quarters of the room raise their hands.

"Three?" A handful of students raise their hands.

"Do you see what I mean? How many of you feel like you're not learning enough in this school?"

Everyone raises their hands.

"I'm glad you all realize that. It's not fair, but it's the reality we face. That's why we need to make the most of our time together—we can't afford to waste it. For some of you, this might be the only chance you get to learn something all day. But remember, we're living in an age where information is all around us, and it's never been easier to follow your curiosity and expand your knowledge.

"You want to be a baker? There's a YouTube video for that. An influencer? There are videos for that too. In fact, much of what I taught this year, I learned online. Look, nobody graduates from high school or college knowing everything.

"Many schools don't teach skills like how to manage money or relationships. Unfortunately, some of our parents didn't get those lessons either. So, what does that mean for us?

"At some point, you need to take control of your learning—become your own teacher. If you don't know a word, look it up in the dictionary.

Stuck on a math problem? There are online tutorials that can break it down step by step.

"The key is to stay curious and keep learning. The more you do, the farther you'll go. All right. Now, I want to open the floor and hear from all of you. It's just one of me, but there are about thirty of you, so I have just as much to learn from y'all as you do from me. I'm brand new to teaching, so help me help y'all. What can I do differently? How do y'all need me to step up to ensure everybody is learning something? Kyree?"

"I think you need to be harder on us," he says.

"Can you elaborate on that?"

"Like you be giving us options. Everybody knows this is the chill class. I can sleep and play on my phone. Am I lying, y'all?"

Silence.

"Y'all can be honest. By a show of hands, how many of you would agree with Kyree that I need to be harder on y'all?"

Surprisingly, the majority of the class raises their hands. I'm flabbergasted. Do they want me to be mean to them? How do I translate "harder" into daily action? I don't have the energy to be a classroom dictator. Perhaps what they really want isn't a cool teacher but someone who will do their job properly—set high expectations, hold them accountable, and provide the structure and discipline I never had as a child.

Growing up, my mom felt more like a peer than a parent because of her addiction. On the surface, I enjoyed the freedom to do whatever I wanted, whenever I wanted, but deep down, I longed for a parent— someone to check my homework, attend report card conferences, and care about my struggles. Like my students, I had enough peers. I needed guidance. Funny, I'm realizing how much I project my childhood onto my students, expecting them to be like the parentified kid I was.

Honestly, I get a huge ego boost from being "the cool teacher." While this earns my students' affection, it doesn't win their respect. Now, I must operate differently and model what it means to be a life-long learner. Doing so will require me to dig deep and cultivate skills I have yet to develop, but I'm willing to do whatever it takes to turn over a new leaf in our classroom. "Okay, anyone else? Ladasia."

"You need to call parents, give some after-school detentions, or something."

"Okay. Thank you. That's good advice. Now, I'll admit I haven't called any parents yet, but I can commit to doing that. What else? Caleb."

"Can we play some games?"

"What kind of games?"

"I don't know."

"All right. I can definitely look into it. I don't want this class to be boring, so I'll make it happen. But will you be excited about every assignment? Absolutely not. Sometimes, in life, you gotta do what you gotta do. It's just a part of the game. I'll try to make the class more fun though. Thanks for the feedback. What else? Nothing?" I pause. "Okay, what type of assignments do y'all like? What can we do to make the class more fun?"

"Can we get some computers?"

"I've been trying to get computers, but they're hot commodities. I can try again, but we might have to do without them."

"Can we do some word searches?"

"I can work on that. I loved word searches when I was in middle school. Raise your hand if you like them too."

Almost the entire class raises their hands.

"Do you hate word searches, Haneef?"

"I don't bang wit dem like that, but I'll do 'em."

"Solid. I can find some word searches."

"Can we do some science experiments, Mr. C.?"

"I would love for us to do experiments. But first, y'all will have to prove to me that y'all can be responsible. Look what happened to the bins and the posters I bought. Maybe we can shoot for every quarter as long as the associated work is finished. By a show of hands, how many of you have ever taken notes?"

Nobody raises their hand.

"Imagine I gave a lecture and had you take notes. How long do you think you could stay focused before getting distracted?"

They start calling out numbers: "ten minutes," "five minutes," "fifteen minutes," and, amusingly, "a minute." The estimates are all over the place, but they are far from the thirty minutes I had in mind during my meltdown lesson.

"All right. Cool beans. That's all of my questions. Do you have any questions for me? Christina."

"Are you going to be our teacher until the end of the year?"

"One hundred percent. My goal is to see y'all walk across the stage in June. So, rest assured, I'm not going anywhere. But you all know that five teachers have already quit, right? The students nod their heads, not looking even slightly shocked. What does everyone think about that? Maria."

"It's sad because, as you said, we don't learn anything."

"Exactly. Who are these students hurting when they make teachers quit? Ciani."

"Themselves."

"Precisely. But no worries. Mr. C. is going to grind it out. Y'all can believe that. I just want all of you to learn something. That's it. And we Gucci. I will never expect it to be dead silent in here, only when I'm speaking. But everyone did phenomenally today, so I know you all can do it. Okay, we have ten minutes left, so y'all can chill it out, and we'll start fresh tomorrow. Good job today. I'm proud of y'all."

They exchange glances, their faces glowing with pride as they acknowledge the discipline and focus they maintained throughout the discussion.

I walk back to my desk. It's the longest I've spent away from it since school started. I can't believe I got through my whole spiel without asking them to be quiet once. It's a miracle.

Once again, I feel hopeful and excited about the possibilities. Today, I made the class a part of the change I want to see. Now, I need to implement the vision with fidelity, hold myself and my students accountable, and keep the expectations high.

When the bell rings, I bid my students farewell. I'm envious they get to go home and chill for the rest of the day. Lucky me, I get to spend the next five hours cleaning airplanes. Woo-hoo.

It Takes A Village . . . and Then Some

—

At the airport, I head straight to the utility closet to pick up my assignment. It's a cramped space, stocked with everything you need to service an aircraft—trash bags, barf bags, hazmat suits . . . you name it. I arrive fifteen minutes early to avoid the changing of the guard. Through the open door, I spot my favorite supervisor, Diane, scanning our shift report like a field commander gathering intel.

I love it when Diane is in charge. Her strong interpersonal and leadership skills always ensure the shift runs smoothly. An army veteran, she brings a level of calm and discipline to this chaotic environment that's unmatched. Selfless is the word that describes her best. If, God forbid, your partner deserts you, Diane will be there to save the day—always willing to jump into the trenches and lend a hand. You don't mind going above and beyond for a boss like that.

"Rique, you're assigned to terminators with Sophia tonight."

"Okay, cool, I appreciate it."

That's another reason I love Diane—she always gives me terminators. These flights stay overnight and depart the next morning. Out of the six jobs I might get stuck with daily, terminators are hands down the best. Taking out the trash for the entire terminal though—that's the worst. You're out in the weather, dodging rats, and every so often a splash of trash juice hits you and leaves you smelling like rotten chitterlings. Terminators are cake compared to that. I've got two tonight, but if my partner agrees to split the list, I'll be down to just one. Sweet—one quick job and the rest of the night off.

Now, don't get me wrong: cleaning a plane from top to bottom is no joke, and you definitely feel it afterward. Both night and morning managers inspect it, so it has to be spotless. All it takes is a couple of cookie crumbs on the carpet to get chewed out. It's crazy how hard they want you to work for $13 an hour these days. Adjusted for inflation, that's like earning 1980s wages. But the freedom to roam the world with the touch of a smartphone makes it all worth it—just as seeing my students' progress makes the challenges of teaching worthwhile.

Tonight, the work continues. I'll take out the trash, disinfect the seats, vacuum the floors, pull up the seat cushions, clean the bathroom, disinfect the trays, stock the bathroom, replace the booze, top up the snacks, wipe down the overhead bins, tidy up the galley, sanitize the cockpit, pull down the shades, and lock it up after Diane signs off on my work.

It takes me about forty-five minutes if I work nonstop, but I usually stretch it out a bit. Cleaning feels meditative. The physical nature of the airport perfectly balances the mental demands of school. I prefer to work alone, but I'm fine with a partner—provided they don't talk my ear off. After school, my will to engage is exhausted. Besides, I've got a ton of homework tonight. I double-check my supply bag to make sure I have everything I need. With a quick nod to Diane, I step out of the utility closet, instantly jolted by the change of scenery.

The blinding lights and endless gate announcements assault the senses, pulling me from the quiet into the buzzing energy of the terminal. The air is thick with the scent of sizzling onions from Tony Luke's cheesesteaks, mixed with the smoky, spicy aroma of Chipotle's grilled meats. I love the rhythm of the airport—the ebbs and flows, along with the endless people-watching potential. But sometimes, the sea of bodies, the relentless beeping, and the rumble of jet engines make this place feel like a pressure cooker about to release steam. That's when I book it to my favorite hiding spot by the training offices.

Like the utility closet, it's a world away from the sensory overload of the gates. It's the perfect place to knock out some schoolwork. We're starting a new chapter in my eighth-grade science class, and I need to do some lesson planning. Fortunately, the airport gives me plenty of downtime. It feels like they're paying me to do my homework, which speeds up my night and helps me stay on top of things in my class.

I ride the escalators up and make my way down the corridor. The arrival screen confirms that all my flights are on schedule. At the training offices, I scan my badge and slip into the hallway. The lights are half dim, and the doors are all closed. It's quiet, so I assume everyone is gone for the evening. I place my book bag on the linoleum floor and slowly descend to join it. My first flight comes in three hours. That should be more than enough time to knock out my homework.

After a lot of trial and error, prayer, and Google searches, I finally have lesson planning down to a science. Well, I do for my eighth-graders. My sixth graders are still a work in progress, but baby steps. I have designed a curriculum that's fun, engaging, and informative. Many of the changes came directly from students' advice about improving our class. Dr. Bloom's influential hierarchy of cognitive skills helped shape my thinking, though I take a more streamlined approach.

Typically, my assignments fall into three categories. I call them levels one, two, and three. The goal of level one is to familiarize students with the key terms featured in the chapter. These words are the building blocks for the ideas students will explore. By mastering them, they lay a solid foundation for deeper comprehension.

Level two assignments focus on applying the information from level one. For example, students might read an article from the online resource CK-12 and answer questions. This helps them contextualize the vocabulary, connect the dots, and see the bigger picture. Finally, level three assignments require students to synthesize what they've learned by creating something or conducting an investigation—mirroring the final stage of Bloom's Taxonomy.

Before I became a teacher, I wasn't too fond of level-one or low-rigor assignments because I thought they dumbed students down, but my feelings have evolved. Low-rigor tasks are essential because they allow students to practice and reinforce foundational concepts and skills. They serve as a gentle entry point, allowing students to learn the basics before delving into more complex ideas. However, level one is just the beginning—a springboard to deeper understanding—and should never be the endpoint in any classroom.

Many teachers fall into the trap of assigning only low-rigor work, leading to student boredom and disengagement. When we don't challenge students with material that pushes their thinking and problem-solving, we rob them of the chance to cultivate these skills. The key is to balance low- and high-rigor assignments, ensuring a range of tasks that guide students from basic understanding to more complex applications. Tonight, I'll focus on creating level-one assignments to help my students master the key terms.

At first, I would spend countless hours sifting through online content, chasing the elusive perfect worksheet. The problem is, there are thousands of them, and it would take a lifetime to sift through it all. On top of that, much of the material is misaligned with my goals. For instance, when searching for a crossword puzzle on cell parts, I might find one with thirty key terms instead of the ten I need, and the definitions rarely match mine.

Consequently, I have taken it upon myself to master the art of worksheet creation, which has made my life a lot easier. Perhaps I'll add "cruciverbalist" to my résumé! Next on the agenda is the classification unit, which introduces terms such as protists, archaebacteria, eubacteria, fungi, plantae, animalia, virus, organism, classification, and taxonomy. Some of these words may seem like Greek to students at first, but by the end of level one, they'll find them much less intimidating.

I create four assignments to help students learn the terminology. First, I design a word scramble worksheet using Education.com. Then, I move on to Discovery Education's Puzzlemaker website to create a word search and crossword puzzle.

Finally, I create a fill-in-the-blank definition sheet, where I remove the two most important words from each definition. I photocopy the assignments, so each sheet has two tasks, and I encourage students to complete both sides. With ninety minutes in class, there's more than enough time to finish everything.

For a step-by-step guide to creating your own word searches, visit TariqueConnelly.com.

Level one is complete once students work with me to ensure they can pronounce the words correctly. I also use this time to assess their understanding of the definitions. It takes me less than two hours to complete all of my worksheets. It took me that long just to find an assignment back in the day, so I'm stoked at my improving efficiency. The floor is wreaking havoc on my backside, so it's time to pull a James Brown and get on up.

With my stomach growling louder than the Cookie Monster, I make a beeline for Chick-fil-A. Hopefully, the line isn't too long. Geez Louise, I don't know what juju they put on that chicken, but folks will line up like it's Black Friday at Best Buy to get their fix. For me, it's the cheddar cheese and waffle fries. It's fast-food heaven. I stroll from Terminal F to the Terminal B/C food court. Shockingly, there are only ten people in line. I pick up my food, top off my Arnold Palmer, and return to my hideout.

I have thirty minutes before my first flight arrives, but it'll only take five to polish off this grub. I fast intermittently, so I'm ravenously hungry by dinnertime. While eating, I receive a text message from Diane: **"Your terminator just landed."**

Shucks. It's early, but I'm in no rush. I'm working my wage. Twenty minutes later, I make my way to the plane. I have timed my arrival perfectly, after all the passengers and flight crew have bounced. I walk up the aisle, scanning the carpet to see how much work I've got ahead of me. It doesn't look half bad. As I return to the front, a woman enters the plane.

"What's up? Are you Tarique?"

"That's me," I say. "Sophia?"

"Yeah. Nice to meet you."

"You as well."

For a second, I get lost in Sophia's beautiful hazel eyes. I'm a sucker for pretty eyes. She's about five-two and wears a company snapback and baggy cargo pants.

"So, you're hanging out with me for the day, huh?"

"Yeah."

"Cool. Well, we got a sweet day. There are only two terminators. If you want, I can bang this one out, and you can do the next one, or we can work together."

"We can work together," she says.

"For sure. I'll start in the bathroom. You got the front."

"I gotchu."

"You have a supply bag."

"Nah."

"It's all good."

I take what I need, then hand it to her, trying not to get lost in her dreamy eyes. I glance down and check out her badge photo to divert my attention. In the process, I notice her last name, *Escarra*.

"Where are you from, Sophia?"

"South Philly. You?"

"I'm from West. I only ask because I was trying to figure out where you got the last name Escarra."

"I don't know. I think it's Spanish."

"Okay, cool. I have two students with the same last name."

"Oh, you're a teacher?"

"Yeah. Maybe y'all are related. Do you know Armani and Kyree Escarra?"

"What! I sure do! That's my niece and nephew!"

"Get out of here! For real?"

"Yeah, why?! Armani be acting a fool, don't she?"

"Well, you know your niece better than I do."

"Yeah, I know she's been feeling herself lately. I try to keep her in check, but my sister can be a handful too."

"I feel you."

"What she be doing?"

"Well, Armani likes to skip class. And when she does grace me with her presence, ten minutes later, she's ready to dip. I try to go easy on 'em."

"Go easy? Armani? Hell to the no! You gotta stay on her ass because she thinks she's grown up. Is Kyree walking out of the class too?"

"No, he doesn't walk out, but he doesn't do any work either. He just plays on his phone all day and wastes time."

"Take his phone away!"

"Nah, we can't."

"Why can't you? I give you permission."

"God forbid I drop his $1,000 iPhone. Who's going to pay for it, because I'm not. And if the district can barely buy soap, you know they're not paying for a smartphone."

She laughs and bats her long eyelashes, accentuating the windows to her soul.

"Have you called my sister?"

"I haven't talked to her yet, but I plan to."

"Well, I'll call her myself because my niece and nephew should know better. My sister might be sweet, but they know I don't play that shit. Armani was at my house last night with her cousin. We are about to chalk that. She will not come over if she can't fix her behavior. You wait until I talk to her. Trust me, I gotchu. If you don't see a change in the next few days, you let me know, and I'll come sit in the damn class myself."

"Cool. Well, I appreciate your help. I'll make sure to hit your sister up too. All right, let's bang out this terminator."

"Say no more."

Working with a partner isn't so bad, especially when they have beautiful eyes like Sophia. We knock out the terminator in a third of the time it would have taken me to do it alone. I'm grateful Sophia and I met, but her question about contacting her sister keeps lingering in my head. I feel guilty for not calling more parents . . . okay, for not calling *any* parents.

I'm squealing on students for not doing their work, and I'm guilty of the same offense. It's a classic case of throwing stones in a glass house. I can imagine my students' mom asking her sister, *Why are you telling me this instead of the teacher?* So, I have to call her before her sister does. I return to my hiding place to make the call.

It's almost eight at night, which is late to call parents. However, if I don't do it now while I'm motivated, I never will. So, I brace myself, block my number, and call Ms. Escarra. Of course, the number is disconnected. I track down Sophia to get the right one. I find her chilling in the food court. Before I say anything, she says, "I texted my sister everything you said and let her know that you'd be calling soon."

"That's exactly why I'm here. The number in the system is wrong, so I wanted to get the correct one from you."

"No problem. I'll give you mine too."

"That's what's up. I appreciate you."

"No doubt. That's my niece and nephew."

I return to my hideout to make the call. I'm glad Sophia stepped in and told her sister what was happening. As the adage goes, "It takes a village to raise a child." I'm a fool for trying to go at it alone. It makes me wonder how many other 'Aunt Sophias' are out there, ready to support my students and my work inside the classroom. I'll never know unless I initiate contact. On the other hand, I'm embarrassed that she beat me to the punch. It makes me feel like a slacker.

I should have reached out long ago, but better late than never. I sit on the hard floor, take out my phone, and make the call. The phone rings several times before she picks up.

"Good evening. Can I speak with Ms. Escarra, please?"

"Who this?!"

"It's Mr. Connelly from Columbia Middle School. I'm Kyree and Armani's teacher."

"Oh my god! I am so sorry. I thought you was one of those damn bill collectors."

"It's all good."

"So, what's the problem?"

"Thanks for taking my call, and I'll keep it brief since it's late. Unfortunately, Kyree and Armani are both at risk of failing science. Armani likes to cut class and hang out in the hallways. When she does show up, she leaves minutes later. Kyree comes to class, but he's always late and needs to complete a lot of work."

"Well, I don't know what you want me to do about that. Shit, if they want to fuck up their lives, let 'em. I'm tired of fighting with Armani and Kyree. I got other kids to worry about."

I would love to suggest pumping the brakes on the gravy train and confiscating their phones, but it's not my place to tell anyone how to raise their child. Instead, I say, "Okay, I hear you, Ms. Escarra, and I understand your frustration."

"Do you have any kids?"

"No."

"Great, keep it that way." I laugh, thinking that I don't need any convincing.

"I'm serious. It's not easy raising kids today. It's harder for me because I'm doing everything by myself. I gotta be their mom and dad."

As much as I sympathize with her plight, I want to tell her that she could be the best mom in the world, but she could never be their dad. But again, that's not my place.

"I gotta bust my ass at work, and I'm tired by the time I come home. Shit, I couldn't watch them 24/7 if I wanted to. I'm trying to get Armani tested because she needs a new IEP (Individualized Education Program). That thing ain't been changed in a month of Sundays."

At that moment, I realize I've never consulted an IEP for any of my students. I only know what the term means because I had one myself. *Shucks.* You don't know what you don't know.

"And Kyree refuses to take his medication, so what you want me to do? But I will try to talk to my kids. Is there anything else? I'm sorry, what's ya name?"

"My name is Mr. Connelly, but the students call me Mr. C."

"Okay, cool."

"No, that's it. I appreciate your time and willingness to help out. If there are any further issues, I'll make sure to contact you."

"Okay, thanks for calling, Mr. C. You're the first teacher from that shitty-ass school that's ever called."

"I'm sorry to hear that. But I'll do better moving forward."

"Okay, thanks again."

"You're welcome. Have a good night."

"Good night." *Click.*

It's a miracle. I made my first phone call as a teacher, and it went a lot better than I anticipated. Even though the results are uncertain, I've done my part, and that's all that matters. Diane texts me to tell me that the last terminator has arrived—it's time to knock this one out of the park and wind down this fourteen-hour day. Lucky me, I get to wake up tomorrow and do it all over again.

THE NEXT MORNING, I sit at my desk, waiting for first period to begin, bracing for the moment the roster chair knocks on the door to hand me a coverage slip. It takes an act of God not to receive one these days. I've covered a class every day since I returned from my day off. It's been over twenty days in a row now. One day, almost thirty staff members called out.

When the lunch ladies don't want to come to work, you know we have a problem. Word must've spread among the substitutes about the state of affairs at our school because they're avoiding us like the plague, which means the honor falls to those of us brave enough to show up. I'm covering so many classes that I rarely make it to McCaffrey's anymore. I hear a knock on the door and tense up.

When I lift my head to see who it is, I'm relieved to find it's Armani Escarra. I open the door.

"Good morning, Armani."

"Good morning, Mr. C. Can I talk with you, please?"

"Sure. What's up?"

"I want to apologize for my behavior. I will stay in class from now on."

"Cool. I accept your apology. Look, I'm not mad at you. I just want you to do better."

Her mouth says, "I will," but her facial expression is saying, *I'm ready to bawl my eyes out.*

"What's up? Why are you looking so sad?"

"Because you got my phone taken away."

"Me!"

"Yeah, you! You snitched! And my mom said I'm not getting anything for my birthday in two weeks."

"And it's my fault?"

"Yeah!"

"That's malarkey." We share a chuckle.

"Sike! I ain't mad at you, Mr. C., because you're the only teacher that cares enough to call."

"I appreciate you saying that. I do care. And I'm willing to do whatever it takes to help you succeed, even if it means snitching. But I'll make a deal with you. Over the next two weeks, if you show up to class on time, complete your work, and stop walking out without asking, I will call your mom and tell her I have seen improvements in your behavior. Deal?"

"Deal!"

We shake hands to make it official.

"Now, don't play with me, because you know I have your mom's and Aunt Sophia's numbers."

"I know. Aunt Fi called and cussed me out last night! Her daughter is my cousin and bestie, so I'm always over their house."

"That's what's up. It's a small world. I'll probably run into your aunt tonight; if I do, I'll tell her we talked."

"Okay, cool. All right, Mr. C., I'll see you later."

"Bet. Peace, Armani."

I close the door and walk back to my desk. Before I reach it, I hear another knock at the door. I turn around expecting Armani; instead, it's the roster chair. My heart sinks.

"Good morning, Mr. C. Here's your coverage slip. Don't look so excited, bro."

I want to tell him to take his sarcasm and shove it.

Instead, I reply, "Okay, then close the door so I can appreciate my last three minutes of solitude."

In the silence, I reflect on my conversations with the Escarra ladies. Frankly, I'm surprised by the quick response. I'm kicking myself for not calling sooner. I probably wouldn't have called at all had I not met Aunt Fi at the airport. During lunch, I go on a parent-calling spree. Of course, half of the numbers are incorrect. *Good grief!* How can you have four numbers on file, and they're all wrong? It's all good though. At least I tried. Once you've given your best, there's nothing left to give.

You Got Got!

———

"WE HAVE TEN MINUTES BEFORE THE TEST begins. Use this time to review, and no talking."

I get the usual mix of subtle nods and blank stares.

"Is the test open-book, Mr. C.?"

"Nope."

"Multiple choice?"

"No."

"How many retakes do we get?"

"How about you review the definitions and stop talking."

"Aight. Aight. I gotchu. I gotchu."

You can cut the tension in the room with a knife. The stress is written all over my students' faces. Well, the half that bothered to show up. The others think they're slick, skipping class right when we're testing. But it's all good—I'll catch them next time. They can't skip forever.

"Okay, time's up. All desks cleared. All you need is a pencil."

"Mr. C., can I borrow a pencil?"

"Trade me something."

"I ain't got nothing."

"Well, you won't have a pencil either." He looks at me like a deer in headlights.

"Give me a sneaker."

"Yoooo!"

"You drawlin', Mr. C., nobody wants to smell his feet," says another student.

"I'll give you my charger."

"Cool. You know the routine."

My teaching coach instructed me to devise a three-step procedure for everything. To get a pencil, students place an item of value in one basket, take a pencil from the other, and return it when they're done. It works like a charm, except when they forget things, but they're improving.

"Does anybody else need a pencil?"

Students swap phones, book bags, and bus cards. Keeping track of it all can be a pain, but I refuse to spend another dime on pencils. A few stragglers trickle into the room.

"What's up, Mr. C.?"

"I'm chillin'. What's up with y'all?"

"We good."

"Y'all late too. Have a seat. We're about to take the test."

"I got time to look at my definitions?"

"No. You missed that opportunity ten minutes ago. I want everybody to spread out. There should be at least one desk in between each student. I shouldn't hear any talking. Don't turn your papers over until I tell you."

"Mr. C., can I listen to music?"

"No."

"But I concentrate better with music."

"I said no."

"Gotchu."

"Does everybody have something to write with? Great, you can get started."

I sit at the front of the classroom, eyeing them like a hawk. If a student looks up, I meet their gaze—a silent warning: don't even think about it. Kids are sneaky, so you have to be one step ahead of them. Occasionally, I walk around the classroom to see how they're doing.

I notice a lot of papers without names, so I say, "Everybody double-check that your name is on the test." If I got a dollar for every time I received a paper without a name, I could pay off my student loans.

"Mr. C., I'm finished."

"I'm done too."

"Are y'all sure? It's only been fifteen minutes. Always check your answers before turning in your test. We still have a lot of time left."

"I'm confident."

"Me too."

"Cool beans."

"Can you mark it now?"

"Sure," I say. I sit at my desk, pull out my trusty red pen, and score the test in seconds.

"Good job, Ladasia. You got a seventy."

"A seventy? Let me see. Ah, man. I'm mad. Are you giving a retest?"

"Take it easy. You got a C. That's not bad."

"Yes, it is. My goal was at least a B. You should give a retake."

"Let me see how everyone else does first."

"Mr. C., can you mark mine?"

"Just give me one second. I shouldn't hear any talking if you're not finished."

"I'm done. Mr. C."

"Me too."

The students begin handing in their papers. With most of them finished, I return to my desk to continue marking the tests. I switch to answer key B.

"Good job, Ciani! You got an eighty."

"Ahh, thank you. What do you want us to do now?"

I didn't anticipate students finishing so quickly. I have no plans for the second half of class. I'm guessing their brains are fried now anyway, so I tell the ladies they can relax. I'm disappointed my overachievers didn't perform better. I was confident Ladasia would ace the exam, but not every student is a strong test-taker. If my most responsible student received a C, that doesn't bode well for the others.

Maybe I should've given them multiple-choice questions instead of asking them to match words to definitions. Who knows? I'm still waiting for three students to finish. I check to see how they're doing.

"Dayquan, what's good? There's nothing on the paper."

"Man, I don't know this stuff."

"You can at least try."

"I already know I'm gonna fail."

"Listen, little brother—like the great Wayne Gretzky once said, 'You miss one hundred percent of the shots you don't take.' So, I want you to try."

"All right, Mr. C. Say less."

Two students hand in their tests.

"What do you want us to do now?"

"Check with me for missing work. If you're all caught up, you can chill for the rest of class."

A few students come strolling in with zero pep in their step.

"Sup, Mr. C."

"I'm chillin'. How y'all feeling?"

"We cool."

"We've got a test, so I need y'all up front. Ladasia and Ciani, switch to the back, please."

"We gotchu."

"What's up, Kyree? I haven't seen you since I met your Aunt Fi at the airport."

"Yeah, my mom told me."

"Keep the noise down. Remember, there are still students testing."

I should have known that once one student started chilling, the others would follow. It's all good—they've earned a breather. The idea that students should work like robots from bell to bell is preposterous, so I let the make-up work slide and start grading. The results? Disappointing.

Only five students pass, and two of those grades are Ds. I don't know where I dropped the ball, but there's a disconnect between what I think I'm teaching and what the students are actually learning. The latecomers hand me their tests. They finish in no time, which surprises me. I mark them immediately. Two performed as expected, but somehow Kyree pulls a perfect score.

I'm pretty sure he cheated—he's hardly ever here. How I didn't spot it is beyond me. These kids are too slick, but I can't judge—I've been there before. I wish I could celebrate the improbable victory, but my intuition won't let me. Instead, my mood sinks, right alongside the average test results.

Several students didn't get one question right. I know they shoulder some of the responsibility, but I can't shake the feeling that I'm to blame. The test feels like an indictment of my teaching ability. For a second, I thought I had cracked the code, but these results prove otherwise. I call Kyree to congratulate him on his "perfect score."

"Come here, Kah."

"What's up, Mr. C.?"

"Congratulations! You got a hundred."

"Word! You lying? Let me see."

I slide the test across the desk, and he snatches it like a winning lottery ticket. Suddenly, he breaks into a happy dance, hamming it up way too much. Now I'm 100 percent certain he cheated, but I still say, "Good job, Kyree."

"Thanks, Mr. C."

"No doubt." Hey, you gotta fake it till you make it, right?

I could see Ladasia and Ciani hanging on to every word. The expressions on their faces say, *That's bull schnitzel.* The day is winding down quickly. I need to enter the results into the system. The deadline to submit interim grades is next week, so I'll stay behind to knock that out. The more I complete here, the less I have to do when I'm not. With just five minutes left, the class is still a mess.

"Let me get everybody's attention. We're not leaving until the desks are straight and the floors are clean."

I place the tests in the top drawer and stand in the doorway to let them know I mean business. I've had it up to heaven cleaning up after them, and there's still a chip bag and crumbs scattered on the floor.

Aniyah screams out, "Pick it up, Saquon! You were the one eating them!"

"Nah, I gave them to DeVonta."

Well, somebody better do it because it's not the janitor's job or mine to clean up after y'all. Jalen finally picks up the bag. Ladasia, like clockwork, grabs the broom and starts tidying up. Finally, the bell rings, setting the captives free.

I lock the door and walk with the students down the stairs. Normally, I'd stay inside to avoid the chaos of dismissal, but everything changed after the accident a few weeks ago. Now, each step toward the doors carries a weight I can't shake, a constant reminder of what happened, pressing down like the heavy autumn air around us.

What began as innocent fun ended in tragedy. Two students were playfully chasing each other when one turned into the street without looking. In an instant, he was struck and killed by a cargo van. Even worse, it happened just after dismissal, and many students witnessed it, leaving the entire community shaken.

Parents send their children to school expecting them to be safe, only for something like this to happen. It's devastating. But amid the heartbreak, my students' resilience has been nothing short of remarkable. Through open dialogue, we built a space for healing, which helped all of us to move forward. Reflecting on it all, one thing becomes clear: the staff at Columbia failed that precious boy and his parents by not maintaining a safe, orderly environment.

As one of those staff members, I can't help but feel some responsibility. Parents should never have to worry about their children's safety while they're at school. But that's the sad reality in the United States today. Since the tragedy, I've made it a point to go outside daily. I replay that day over and over, wishing I could have done more to support and prevent such a huge loss.

But I can't rewrite the past. Some things are beyond my control. It's better to focus on what I can change, like making better decisions moving forward. These days, the dismissal's cray, but not cray-cray like it was at the start of the year. Students skedaddle in no time with a little friendly cajoling. Once the coast is clear, I head upstairs to finish marking tests and entering grades. If I manage to complete everything, I might actually have a weekend free of schoolwork, which would be a miracle.

I insert my key and feel the knob turn. I twist it, only to discover that the door is already open. That's strange—I definitely locked it. A sense of unease creeps in as I rush to my desk, heart pounding, each step amplifying my anxiety. When I spot my computer sitting untouched, a wave of relief washes over me. For a moment, I think everything's okay. But when I open the top drawer to grab the tests, my relief crumbles— the drawer is empty. I check the other drawers, just in case. Nothing.

I check the top drawer again. Still nothing. Then it hits me like a gut punch—I've been violated. One of these little mofos broke into my classroom and stole all the frigging tests. My stomach flips. I grip the edge of the desk, trying to steady myself.

It's not just the tests—it's the nerve, the breach, the boldness. It feels like somebody broke into my home. I sit there, frozen, trying to make sense of it all.

On Monday, I wait for most students to arrive, then tell them we're retaking the test.

"What?" says one student.

"Why?" says another.

I wait for all the ruckus to calm down.

"As I'm sure some of you know," I say, "somebody broke into our classroom and stole the tests."

"For real, Mr. C.? You lying."

"I wish I were, but I'm not."

"So, we're going to retake it today."

"That's not fair! We didn't steal the test. Why do we have to suffer?"

"Well, that's life. Desks cleared—now."

I know this is ridiculous, and most students won't do well. However, I want to prevent the sticky-fingered student from pulling this shenanigan again. Of course, the results are practically the same, with one exception. Kyree, who received 100 on the first test, does horribly on the second.

He asks me, "Mr. C., how did I do?"

"How do you think you did, given you got a hundred on the first test?"

"I think I got another hundred."

"Seriously? You must've studied a lot, huh?"

"I did."

"How did you study?"

"Huh? I looked at the words."

"Okay. Well, I'm sorry to tell you, but you got a twenty."

"You lyin'?! Let me see."

I show him the test. He's completely stunned. "I don't get it. These are the same answers from the last test. That's that bullshit, man!"

I give him the look.

"I'm sorry, Mr. C., but you know I got a hundred on the first test. You should count that jawn! Ain't my fault you got got!"

"You can thank one of your classmates for that. And you probably know who did it."

"Yooo! No, I don't—that's cap! I don't know anything."

"Then why are you laughing?"

"All right, I do know who did it, but I ain't no rat."

"Since no one's talking, we all have to pay the price."

What Kyree didn't know is that I had created two versions of the test. All his answers were correct—just not for the exam he took. I'm still surprised at how far students will go just to avoid failing. Ironically, it shows me that they care and are concerned about their grades. I only wish they could channel that energy into something more constructive—like studying. With all the tests in hand, it's time to get back on my soapbox and deliver a reality check.

"Listen up! I can't stress enough how disappointed I am that someone—maybe one of you—would break into this classroom and steal those tests. It was only our first test. I knew many of you would struggle, and that's okay. As long as you're trying and putting your best foot forward, you will never have to worry about failing my class. But lying, cheating, and stealing? I will not tolerate.

"Now I don't even feel safe leaving my stuff in here. And I shouldn't have to feel that way. So, whoever stole those tests didn't just disrespect me; they disrespected all of us. And it's not cool. Whoever you are, you better chalk that behavior ASAP, and if it's your homie, you can tell them I said it.

"At the end of the day, your character matters more to me than your grades. This test? It won't matter in the long run. But your character and your habits? Oh, those matter. So make sure the choices you make today match who you want to be tomorrow—because trust me, you'll be adults before you know it."

I let my words marinate for a few seconds. In the silence, I remember one of my favorite quotes. I tell the class I want to share it with them. I write it in big blue letters on the dry-erase board:

Watch your thoughts; they become words.
Watch your words; they become actions.
Watch your actions; they become habits.
Watch your habits; they become character.
Watch your character; it becomes your destiny.

"Think about that for a second. Again, it's bigger than biology. The choices you make today lay the foundation for your tomorrow—choose wisely. All right. That's enough of that. Let's keep it pushing. By a show of hands, how many students studied for the test?"

Only Ladasia raises her hand. This doesn't surprise me.

"How did you study, Ladasia?"

"I just read the definition on the crossword puzzle."

"Gotchu. Did you have someone test you?"

"No."

Suddenly, I realize it's not that the students couldn't pass the test; the issue is no one ever taught them how. I told them to study, assuming everyone knew what that meant. Unfortunately, I was wrong. I was suffering from what's known as the curse of knowledge.

The curse of knowledge occurs when someone who understands a concept struggles to communicate or explain it to someone with limited or no knowledge. It happens because we forget what it's like not to know and mistakenly assume others share our level of understanding.

I began studying in elementary school, so I automatically assumed my students had similar opportunities. But now, I realize they haven't. I never saw studying as a skill that needed to be taught, but it's clear to me that I need to break it down for them. I can't ask them to hit a home run without providing the bat, ball, and techniques to do it. To do otherwise is to set them up for failure.

"Okay, thanks for the feedback, Ladasia. I know many of you asked for a retake, but it doesn't make sense now."

"Ahh, man. Why, Mr. C.? You said we could."

"No, I said I would consider it, but hold on a second. Instead of giving a retest, I will drop the lowest test grade from this quarter. So, you still have a chance to turn things around. The responsibility is yours. I can give you the tools, but it's up to all of you to use them. How many of you still have the worksheets from this chapter?"

"What worksheets?"

"The crossword, word scramble, fill-in-the-blank, and word search." Only five students raise their hands.

"You never returned my worksheets, Mr. C."

"For real?"

I reach my desk, flip open a folder, and there they are—graded worksheets I forgot to hand back. Annoying? Absolutely. But I won't dwell on it. Mistakes happen, and while they may be frustrating, they don't define me; they refine me. With a growth mindset, setbacks are simply lessons in disguise. And today's lessons are clear: Teach study skills, return assignments on time, and remember—growth isn't always linear, but it's always worth it.

Chapter 10

Travelerapy: Goa Edition

———

THE LUNCH BELL RINGS. THE EIGHTH GRADERS BUST out of the cafeteria like it's the last day of school. The energy in the building has been bonkers all day. We are days away from winter break, but the students are already there mentally. Sadly, we lost another teacher yesterday. He was placed on leave after defending himself against a student's attack.

To make matters worse, instead of helping the poor soul, several students pulled out their phones to record the event. What should have been a moment of compassion turned into voyeurism. It's heartbreaking that we live in a time where capturing someone's misery takes precedence over offering a helping hand.

I've tried explaining that not all attention is good attention, but the allure of viral fame is still too intoxicating, even with a snowball's chance in hell of it ever happening. I race up the stairs, but the eighth graders barrel after me like bulls in Pamplona, their wild energy a stark contrast to the weight of what's unfolding around us.

When I reach the second level, I bump into one of my students, Aaron.

"What's up, Mr. Connelly?"

"I'm chillin'. What's up with you, Aaron?"

"I'm good. What we doing today?"

"We're going to watch a video, then discuss it afterward. And you'll answer some questions."

"Oh, okay, cool. So, we're not doing a Kahoot! today?"

"Come on. You already know. We do Kahoot! every day unless we have a test."

"Say no more."

As we climb the stairs, I think about how much Kahoot! has transformed my classroom. It's an online quiz game where students compete in real time, answering multiple-choice questions for points. What used to be a "Do Now" with varying levels of participation has turned into daily Kahoot! sessions, where nearly every student participates. The best part? The students don't even realize how much they're learning because they're too busy having fun. I've seen a huge boost in enthusiasm and test scores. By the time we reach the top of the stairs, I'm already imagining the excitement that'll fill the room when the game starts.

Students can play solo or team up with classmates, as long as they have a smartphone or computer. Thank God I finally scored some laptops last week. After so many teachers quit, the math and science lead, Mrs. Mayfield, was forced to pick up an extra class, and she'll be using my room for the honors. It turns out, when she suggested I use outdated magazines to "keep the students busy" at the start of the year, she was secretly hoarding brand-new laptops for the one class she taught.

At first, she would take the computers with her after each class— until I pleaded with her to leave the cart behind. It's a shame I had to ask, but I'm not too proud to beg. Computers aren't a panacea for educational inequities, but when used thoughtfully, they can support learning in powerful ways. The verdict is still out on whether they're more of a blessing or a curse.

But I will tell you one thing: some resources are better than none. After playing Kahoot!, I confiscate the computers. The students know they can only get them back once all their work is done. Surprisingly, this tactic works like a charm, motivating students who wouldn't even pick up a pencil before—well, that and all the candy I shower them with.

At first, I made it rain Snickers, Starburst, Reese's Cups, Mr. Goodbars, Almond Joys, and Skittles—but I realized they were a dental disaster, so now I stick to Jolly Ranchers. Some students don't care for candy, so I also offer stickers, coloring books, and school supplies.

As we exit the stairwell, I try to locate my keys while Aaron talks incessantly.

"Mr. C., do you watch anime?"

"Nah. That's your thing?"

"Yeah, I draw characters too. Check out this Naruto I drew in first period."

"Let's wait until we get settled in class."

"No doubt."

We round the bend in the hallway, me on the left by the doors and Aaron on the right near the windows. He chatters nonstop as I dig through my pockets for my keys. Finally, I find them and glance at him to show I'm listening.

The second he takes a breath, I rotate my torso, glance ahead—and then, *bang!*

A student flings the door open, catching me completely off guard. My head collides with the unforgiving edge, pain shooting through my skull as my eyebrow splits open. Stars flash in my vision, warm blood running down my face. For a moment, all I can do is stand there, stunned, the hallway spinning around me.

"Oh, my god, Mr. C.! Are you okay?"

"I'm cool. Calm down. Does it look bad?"

"Yeah! You leaking!"

"All right, no worries."

We make it to the classroom, my head still throbbing with every step. Inside, I grab a few Kleenexes from my desk to stanch the bleeding. There's so much blood that after a minute, I have to ditch the flimsy tissue for the sturdier brown paper towels. I'm guessing I'll need stitches. As I pack my things, the other students start arriving, and the moment they see the blood, they start freaking out.

"OMG!"

"What happened, Mr. C.? Are you okay?"

"Please, have a seat, y'all. I'm cool, but I have to go to the hospital. I'll get someone to cover the class. Just chill for a second."

I call the office. The assistant principal picks up the phone. I guess the secretary needed a break too.

"Good afternoon, Principal Montgomery."

"Hey, Mr. C.! How are you?"

"I could be better. I need someone to cover my class. I had an accident."

"I'm sorry, Mr. C. Unfortunately, we don't have anybody to cover right now. We're severely understaffed today." *What else is new?*

I take a deep breath to compose myself.

Finally, I respond, "My head is bleeding and I need to go to the hospital, so please send someone ASAP."

Amanda, from the City Year office next door, hears everything and offers to watch my class until someone arrives.

"Thanks, Amanda. I appreciate it."

"No worries, Mr. C. Take care of yourself!"

"No doubt. Peace, everyone, and enjoy your break."

"Break!? You're not coming back tomorrow, Mr. C.?"

"It's three days until winter break. It might take me that long to get my stitches out, so at the very least, I'll be back after the break."

"Ahh, man! I'ma miss you, Mr. C."

"I'm going to miss y'all too. Y'all better be good. See y'all when I get back. And don't let anybody destroy our classroom. All right, I gotta go. Peace, everybody."

The students look devastated, like I'm leaving for good. I do dream of joining the FIRE movement someday, but that's not in the cards right now. Still, it looks like fate's giving me some extra time off—I could really use a break. I exit the classroom and head toward the office, passing a few students from my other classes along the way.

"Mr. C., what happened? Somebody knocked you out?"

"You got jokes."

"Let me see it."

I take the blood-soaked towel away from my eyebrow and hear a collective "Ew" from the students. Then, I walk inside the teachers' lounge to check it out myself. The blood makes it look worse than it is, but it's still a pretty nasty gash. Wow, this place has literally cost me blood, sweat, and tears. Now I have the honor of having it etched into my face forever. *Awesome sauce.*

As I enter the office, the assistant principal quickly apologizes, realizing the gravity of the situation. She gives me the address for Accord Hospital, which is about fifteen minutes away by car.

"You don't have to go there if you don't want to. Here's the number for workers' compensation too. You take as much time as you need. All your days are covered, so you don't have to worry about using your sick days."

Please don't encourage me.

I walk out of the building feeling pissed that I probably have to get stitches but relieved that my winter break is beginning earlier. It's a shame it had to start this way, but everything happens for a reason.

At the doctor's office, I sign in at the glass window. The office is empty, so I'm assisted immediately.

"Ew, somebody had a boo-boo. What happened?"

"I'm embarrassed to say, but I walked into a door. I wish I had a more exciting tale, but that's all I got."

"Okay, we'll get you all cleaned up."

"Thank you."

"We've been getting a lot of activity from your school lately. What's going on there?"

I think, *Where do I even begin?* Before I can utter a word, I break, and the tears start flowing like a waterfall, unleashing a torrent of emotions I can no longer contain.

"Why? Why? Why does it have to be so hard?"

All the trials and tribulations culminate in this moment. It takes me a couple of minutes to compose myself. The receptionist hands me some tissues. I apologize to her for losing it.

"No, baby. I understand. Teaching is a labor of love. My hat's off to you because I couldn't do it."

The receptionist directs me to another part of the building, where I'll receive my stitches. The hospital has seen better days. The place feels more like an asylum than a hospital, but I can't risk waiting to see a doctor. I don't want the cut to get infected. Minutes later, the nurse calls my name. She asks me to follow her into the examination room, where she weighs me and takes my vitals.

"Okay, sit tight, and the doctor will see you shortly."

Before long, a demure lady walks into the room.

"Good afternoon, sir."

"Good afternoon."

"We had a long day, huh?"

"That's putting it mildly."

"Well, I'll get you all stitched up and on your way, but first, we need to numb you up."

"Okay. I figured I would need stitches."

"Yeah, the gash is too deep. You want it to heal nicely to minimize scarring. Don't worry. I'll take care of you."

"All right. Don't jack up my stitches. I'll have to wear this scar for life."

"No worries."

As she approaches, I read her badge and notice she's only a resident. Am I just practice? I don't know, but I don't have the energy to argue, so I shut up, close my eyes, and flinch as I feel the needle slowly inserted above my brow.

"I'll return in about ten minutes."

"Okay, thanks."

I begin tapping my head to see if I have any sensation. The anesthetic kicks in almost immediately, and the sharp sting fades into a comforting numbness. I'm still dreading stitches, but what other choice do I have? My heart drops when I hear the door open.

The resident wastes no time: "You should be good now." She takes the needle out of the packaging and gets everything set up. "Are you ready, sir?"

"Well, as ready as I'll ever be."

"Okay, this shouldn't take too long. Just let me know if you feel anything."

Fortunately, the job takes less than five minutes.

"Do you think the scar will be noticeable?"

"No, I don't think so. Just make sure you take care of it."

"All right, thanks for your help."

"That's what we're here for."

When I get back to my car, I remove part of the bandage to check out my stitches. They don't look half bad. I'll have to return Friday to get them out, so I won't be required to return to school until after the break. With so much time off, I can take a proper vacation. At this point, traveling isn't a luxury—it's *Travelerapy*. The only question is where should I go.

It'll be New Year's Eve, so I have to find somewhere special to celebrate. Last year, I rang it in dressed in all white, standing on Copacabana Beach in Rio de Janeiro. That'll be hard to top, but I'm down to try. When I arrive home, I dive into planning. I hop online and start googling the best places in the world to celebrate New Year's Eve. The first link catches my eye, so I click it without hesitation.

Naturally, New York tops the list, but I've already checked off the Times Square ball drop during my NYU days. Sydney, Cape Town, and Las Vegas? Been there, done that. Now, number five: Goa, India. Bingo! India has been on my radar since I started practicing yoga and exploring Buddhism, but reading Elizabeth Gilbert's *Eat Pray Love* kicked that desire into overdrive. This might be the perfect opportunity. I hope I can get a visa in time. After a quick check on the Indian embassy's website, I find an expedited electronic visa option. I apply immediately.

DAYS LATER, I step off the plane at Goa International Airport. Warm, humid air envelops me like a blanket, a welcome contrast to Philly's icy chill. The sun melts away the last traces of winter as I make my way through the bustling terminal and out to a waiting taxi. The ride to Wonderland Hostel is a blur of winding roads and glimpses of palm-fringed beaches. When we pull up, I take in the open layout, outdoor kitchen, and bohemian décor. Not bad. For once, a place actually looks like it does on the internet.

From the moment I walk in, I feel right at home. Some hostelers lounge in hammocks, while others flow through yoga poses—each under the lingering spell of hippies from yesteryear. This is my tribe. I love the backpacking community. It's the most interesting, free-spirited group of people I've ever met, and it doesn't take long before we're swapping stories and laughing like old friends. That's the beauty of this life: in no time, strangers become family, moments become memories, and memories become stories you carry forever.

It's proof that home isn't just a place. It's the people who shape our journey. I'm grateful for the soul family I find abroad, a connection that often feels elusive back home. Tonight, the air buzzes with excitement as we gather beneath the starlit Goan sky, preparing to head to Hilltop for the island's biggest rave to ring in the New Year.

Coincidentally, the area where I grew up in West Philly is also called Hilltop, which adds to the feeling that I'm meant to be here. My squad includes Anna from England, Maria and Lydia from Spain, Tiago and Alicia from Portugal, Shabeeb and Rajesh from India, and Benny from Israel. Our crew reflects the eccentric spirit of the rave.

As we arrive, trance music thumps from the packed parking lot. Stepping out of the taxi, a local offers me a wristband for $30—less than a third of what I paid for mine. I feel a twinge of regret but remind myself: will the extra money matter five years from now? No. So why stress about it now?

My heartbeat syncs with the pulsing bass line as we near the entrance. Inside, the dance floor greets us—an explosion of neon lights, laser beams, and psychedelic visuals. The crowd is a mix of locals and travelers wearing everything from kurtas to body paint.

As the year winds down, the air thickens with anticipation. With ten seconds to go, the crowd unites in perfect harmony as our voices rise in unison.

"Three, Two, One . . . Happy New Year!"

The clock strikes midnight, and the sky erupts in fireworks. My crew and I exchange hugs with each other and strangers alike, embracing the birth of the new year. Cheers and laughter fill the air, sending the party into overdrive.

The energy surges with music, dancing, and camaraderie, carrying us into the early morning. As the first light spills across the horizon, a deep sense of gratitude washes over me for this unforgettable evening with kindred spirits united by rhythm and revelry. I take one last glance at the glowing sky, savoring the night's magic before it fades. With joy still humming in my chest, I leave Hilltop, carrying memories that will bloom forever in the garden of my heart.

See exclusive pictures and moments from this chapter here:

TariqueConnelly.com/Goa

Chapter 11

System Asininity

———

THE SCHOOL DOORS CLOSE BEHIND ME BUT THE whispers of the Arabian Sea still stir in my soul. The exhaustion has lifted, replaced by a quiet, steady energy. Even the air feels lighter, mirroring the lightness in my body. Hope fills me as I look forward, excited for the new beginning.

I walk toward my classroom, soaking in the solitude. It's a welcome change from my last stroll down this corridor, when I learned doors don't respect personal space. This time, no unexpected collisions—just the quiet relief of finding my classroom intact with no broken furniture, ripped posters, or expletives marring the board. Nice. I settle in, set my bag down, and take in the last moments of stillness.

The bell rings, and in an instant, the floodgates open—kids spill into the hallway, their laughter and chatter surging through the air. A few students rush in, their faces lighting up the moment they see me.

"Hey, Mr. C.! Welcome back!"

I smile. "Sup, Ladasia! Sup, Ciani! Sup, Steve!"

"OMG! We thought you quit! We missed you!"

"I missed y'all too!"

Ciani narrows her eyes playfully. "Stop lying, Mr. C., you did not miss us."

"I'm serious. I did miss y'all."

"Where were you?"

"I went to India and Qatar."

"For real? Where's Qatar?" says Steve.

"It's in the Middle East, near Dubai and Saudi Arabia."

He grins. "Wow! I want to travel one day."

"You will. Trust me, it's the best education. If you could go anywhere, where would you go?"

He taps his chin. "I don't know. Let me think about that for a second . . . Jamaica. I would go to Jamaica."

"I want to go to Miami," says Ciani.

"What about you, Ladasia?"

She shrugs. "Maybe, like, Japan."

"That's what's up. And y'all will! Was everyone good while I was gone?"

"Yeah, we were chillin'."

I glance around. "The class doesn't look like a tornado blew through it, which is great. What happened to the computers?"

"Mrs. Mayfield took the cart," Steve replies.

"It's all love. We'll work it out."

It feels great to be back. The students probably thought splitting my head open was the last straw, but I promised I'd be there to watch them graduate in June, and I meant it. These days, their energy feels a lot more laid back. Maybe they're feeding off my Indian vibe, or maybe they're afraid I'll quit if they cut up again. Whatever the reason, they've been on their best behavior. It's like I'm teaching an entirely different class.

I should be happy they no longer sprint around the room, curse like sailors, and record TikTok videos like it's their job. Yet, somehow, I miss the chaos. The ninety minutes move like molasses now. It's like the whole class is tranquilized.

I even ask them sometimes, "Why are y'all so quiet?"

"We're just chillin', Mr. C."

"Gotchu."

The bell rings, and I trail behind the students, bracing myself for the madness of the hallway.

As I make my way to Mrs. McCaffrey's class, I run into my buddy Ms. Kennedy. She's about thirty years old, stands about five-ten, and likes to wear heels, making her tower over me like a supermodel in stilettos.

"Good morning, Ms. Kennedy."

"Hey, Mr. C.," she responds in her sultry alto.

"How are you feeling today?"

"I'm stressed!"

"What's up?"

"I'm running out of time. I have to pass this damn Praxis, or I'll be looking for a new job next year."

"What's stopping you?"

"I can never find the time to study. How can I when I'm always here? Even when I'm not here physically, I'm still here mentally."

"Facts. I thought you had to pass the Praxis before you could teach."

"No, the district gives you three years but allows you to teach on an emergency permit."

"Word?"

"Yeah. The only thing you need is a bachelor's degree."

"Gotchu. How many classes have you completed?"

"None. I don't have the time! It's impossible! And I still have to care for my son while working my side hustle."

"Sis, you are grinding."

"I have to. I'm a single mom."

"I salute you, queen."

"Thanks. I appreciate it. Let me get this class started. Later, Mr. C."

"Peace, Ms. Kennedy. And good luck studying for that test."

It's a minute before the bell rings. I hurry to make it to McCaffrey's class on time. Once the independent work begins, I disappear to the back to check my emails. The principal finally released the new schedule for the third quarter. The second-semester schedule came with the surprise of an additional class.

Of course, it was the most challenging class in the building. Never mind; I'm still brand new and winging it. I start thinking about my conversation with Ms. Kennedy and wonder how many other teachers are out there on emergency permits, masquerading as real educators with no training. The problem is more widespread than I thought.

It's no wonder students are struggling—we're just glorified babysitters. But if not us, then who? Someone has to replace all the baby boomers retiring. It's just a shame that the bar is set so low—*do you have a pulse? You're hired!*

The decline in teacher quality is a symptom of a much larger issue: our education system, once the great equalizer, now perpetuates inequality by underfunding schools and pairing teachers with the lowest qualifications with students who have the greatest need.

This is why the American Dream is fading, reduced to little more than a fantasy for so many. Without a solid educational foundation, particularly for the most vulnerable, upward mobility becomes an illusion, not a real possibility.

The prosperity the US enjoyed after WWII is slowing, and the education system, once a key driver of that success, now reflects this decline. Whether it's life expectancy, quality of life, or maternal mortality rates—where we consistently rank lower than other affluent nations—it's clear that the cracks in our societal foundation are deepening. Education may not be the root cause of these issues, but it certainly plays a role in widening them.

At the heart of this challenge is the shortage of qualified teachers. Without enough skilled educators, students miss the chance to develop critical thinking and life skills essential for shaping their future. This isn't just about education—it's about their ability to live purposeful, fulfilling lives. Nine out of ten kids in the US attend public schools, so the fate of our schools is the fate of our nation. And when students' opportunities are limited, so is the country's potential.

Despite the weight of it all, it would be so easy to coast through the day, doing the bare minimum. No one would notice. Thank God for intrinsic motivation. The only reward I get is more work, but it's all good because my students are worth it.

I click on the link for the new schedule and find my name. My sixth- and seventh-grade classes have changed, as expected. Everything looks fine until I reach my last two periods, where my eighth-grade class should be. Instead, I see "school use," which means I'll be the designated substitute for those periods. That's ridiculous.

I keep scanning the schedule and notice that my class has been assigned to Mr. Tanaka, the teacher who was on leave after a student attacked him. I immediately shut my laptop, tell Mrs. McCaffrey I'll be right back, and speed-walk to the principal's office.

My heart is beating through my chest. This has to be a mistake. Surely, the principal wouldn't take the students away from me after all the hard work I've put in. I walk into the main office and ask if I can see the principal. The secretary rings her, gets the okay, and says I can let myself in.

"Good afternoon, Mr. Connelly. How can I help you?"

"I noticed I'm no longer teaching the eighth graders. Please tell me that's a mistake."

The principal shifts in her chair, gaze briefly darting away before meeting mine.

"No, that's the schedule for the third marking period."

"I can't believe this. You know how hard I've worked with them."

She exhales sharply. "It was a tough decision, but necessary. Because of the incident with Mr. Tanaka, he can no longer teach seventh grade."

"What does that have to do with us? Why are we being punished for something that happened in another grade?"

She rubs her neck. "Look, I understand your frustration. But this was the best solution we could come up with, given the circumstances."

I stare at the ceiling, anger knotting my thoughts. "But why now, with half of the year already gone? Once again, I'm being set up to fail."

Her gaze sharpens. "I'm sorry you feel that way, but we have to do what's in the best interests of our students."

"The students? This has nothing to do with them."

"Well, that's your opinion."

I lock eyes with her. "You know they won't take this well."

She shrugs. "Kids are resilient. They'll be all right."

I don't reply. I walk out, the door clicking shut behind me. My jaw clenches, hands balled into fists, frustration boiling over in my chest. Each step echoes in the silence, the weight of helplessness pressing heavier with each sound.

As I round the corner, something catches my eye. Through the half-open door, I spot my eighth graders in another classroom—laughing, chatting, unaware that our amazing journey together is coming to an end.

I knew I would have to break the bad news to them at some point. I didn't expect to have to do it now. I slowly enter the room. The students greet me enthusiastically, but my subdued response conveys that something is wrong. They have a substitute teacher babysitting them. I introduce myself and ask her if I can have the floor.

"Sure, it's all yours," she says.

"Everybody, have a seat."

I inhale deeply and then exhale audibly.

"I got some bad news." Tears well in my eyes and fall like gentle rain as the weight sinks heavy in my stomach. I take a deep breath, knowing there's no easy way to say this.

"Unfortunately, I'm no longer your science teacher."

"What!? Why? You're leaving, Mr. C.?"

"No, I'm not leaving. They've decided to switch the class to Mr. Tanaka."

"Man, that shit is ass. I'm cutting his class every day," responds Kyleem.

I give him the look.

"My bad."

I notice Ladasia wiping tears from her eyes, which makes me even sadder.

"Look, I want y'all to know how proud I am of all of you. Teaching is the hardest job I've had in my life, but watching y'all mature and make strides has made it all worthwhile. I was just thinking today about our class and how far we've come. Man, y'all used to get on my nerves. But once I improved and stepped my game up, y'all did too. And each day since has gotten better and better. Now, they want to throw salt in our game right when we're coasting.

"Real talk: y'all changed my life. Y'all helped me not only to become a better teacher but also a better man, and for that, I thank all of you. I don't have kids, so this is the closest I've come to experiencing parenthood. When I look at y'all, I don't see strangers—I see myself. I see my nieces and nephews, and I want the best for y'all just like I would for them. And I'm sad I can no longer be that for y'all."

Silence fills the air as the weight of the last line lingers. Then the most important lesson of the year commences.

"If you remember nothing else I've said this year, remember this: You're loved. You're special. And with hard work, you can achieve amazing things—even when the odds are against you. I'm living proof that it's not where you start, but where you finish. Don't ever forget that. I'm really going to miss y'all."

Suddenly, the door swings open, and every head snaps in that direction. The roster chair and one of his minions barge in, obliterating the vibe. The students can't stand him, and neither can I. How absurd that the school's biggest bully is a grown man, probably once a bullied child himself. Around here, he's the enforcer, ruling with an iron fist. He's probably come to make sure the students aren't running the substitute into the ground.

I wrap up my spiel by telling the students, "If you ever need me, you know where to find me. I'm sorry things turned out this way, but that's life. The only constant is change. All we can do is roll with it. All right, peace y'all."

I'll never forget the devastated looks on their faces. It was like the ground beneath them had suddenly shifted. I can't shake the feeling that I'm abandoning them, that I've let them down. Still, I have to accept that some battles can't be won. The system made it impossible to see this through, no matter how much I wanted to.

So, in the words of Reinhold Niebuhr, "God grant me the serenity to accept the things I cannot change, the courage to change the things I can, and the wisdom to know the difference."

The students always worried that I would leave them. I told them they had nothing to worry about, but I was wrong. I wasn't just their teacher; in many ways, I was a father figure. And now, it feels like I'm being torn away from my family, leaving behind a void I never realized I filled.

Since the switch, my students come to see me every day. They constantly complain that Mr. Tanaka can't teach, control the class, or speak proper English. Now that they know what it's like to learn and be challenged, they can never be bamboozled again.

Ladasia even started a petition that every student signed, demanding the principal reverse the decision. Sadly, it was to no avail. What's wild, though, is that I'm generally free during the two periods I used to teach, so my days often end around one o'clock.

With the extra time, I'm finally completing my school-related work at school. It feels amazing to create boundaries between my professional and personal life. The additional time allows me to find cooler assignments for my other classes. My seventh graders are performing experiments now. One day, while they were investigating, a few of my eighth graders walked in. They were livid.

"Mr. C., that's not fair! We never did any experiments."

"Well, it took me a whole semester to get y'all to sit down and stop running in and out."

"Facts."

"Now, get back to class."

"Can we just stay in here with you?"

"No."

"But we're not learning anything!"

"There's always an opportunity to learn something if your mind is open and your mouth is closed. Now, go back to class."

"Bye, Mr. C."

"Peace."

Days later, there's a knock on the door. It's Mr. Tanaka.

In utter despair, he asks me what my "secret sauce" is. I try to explain that it essentially boils down to building relationships with students. Most importantly, I engage them in the process. I always ask for their feedback and use the information to refine my approach. The most important lesson teachers can impart to students is how to become life-long learners. And the best way to do that is by modeling that mindset daily.

"Well, can you stop by and give me a hand sometimes?"

"Sure," I respond. *Yeah, right.*

A part of me is still seething about the principal's asinine decision. Sometimes, I peek into his class to witness the bedlam before napping in my car. It's not that I don't care, but I warned the principal that the students wouldn't take this well, and she told me to "kick rocks." Now, Mr. Tanaka has to tough it out. Besides, he only teaches two classes anyway.

WEEKS LATER, ONE OF MY FORMER STUDENTS, STEVE, runs into the class and says, "Mr. C., we're coming back! We're coming back!"

"What'choo talkin' 'bout, Willis?"

"Huh? No, seriously, you're going to be our teacher again."

"How do you know?"

"Because we made Mr. Tanaka quit."

"No way? Seriously?"

"Yup," he says, with a sense of pride scrolling across his face.

"That's ridiculous."

Leaving now means Mr. Tanaka will lose his summer pay and tenure with the school district. I can't believe it. How do the students know before I do?

Sure enough, the principal informs me that afternoon: the students are returning. I wish I could say, "I told you so," but I didn't anticipate them making the poor guy quit. A small part of me is flattered that the students missed me so much that they'd move heaven and earth to bring me back. But another part of me is livid that they caused another teacher to resign.

I'm also pissed because they should've never been taken from me in the first place. Now, what am I supposed to do a week before spring break? After the holiday, there are two weeks of testing, followed by Memorial Day and the start of graduation practice. The school year is basically over.

The students show up the first day, clearly ecstatic to be back home in my class, but I don't share their enthusiasm. I tell them how upset I am that they made Mr. Tanaka quit.

"I'm never going to celebrate y'all doing wrong. Wrong is wrong. Now, we're supposed to just pick up where we left off? It doesn't work like that. I've had no time to prepare, and we're about to be off for spring break. What y'all expect me to do? So, forget about it. We aren't doing anything. Y'all can relax. We'll pick it up after the break."

On one hand, I'm glad they're back; on the other, I miss my shorter schedule. But the only constant in life is change, so I have to flow with it. It takes me a day to get back on course. I just had to take a sledgehammer to my pity pot. The students insist Mr. Tanaka didn't teach them anything, so I pick up where we left off. With so little time left, I won't be able to cover the last quarter of the eighth-grade science standards.

Teaching all the material under normal circumstances would be challenging, but now it's impossible. Consequently, they won't know some of the material for the state science test. That's a bummer. Regardless, all I can do is my best. Once you've given your best, to hell with the rest.

Chapter 12

Crashing Graduation

——

G RADUATION DAY. I MADE IT. I TAKE A MOMENT TO reflect in my car. It's hard to believe how far I've come—how many times I thought I wouldn't make it, yet here I am. The Carl Jung High School parking lot buzzes with energy as families gather for the ceremony, balloons and flowers in hand, cell phones raised to capture the moment with their loved ones.

A wave of joy washes over me as I approach the finish line, ready to embrace the closure this moment brings. With just twenty minutes to go, I step out of my car and immediately spot a few of my students lingering outside, their faces lit with anticipation.

We chat for a moment, their excitement contagious as they proudly rattle off the high schools they're heading to. Just as I'm about to ask where another student's going, a colleague interrupts: "You must return to school immediately. The roster chair said you're not authorized to be here."

I knew he had something to do with this.

"Okay, cool. I'll be on my way." *Yeah, right.*

I sit in my car, waiting for the festivities to begin. There's no way I'm skipping this graduation. I wouldn't miss it for the world.

I just have to figure out how to crash it without a ticket. I see a group of late teachers entering the side of the building, so I flash my badge and join them. But instead of sitting in the front, I sit in the back and blend in with all the other family members—right where I'm supposed to be.

The time has finally come. The crowd's noise begins to fade as I watch, heart pounding in my chest. I've waited for this moment all year. And then, there they are—my students. They step onto the stage, their faces a mix of pride and disbelief. Tears fill my eyes. I rise to my feet, bearing the weight of the promise I made to them in my chest. I said I would be here, and they will feel my presence.

Most families scream when their kid's name is called. Well, I've got about thirty of them, so I start cheering louder than a tween at a Taylor Swift concert.

"Go, Ladasia! I see you, Steve! Do that, Ciani!"

I can feel people looking at me like I'm crazy. Even my students shoot me confused looks, like—*Why is Mr. C. in the audience? And why is he screaming like a madman?*

But none of them have the faintest idea what it took for me to stand here today. And while I rejoice in my students' achievement, I'm also celebrating my own hard-fought victory. The roster chair spots me screaming at the top of my lungs, and I see the annoyance flash across his face. Sure, I'm being loud and ghetto, but what can I say? I'm from the projects. It's in my blood.

With the last name called and my voice hoarse from all the cheering, I make my way to the exit, a deep sigh of relief escaping me. The hardest part is over, and the weight of the year lifts off my shoulders. Next year, I'll officially join the Teacher Residency and head to high school— where I truly belong. But for now, it's time to dust off this passport and indulge in one of the best perks of being a teacher: a well-deserved summer off. Believe me, we earn it.

I'm on a mission to challenge the status quo in our schools and shine a light on what really happens in the classroom. If this book has resonated with you, your review can help others discover this story and join the conversation.

Scan the QR code to post your review and sign up for my newsletter at **TariqueConnelly.com**. Together, we can raise awareness, spark change, and make a difference in education.

PART TWO

Chapter 13

Kicked Out for Showing Up

———

IT'S THE FIRST DAY OF SUMMER VACATION, AND ALL I crave is sleep. But Creamy, my furry alarm clock, is already yowling at 5 a.m. She's carrying on like I owe her rent—cursing me out in kitty. Where's a whisker whisperer when you need one? Cats are supposed to be chill, low-maintenance, and independent—not Creamy. She's a diva with my heart in the palm of her paw, and she knows it.

After chasing her away for the third time, I finally get out of bed to feed her. I couldn't sleep much anyway. Maybe it's the excitement of my first summer off, or perhaps it's the anxiety of not having a job lined up for next year. Go figure. As much as I want to start my American detox, I can't travel with peace of mind unless I have all my ducks in a row back home. So, today will be an administrative day in preparation for the next school year.

At nine o'clock, I call Keisha Jenkins, the hiring coordinator who set this whole experience in motion. We haven't talked much since I was hired—just when I've called to complain—but I'm sure she'll be glad I stuck it out.

"Good morning, Keisha! It's Tarique."

"Good morning, Tarique. How are you?"

"I'm well. Thanks. And you?"

"I'm okay. How can I help you?"

Huh? She knows exactly why I'm calling. But I play along anyway.

"I want to get the ball rolling on the Teacher Residency. Currently, I'm listed as a full-time employee, so my first concern is how I can get redesignated as a teacher resident?"

"Oh, Tarique, I'm so sorry. I thought you received the email about the changes to the residency."

"Changes? What changes?"

"Unfortunately, the new director isn't allowing teachers on emergency permits to become teacher residents."

"What? You've gotta be kidding me. Why?"

"Tarique, I had nothing to do with the decision. I'm just the bearer of the bad news."

"Well, it's a shame I had to call you to get it. This doesn't make any sense. I only worked at Columbia on an emergency permit because you asked me to. I thought I was doing y'all a favor. Bad enough I was lied to and told I'd be an assistant, then made a full-time teacher—now you're saying that somehow disqualifies me? That's absurd!"

"Look, Tarique, I get it. You've got every right to be upset. That said, Columbia would love to have you for another year if you're interested."

"Oh, so that's what this is about. You guys want to twist my arm so I'll stay at Columbia. Well, that's not happening. I'd quit before I ever set foot in that school again."

"Understood. That's your call."

"How am I supposed to earn my teaching credentials now?"

"Oh, no worries. There are plenty of schools with teacher certification programs."

"And who's paying for it?"

"That's your responsibility."

"Yeah, right. Not happening." There's a three-second silence. "I can't believe this. The district talks all this game about needing more teachers. Now, y'all are pushing me out the door."

"Well, Tarique, when we spoke throughout the year, you communicated to me in no uncertain terms that you were unhappy, so I assumed you would be making other plans."

"Yes, the year was tough, and there were days I wanted to walk away. But I'm not a quitter. I'm a man of my word—unlike the district, which clearly doesn't honor theirs."

"Look, Tarique, this wasn't my call to make."

"Okay, then I need the name and email of the person whose decision it was because this is ridiculous. I only worked at the school because you asked me to. Now you're making it seem like I did something wrong."

"Are you ready?"

"Yes." She hastily gives me the new director's name and email.

"Is there anything else I can assist you with?"

"No."

"Take care, Tarique." *Click.*

I've never felt so used and disposable in my life. Keisha, more than anybody, knows how hard I worked, from the Praxis through the school year. She single-handedly hyped me up to go to middle school—the last place I wanted to be—only to turn around a year later and give me the finger. She could've at least said "let me see what I can do."

However, I can understand their logic. First, placing me in the Teacher Residency Program would create a vacancy at Columbia. With Mr. Tanaka and me gone, they're already down two science teachers. It's robbing Peter to pay Paul. Furthermore, the Teacher Residency was designed for career changers with zero experience, providing them a gradual entry into the classroom. I already have a year under my belt. Why would they pay me nearly my entire salary to shadow someone now?

Still, that doesn't make it right. They made a promise—and I've got the receipts to prove it. It's obvious they're trying to force me to stay at Columbia. Having someone who can teach, manage a classroom, and relate to students is like striking gold. But the system is broken, and I won't keep breaking myself to fix what others refuse to repair. I can't save the world just to lose myself.

From the beginning, I only wanted to work with high schoolers. Older students are more my speed. I can talk and reason with them. Middle-school energy is just too frenetic for me. I took the first year on the chin, trying to help out—but look where that got me.

So, there's about an ice cube's chance in hell I'll go back. My former colleagues say, "But what about the students?" My reply: "But what about my happiness, support, and quality of life?" *Oh, right, nobody gives two figs about that.*

The students aren't to blame—they're innocent here. However, Columbia's administrators are a different story. Time and time again, they've made a challenging job more difficult. Forget offering a little support; instead, they sabotage and undermine my efforts by doing whatever they think works for the moment, like taking my students away in the third semester, only to send them right back a month later. So, if my teaching career is contingent upon working at Columbia—I quit.

I log into the school district's website and immediately resign. No hesitation. I know my worth—the students deserve better, and so do I. So I walk away—no guilt, no second-guessing. But I'm not ready to give up the fight just yet. I email the new director, explain everything, and let her know I've resigned. The next day, she asks for more details.

I send her a lengthy email, detailing my experience from the Praxis to the school year, along with all of my correspondence with Keisha. Then I wait. Two days pass. No response. I try not to overthink it, but of course I do. I keep checking my inbox, hoping for a sign. And then, finally—her name pops up. I click, heart racing, bracing for the verdict—my teaching career hanging in the balance. If she says no, that's it. I'm done. I'm not about to pay for a certification out of pocket.

I read, adrenaline surging. Then, I spot the words that make everything all right:

Congratulations and welcome to the Teacher Residency for the 2019–20 school year. I block out everything else. That one word—*Congratulations*—is all I see.

Awesome sauce.

They would've been out of their minds to let me go, given their recruitment challenges. The following day, I receive an email from Keisha welcoming me into the Teacher Residency Program. I don't even bother responding. My next task is following up with the recruiter at Temple University.

She already has my application, résumé, transcripts, and letters of recommendation. I just need to know when classes are starting. Instead, she tells me there have been some changes there as well. Here we go again.

She says, "Upon reviewing your transcripts, I noticed you hadn't taken any science courses. Unfortunately, completing all core biology classes is now a prerequisite for residents in our program. So, you must take those first."

"But I already have a year of teaching experience. I know the content like the back of my hand. I also passed the Praxis with a score well above the cutoff. That's not enough?"

"Sadly, it isn't."

"Well, thank you for your time."

Just like that, my Temple dreams go up in flames. That leaves me with one last option: the Relay Graduate School of Education.

I've never heard of Relay, so I do some internet sleuthing. What jumps out is that it began as Teacher U, a program created by charter school leaders in partnership with Hunter College. Later, it was rebranded and accredited as Relay, an independent graduate school training and certifying teachers.

Relay's branding cleverly masks its charter school roots. From the outside, no one would guess the two are connected. So, the private education sector isn't just redirecting funds from public schools when students leave—it's also cashing in by training their teachers. Nice. Kudos to them for keeping those coveted tax dollars flowing.

I'm a capitalist at heart, so I have no qualms about the private market stepping in with a *potentially* better mousetrap—as long as there's accountability and the training is solid. Besides, with a year of experience under my belt and now working with high schoolers, I feel confident that I can weather any storm.

Regardless, Relay is the cheapest, quickest, and, frankly, my last option for securing my teaching credentials, so it's either Relay or the highway. Sure, I might sacrifice some rigor, but I already have the cake; I'm just looking for a little icing on top.

I call to speak with one of the recruiters. Surprisingly, most of the information from last year is still valid, which feels like a small miracle. The only difference is that the master's in the second year isn't free. It'll cost about $3,000. That's a pittance compared to my NYU tuition, which I'm still paying almost twenty years later. I can knock out my Relay tuition now. Let's hope the value of the training is worth more than I'm paying for it. The X-factor will be my mentor teacher; if they're experienced, I should have plenty to learn from them.

The program structure is straightforward. There are a couple of classes at night and one during the school day. I will gradually take on more responsibilities as the year progresses, through a structured on-ramping process. Then, the following year, I'll earn a master's degree while teaching independently. The master's degree is essential because it will give me a $5,000 pay bump on top of our annual raise.

If I play my cards right and earn thirty additional credits over the next ten years, I can top out at $93,000—and that's with summers off! The only question is whether I'll survive ten years. I ask the recruiter about Relay's lack of accreditation in Pennsylvania. She says, "There's nothing to worry about because the school is accredited in New Jersey, and they have reciprocity with Pennsylvania."

"Cool beans. How do I get started?"

Chapter 14

Don't Drink the Kool-Aid

———

TWO MONTHS LATER, I WALK INTO ALAN WATTS Charter for an "intensive" three-day summer course. Immediately, I'm struck by all the melanin in the room. I've been reading about the dearth of teachers of color for years, so to see so many under one roof is inspiring.

Scanning the room, my eyes land on Dr. Richardson, the dean of Philly Relay. I recognize her instantly from her profile picture on the website. Petite, with long faux locs cascading down her back, she moves through the crowd with ease, her presence magnetic. She greets each person with warmth, making everyone feel welcome.

Still, it's ten minutes past showtime, and I'm starting to fume. If there's one thing I can't stand, it's tardiness. We only have three days to prepare for the school year and we're already wasting it. I have to remind myself that not everyone values time in the same way. The clock ticks, but no one seems to notice. The minutes stretch on, each one feeling longer than the last, until finally, the show begins.

The bigwigs kick things off with introductions, outlining the day's agenda and offering their standard speeches. Then, we're instructed to form a circle and share our name, subject, school, and favorite summer memory. A quiet tension fills the air as everyone looks around, unsure who will speak first. Sensing the hesitation, I decide to break the ice. "I'll go first," I say, offering a quick smile to get things moving.

"My name is Tarique Connelly. I teach biology." I can tell people are surprised—I guess I have "gym teacher" written all over me. "Unfortunately, I don't have a school yet. My top two memories this summer were playing a bodyguard in *Creed II* and creating a vlog where I explored new places and ended each video with a song."

"Wow! Where did you go?"

"I went to thirteen spots: Croatia, Kauai, Kazakhstan, Colombia . . . I was all over."

A mixture of awe and envy scrolls across my colleagues' faces. Their expressions say, *How do we ever top that?* We spend the next five minutes going through the motions. Seconds after wrapping, we're immediately put back into groups to discuss our motivations for becoming teachers. I gather they keep us talking to each other because they have so little to say to us.

I don't hear an original word from the administrators the entire day. They usually stick to the script on the screen and read to us like we were toddlers at story time. If I got a dollar for every buzzword, like *equity, anti-racism, social justice,* and so on, I could buy a Bentley. Meanwhile, I haven't heard anything about lesson planning, classroom management, or best teaching practices.

I look around the room, wondering if anyone else is as underwhelmed as I am. However, most residents seem to be guzzling the Kool-Aid with no qualms. Relay's leadership frames teaching as a social justice mission, which tugs at the heartstrings but obscures the reality of the situation. Students don't need saviors—they need skilled, qualified teachers.

It doesn't take long to realize that most of my colleagues teach in charter schools, which makes sense, given Relay's strong connection to them. The bigger shock, though, is discovering that none of the charter residents have passed the Praxis and are still being allowed to teach. Silly me for thinking I was the only one thrown into the deep end. Now, I see how the system sets countless others up to fail in the same way.

Charter residents also teach solo from day one, but at least they get lesson plans—a luxury I envy. Sifting through mountains of content to craft engaging assignments is incredibly time-consuming, but the payoff is lessons that truly resonate with students. Thankfully, with an expert teacher guiding me this year, I can focus on working smarter, not harder.

The next two days are much the same. If I didn't have experience or a partner, I would be freaking out right now because I haven't heard anything useful that could've helped me on my first day of class. I keep looking at my colleagues thinking, *You have no idea what you're getting into.* Out of nowhere, I hear something ridiculous and scan the room to see if anyone reacts.

I lock eyes with a brother who looks like Tommy from *Martin*. We side-eye in unison. Finally, someone else who's critical of all this rah-rah. We shake hands after the let-out. His name is Terrence. He teaches English. I can tell he's not from Philly by his accent. We chat in the parking lot, out of earshot of our colleagues.

"Can you believe all this crap we're hearing?" he says. "It's all fat and no substance."

"Agreed. I can't think of a single valuable thing I've learned over the past three days. It's torturous."

"Bro, I know. I knew I couldn't be the only one feeling this way."

"Nah, bro. I feel you."

"Do you know Caitlin?"

I smirk, realizing who he means. "The girl with the colorful hair?"

"Yeah. She's on the same page as us."

"Do you mean she hasn't drunk the Kool-Aid?"

"Nah, bro!" We both share a laugh.

Terrence and I plan to stay in touch throughout the year. His sister is a seasoned teacher, so I hope she can be a valuable resource as well. Overall, I'm feeling hopeful. I didn't expect much from the "summer intensive," so I'm not surprised by how it turned out. But my heart breaks for my colleagues who will be blindsided by what's ahead—the long days, overcrowded classrooms, dwindling resources, and the constant struggle to inspire students who may feel just as lost as they do.

I'm just hoping to secure a great mentor teacher. The process is opaque, and the residents have nothing to do with it. It's a week before school starts, and I'm still waiting to hear something. I wouldn't be surprised if they told me at the last minute that it's a no-go, which would align with my experience thus far.

I wish I could interview my mentor teacher to see if we're a good fit, but now just having one feels like it'll be a miracle. My anxiety is going into overdrive. I hate feeling like someone else is pulling the strings of my life. Every step of this process has been unnecessarily complicated and stress-inducing.

Finally, two days before school starts, I receive an email assigning me to John Taylor Gatto High School's Magnet program—and I'm ecstatic. I'm lucky because teacher residents are typically not allowed to work in selective schools or programs. Our contract stipulates that we must work only in high-need schools. I'm not sure who worked their magic, but I couldn't be more excited to teach in an environment where students are invested in learning from day one.

Now, I can focus more on instructing instead of classroom management. I check out the school's standardized test scores. They leave a lot to be desired. Like most high schools in Philadelphia, most students scored in the basic and below-basic categories in biology, math, and reading. However, 10 percent of students got advanced scores in biology. I'm guessing these are my magnet students. My goal is to triple that number and make sure the rest at least score proficient. It won't be easy, but I'm excited to prove what's possible when teaching is driven by love, creativity, and proven strategies.

Chapter 15

She's Got a Ph.D.

———

I ARRIVE THIRTY MINUTES EARLY AND SIT IN MY CAR, watching students trickle in through the morning haze—some walking, others stepping off SEPTA buses. Their casual energy stands in stark contrast to the tension coiling inside me. A few smile with anticipation; others shuffle along like extras on *The Walking Dead*. In their faces, I see the future—not perfect, but powerful, each one brimming with possibility. I take a slow breath, letting the morning settle. Finally, it's time to shake, rattle, and roll.

Cool air brushes my skin as I step out of the car and make my way toward the building. I step inside, and chaos greets me. Students stream past, voices collide, doors bang in rhythm. I weave through the crowd, each step tightening the tension inside me.

The office comes into view. I push open the door and take in the spectacle. After signing in at the front counter, I approach one of the six assistant principals, who looks up from a stack of papers, eyes wide.

"Good morning! My name is Tarique Connelly. I'm a teacher resident with Relay."

"Good morning." He looks at me like a deer in headlights. "I'm sorry, who did you say you were with again?"

"I'm a teacher resident with the Relay Graduate School of Education."

"My apologies; I can't say I have heard of them."

He tells me to sit tight while he checks with the other administrators.

Seconds later, he says, "You're a student teacher! Now I get it. Okay, we have to figure out who you're working with. What subject do you teach?"

"I teach biology."

"Hmm, okay." *Don't look so surprised.* "So, you'll be working with the science lead, Mrs. Nettles. She's running a little behind today, but feel free to relax in the teachers' lounge."

"Thanks, I appreciate your help."

"My pleasure. Welcome to Gatto."

I make a beeline for the lounge.

The hallways teem with students looking just as lost and confused as I am. I knew this was one of the biggest schools in Philly, but nothing can prepare you for 2,000 students moving in concert. It's sheer pandemonium. I finally make it to the lounge and wait. Thirty minutes pass. No sign of my partner. I glance at the clock, then around the empty lounge. Did I miss something? Am I in the wrong place? I sling my bag over my shoulder and head back to the office to figure out what's going on.

"She hasn't arrived yet," the AP says. "Don't worry. I'll let her know you're there."

"Okay," I reply, trying to sound more relaxed than I feel.

I head back to the teachers' lounge and wait. And wait. It's awkward just sitting here, not knowing when—or if—she'll show up. There are definitely better ways to start our partnership.

Almost an hour later, she strolls in like it's nothing.

"Are you Mr. Connelly?"

"That's me."

"Hello, I'm Mrs. Nettles. Nice to meet you."

We shake hands. "The pleasure is mine."

"So, I hear you'll be with me the entire year, eh?"

"Yeah, that's the plan."

"Well, it would've been nice if they'd told me earlier."

"Oh, that's unfortunate."

I could tell she wasn't happy to see me—now I know why. I'm not mad at her because I'd be upset, too, if I were told to train someone without warning. However, I'm still hopeful we can build a fruitful partnership. It's fantastic that there are two of us. There's no reason the school year shouldn't be smooth sailing.

"Where are you getting your teacher's license?" she asks.

"It's called the Relay Graduate School of Education."

"One more time?"

"The Relay Graduate School of Education."

She squints. "Oh, I've never heard of that school."

"Why am I not surprised?" I say under my breath.

"Do you have any teaching experience?"

"Yes, I taught sixth-, seventh-, and eighth-grade science last year at Columbia."

"Nice. Were you pre-med in college?"

"No, I studied music business at NYU."

"Music business?"

"Yup!"

She laughs. "Okay, do you have any science background?"

"I don't, but I studied a lot and passed the Praxis."

"But you've never worked in a lab or taken any science courses?"

"Nope."

She frowns. "I find that so weird. How do they expect you to teach science without any formal experience?"

"Technically, if you count last year, I'm not walking in with zero experience. How about you?"

"I have a Ph.D. from UPenn."

Then what are you doing here?

"Nice," I reply.

"I studied dentistry but came back a few years ago to earn my teaching credentials—so hearing you don't have any formal training is . . . surprising, to say the least."

The walk to her classroom takes forever. Every step feels like I'm marching toward judgment. Inside, Mrs. Nettles sits at her desk, and I sit at a student's desk in front of her. I draw a breath, steady myself, and let the words come out measured and sure.

"I understand your concern about my experience. But rest assured, I have a good grasp of the material and continue to learn daily."

"Well, that's not going to work for me. I've got too much going on right now. I'm already teaching three classes, running professional development sessions, buried in paperwork—and on top of all that, I'm a single mom going through a divorce. I can't take on any more responsibilities."

"I totally hear you. That's a lot to carry on your own. But maybe I could help lighten the load. I could handle the day-to-day stuff—grading, attendance, planning—so you don't have to shoulder it all alone. I'm here to support you, not to add stress."

She lets out a short sigh—somewhere between skeptical and resigned.

"Okay, so what's expected of me?"

"Well, you're required to train me."

"I thought you were already trained."

"No, I completed last year without any training, so I'm eager to learn whatever I can from you. I already have a good foundation. I want to build on it, so I'll be watching and observing—"

"Watching and observing?" she cuts in. "See, that's the problem. I need someone who's ready to jump right in from day one. Ms. Crawford's student teacher from Drexel is starting immediately."

"Look, I'm flexible. I just want to learn as much as possible. That's it."

She hesitates. "Listen, it's not that I don't want to help, but I can't train you and take care of my other responsibilities. It's just too much."

"Listen, the training will be minimal. I'm just interested in learning best practices and any other teacher wisdom you can share. Don't worry. I will be an asset to your class. You can trust me."

"I'm just being honest with you, Mr. Connelly. I don't have the time to train you. I'm sorry. I wish I could."

Yeah, right.

"Can you find another mentor?"

"I had no say in finding you, so I doubt it."

"Okay." She takes a deep breath.

Finally, she says with a shrug, "Let's just see how things go."

"Cool beans. I appreciate you giving me a shot. That's all I can ask for."

"No problem. So, tell me more about this Relay program."

"Oh, it's super sweet. I'll earn my license after working with you this year. That's free. And we get a salary. Next year, I'll run my own class and receive my master's for three thousand dollars."

"Are you serious?"

"Yes."

"Three thousand dollars?" She stares at me in utter disbelief.

"I wouldn't be here otherwise."

"Why wasn't this program available when I was at UPenn?"

Judging by her reaction, she's definitely sipping some haterade. I felt similarly working at the front desk of the Ritz-Carlton after graduating from NYU. I didn't need my degree to do the job.

On the other hand, I didn't go to NYU just to get a job; I went to expand my human capital. Mrs. Nettles interrupts the incessant chatter in my head and says, "The students will be arriving in a few minutes. The game plan is to do introductions, a few icebreakers, and review the syllabus."

When the bell rings, the students come streaming in. This takes me back to my first day at Columbia. The only difference is that these students are already in chill mode. I know they'll be great to work with. The room is silent as Mrs. Nettles takes the roll for the first time.

Afterward, she introduces herself to the class. The room remains quiet. Then, she says, "We have a special guest. I'm not sure how long he'll be with us, but I want to give him a chance to introduce himself."

Shucks. She's still plotting to get rid of me. I stand up and walk to the front of the class.

"Good morning, everybody. My name is Mr. Connelly, or you can call me Mr. C. I'm excited to work with all of you this year. I'm from West Philly, so when I see y'all, I don't just see some random group of kids. I see myself. I know what it is like to sit in those chairs, but I also know what it's like to live the life of your wildest dreams—and I want to help all of you do that.

"I went from a high school dropout to a college graduate, and finally to a world explorer traveling to over sixty countries, from the Bahamas to Bora Bora. And if I can make my dreams come true, I'm one hundred percent confident that all of you can too, and education will be the key to getting you there. So, thank you so much for your time and attention. And let's have an incredible school year."

Suddenly, the class erupts in applause. Mrs. Nettles looks stunned.

"Wow! Okay. Someone has fans."

"Oh, I didn't tell you . . . I'm a professional speaker too."

"I see."

Hopefully, this sways her in my favor. She asks me to hand out a worksheet. She tells the students, "This is one of the most important lessons of the school year. It's something that you can use for the rest of your life to help you become successful. Today, you are going to learn your unique learning style. The way you learn best. Take your time and answer the questions truthfully."

I guess Mrs. Nettles never learned during her elite Ivy League education that the theory of learning styles has been debunked. There's no evidence that tailoring lessons to students' learning preferences improves academic outcomes, yet many educators still buy into that malarkey. Still, I'm hoping that now that she's seen me in action, we can move forward and have a great year.

The next day, I receive an email saying that I'm being reassigned. What a bummer! I need a miracle because I don't want to leave this school. It already feels like home. The students are respectful, well-mannered, and eager to learn. There are no fights, the facilities are well-maintained, and the school culture is sweet. It feels utopian compared to my early days at Columbia.

There's no point in trying to reason with Mrs. Nettles any further. Remember, she has a Ph.D.—a player-hater's degree. I attempt to meet with the big boss, which is like scoring a meeting with the pope. My last hope is to talk with one of his six assistant principals. The AP who helped me on my first day offers to meet with me. I spend five minutes pleading my case.

"Her biggest gripe is that I don't have a science background. And I get that. But what I do have is a deep love of learning. I'm a lifelong student. There's not a day that goes by that I don't spend at least an hour or two reading. I taught myself guitar, Spanish, and passed the Praxis in a month. And I'm from Philly, so my cultural competence is impeccable." The AP seems sympathetic. He compliments me on my passion and experience.

Then he says, "I can tell you're a tremendous asset, and it would be a shame to lose you, but unfortunately, that decision isn't in my pay grade." Of course it isn't.

I continue showing up to Gatto. It's only been a fortnight, but I've already become fond of the students, and Mrs. Nettles hates it. We play nice, but I know she can't wait until I'm gone. On a Thursday evening, her wish is granted. Dr. Richardson finally emails me my new assignment. I will be working at Agape High School. How I managed to land another magnet school is beyond me.

Back in the day, there were only a few of them, like Central, Masterman, and George Washington Carver. It's not uncommon for students to go from these schools to the Ivies. The big difference between a magnet and a traditional school is the range and quality of classes students can take. For example, the highest level of math I took at my alma mater, Overbrook, was Algebra 2.

Central has calculus, trigonometry, elementary functions, and analysis and approaches. And if that's not enough, many classes have an honors, IB, or AP option. Want more? La Salle University is right next door, ready to devour your adolescent attention and load you up with more degrees than a thermometer—and the debt that comes with them.

Hopefully, Agape gives students access to rigorous classes too—classes that actually prepare them for the future.

Out of curiosity, I look up their test scores—and I'm shocked. Most students score in the basic or below-basic categories in math, reading, and biology. Biology is the worst: 70 percent of students scored below basic. That's not a gap—that's a crater. Of course, standardized test scores don't tell the whole story, but they do provide a snapshot of certain academic skills. Hopefully, I can help them move the needle.

On the bright side, my commute has been cut in half. But sadly, I won't get the chance to say goodbye to my Gatto squad. I feel like I'm abandoning them, but that's the way the cookie crumbles. As I said, the only constant in life is change. You can either swim against the tide or you can go with the flow.

Chapter 16

New Level, New Devil

——

MORNING LIGHT SPILLS ACROSS THE CITY AS I cruise toward Agape High, a cool breeze slipping through the cracked window. The streets stir softly, the city still rubbing the sleep from its eyes. I glide through green lights, past shuttered bodegas and weathered row homes, the stretch ahead wide open. There's a lightness to the drive, to the morning, like something heavy finally let go. Maybe it's a sign the worst is behind me. Then again, you never know what's waiting around the next bend.

I ease toward a red light, and the school comes into view. Its plain brick is softened by the early glow. Out front, students are scattered along the pavement, some standing alone, others chatting in small groups as they wait for the doors to open. Everything looks calm. Normal.

When the light turns green, I coast past the front entrance and into the back lot. A few cars sit quietly in the shade, their silence blending into the hush that hangs in the air. I cut the engine and lean back, letting the calm settle around me. It feels like an invitation, so I close my eyes for a meditation to set the tone for the year ahead.

I begin by whispering my intentions: to make an impact, to use my gifts, and to be a blessing to my community. As I sink into the silence, I let everything go. Only my breath remains, steady and slow, anchoring me in the stillness.

Twenty minutes later, "Pie Jesu" begins to play, gently calling me back from my sweet surrender. I take a breath and open my eyes. I sit with the silence a moment longer, suspended between stillness and motion. Time seems to pause, just for a heartbeat, before life resumes outside my windshield.

Across the lot, I spot a handful of kids spread across the blacktop. Wait—they're tiny. Like, elementary school tiny. What's that about? I grab my bag from the passenger seat, open the door, and head in that direction. As I pass the munchkins, the lettering on their shirts comes into focus: Nietzsche Charter. Then it clicks. These aren't my students. We're just sharing the same building.

Hallelujah!

This place has lived many lives. Decades ago, my brother went here, back when it was still a middle school. Now, it's something else entirely. Schools these days flip identities like pancakes. And with the looming demographic cliff, that churn is only expected to accelerate, leading to more closures, more consolidations, and, sadly, fewer opportunities for students.

As I near the entrance, I scan the side of the building for any trace of the pool my brother used to rave about. I wonder if it's still there— whether students today still get the chance to learn how to swim, or if that's one more essential skill quietly phased out, like so many others.

That question makes me think about the role swimming has played in my life. More than just how to stay afloat, it taught me how to stay calm, keep moving, and trust myself, even when I was out of my depth. What began as a life skill blossomed into a deep love for the water itself and for the worlds that free diving and scuba diving opened to me.

Now, each time I slip beneath the ocean's surface, I'm not just swimming. It feels sacred. Every movement is deliberate, the noise above replaced by the rhythm of my own breath. In the deep, I find a peace the surface world can't reach. There, in that ancient current, I connect to something older than memory, a breath that flows through the earth and all that lives. A quiet communion that whispers: I belong to it all.

And that's what makes it so difficult to accept—that something this vast, this powerful, this life-giving, is out of reach for so many. We live on a planet of water, yet far too many students never learn how to move through it. So they grow up never knowing what it feels like to be calm in the deep, to move with confidence where fear once lived.

This isn't an oversight. It's the result of a system that was never meant to prepare them for life, just to obey, never to be free.

So the question becomes: What would it take to build something better? An education that doesn't just fill heads with facts but builds real skills that foster resilience, awareness, and a deeper connection to the world. The kind that helps students not just survive but thrive.

Just as the vision takes shape, reality rushes back in. I step through the entrance into the vestibule, where students file through metal detectors one by one, placing their bags on the belt like travelers at a TSA checkpoint.

I walk down a short flight of stairs and into the empty main office. A lone woman is holding down the fort, talking to someone on the phone while the other lines buzz.

"Okay, hold on for one second, please," she says, probably praying they hang up when one second becomes one thousand. She puts the call on hold and turns to me.

"Good morning. Thanks for your patience. How can I help you?"

"Good morning. My name is Mr. Connelly. I'm a new teacher."

"Welcome, Mr. Connelly. I'm Mrs. Robinson."

"Nice to meet you, Mrs. Robinson."

"The pleasure is mine."

"By chance, do you know where I can find the principal?"

"She's usually out front greeting students. I would try there."

"Okay. Thanks."

"You're welcome. Have a good one."

"You as well."

She takes a deep breath before braving the phone lines again. I admire her ability to stay so friendly and poised. I exit the office and head up the short flight of stairs.

When I reach the top, I spot a woman across the lobby, her back to me, laughing and chatting with students. It takes me a second to realize it's the principal. Her profile pic must be from college. My first impression is that she's highly personable and warm, and she has a great rapport with the students. I can also hear her from a mile away. But in this business, it's better to have a big personality than none at all.

"Good morning, Principal Ross. I'm your new teacher resident, Mr. Connelly."

"Good morning, Mr. Connelly. Welcome to Agape!"

"Thanks for having me."

"Oh, my pleasure. Just give me five minutes to finish greeting students, and I'll be right with you."

"No problem. Take your time."

I love that Principal Ross isn't sequestered in her office barking orders like a dictator. She's a leader on the front lines, marshaling her troops in the battle for their minds. I overhear her telling a student that "she's cutting up." What? Could it be? A leader with personality *and* cultural competence? Watch out! I'm suddenly excited about the possibilities.

The bell rings. She thanks me for my patience and leads me to her office. A short walk and one narrow hallway later, we arrive.

I follow her inside. She sits at her desk, glances at her laptop, and lets her attention drift for a moment toward whatever's on the screen.

"I'm sorry, Mr. Connelly," she says, clicking at the keyboard. "Just give me one more second."

"No worries. I understand. A principal's job is never done."

"Tell me about it."

She finishes typing, rotates her chair, and gives me her undivided attention.

"Again, welcome to Agape. You'll be working with our science lead, Mrs. Srinivas. She's got a lot of experience and will be a great mentor."

"Awesome. I'm looking forward to meeting her."

"I can walk you over to her classroom now, unless you have any questions."

I was always taught during interviews to have at least one question. Of course, this isn't an interview, but Agape might be my forever school, so I want to make a good first impression.

"Sure, I have a question. I looked up Agape's Keystone scores. The results surprised me."

"You and me both," she interjects, which I find hard to believe.

"What happened?"

"We have a lot of English-language learners and foreign students, which drags down our scores. We've also had issues finding qualified teachers. But yes, it's a huge improvement area, and I hope you can help us with that."

"I would love to. I taught all last year, so I have a few tricks up my sleeve."

"Excellent. Anything else?"

"No, that's it."

"Okay. Let's go."

We step out of the office, and I'm awestruck by the hallway's tranquility. It's a world away from Columbia, where my teaching journey began. I marvel at how far I've come in just a year. Principal Ross greets every student we pass, calling many of them by name. That's the beauty of a smaller school—it's easier to build relationships and foster a sense of community.

Soon, we reach Mrs. Srinivas's classroom. Principal Ross knocks once, then steps inside. I follow close behind.

"Good morning, Mrs. Srinivas. Good morning, scholars," she says with a warm smile.

"Good morning, Principal Ross," the students reply in unison.

Wait—are we still in Philly?

Mrs. Srinivas, sweet as pie, greets Principal Ross with a warm hug. Her slight frame reminds me of my grandma. Her glasses give her a scholarly air.

The room stays calm as Principal Ross steps forward and addresses the class.

"I want to introduce everyone to Mr. Connelly," she says. "He'll be with us for the year, and I expect you to show him the same respect you give Mrs. Srinivas. Once again, welcome to Agape, Mr. Connelly."

"Thank you."

"You're in good hands," she says with a smile, then exits, the door closing behind her as Mrs. Srinivas watches and beams.

Then she says, "Mr. Connelly, would you like to introduce yourself?"

"Sure."

"Good morning, students. My name is Mr. Connelly, or you can call me Mr. C. I'm excited to be here with all of you. I'm from Philly, so this feels like home. I buy my potato greens at Theresa's Kitchen, not too far from here."

"Potato greens? What do you know about potato greens?" a student with a thick Liberian accent asks.

"Are you kidding me? I'm Liberian, bro. It's in my blood."

"For real?! You're Liberian!"

"Facts. Well, half. My father's from Nimba."

"No way? I'm from Nimba County, too!"

"Stop playing! Where?"

"Ganta."

"That's wild! I pass through Ganta on my way to Vayenglay all the time."

"Wow! That's lit!"

Soon enough, other students start chiming in.

"I'm Ghanaian."

"I'm from Guinea."

"I'm Ethiopian."

Cool beans! We've got about a quarter of the motherland represented in class. That's super cool.

Racially, Agape is pretty homogeneous, but ethnically, it's highly diverse. As a first-generation US citizen on my father's side, I feel right at home. There's an unspoken bond between children of immigrants, the feeling of being caught between two worlds, carrying the expectations of one while trying to find your place in the other.

Wanting to build on that connection, I ask, "How many of you have family from another country?"

Almost the entire class raises their hands. Nice! I glance at Mrs. Srinivas. She watches with muted irritation. Her face says, *Stick a fork in it.* I take the hint.

"Well, I look forward to getting to know everyone. And if you ever need help, don't hesitate to reach out. That's what I'm here for."

I turn to Mrs. Srinivas. "It's all yours."

She wastes no time reclaiming the throne. "Okay, students, let's get back to work. Remember, we're having our first test on Monday. Make sure you complete the reading and the questions at the end of the chapter."

I walk the room, trying to get a sense of what they're learning, but I don't have the slightest idea. Some are still on chapter one, while others are working on chapter two. What exactly does the exam cover? And if there's a test on Monday, wouldn't Friday be the obvious day to review? As I make my rounds, I can feel Mrs. Srinivas watching me like a hawk.

Five minutes before the bell, she reminds the class again to study over the weekend. I wait for her to offer some kind of strategy, anything to help them actually prepare, but it never comes. It's that familiar curse of knowledge: when something feels obvious to you, it's easy to forget it might not be obvious to everyone else. But I can't judge because I've made that mistake myself.

The bell rings. Backpacks zip, chairs scrape, and students pour into the hallway. Once the room clears out, I decide to play nice.

"So, Mrs. Srinivas, you're from India, right?"

"Yes, I am."

"Cool. Which part?"

"I'm from Gujarat."

"Nice, my good friend Priti Patel is Gujarati."

"Okay," she replies.

"I was just in India this past New Year's Eve."

"Hm? Where did you go?"

"I visited New Delhi, Agra, Jaipur, and Fatehpur Sikri, then flew to Goa for New Year's Eve."

"Sounds nice," she says, though she looks unimpressed. Her vibe is saying: The school day is over; please go home. I oblige.

"Well . . . it was nice meeting you, Mrs. Srinivas. Enjoy your weekend."

"You too, Mr. Connelly."

"Thanks."

ON THE FOLLOWING MONDAY, the students take the test and perform horribly. Mrs. Srinivas tells them they can get extra credit by looking up the correct answers in the textbook. As they work on the corrections, one of my Liberian buddies asks me if I can explain something to him.

Prince says, "I don't understand why I got this question wrong if the book says I'm right."

"Let me take a look at it."

The question:

Which sequence of terms progresses from the simplest to the most complex?

1. cells, tissues, organs, organ systems
2. tissues, organism, cells, organ systems
3. cells, molecules, organ systems, organs
4. molecules, organelles, cells, tissues

The correct answer is option four. But the textbook diagram matches option one, which is what Prince recognized. Molecules and organelles hadn't been introduced yet, so he went with what looked familiar. Mrs. Srinivas probably pulled the question from some random resource without checking for alignment.

"Should I ask Mrs. Srinivas to change it?" he says.

"I would. Number one should be marked correct too, unless she went over biochemistry and organelles."

"Nah, bro, she didn't."

The student immediately walks up to Mrs. Srinivas to contest the answer.

"This one should be right," he says, pointing to his paper.

She reads the question, glances at her answer key, and replies, "The correct answer is number four."

"Then why did Mr. C. say it can also be number one?"

What? That little booger. Why did he have to bring me into it? She nonchalantly brushes aside the statement and chuckles.

The bell rings, and the students begin to exit the classroom.

"Let's talk about it tomorrow," she says. "Have a nice day, Prince."

Mrs. Srinivas then asks me, "Mr. Connelly, what was he talking about?"

"Let me show you."

I turn to the biology textbook page describing how living things are organized. The diagram illustrates the structure and relationship between a cell, tissue, organ, organ system, and organism. There's no mention of molecules or organelles.

"This is why Prince was confused," I say. "Answer one is more in line with the diagram in the textbook."

She studies the page for a moment. Her face tightens. She knows I'm right.

"Okay, fine," she snaps. "But what difference does it make? I'll give him the points. Then what will he have? A sixty?" She laughs, sharp and dismissive, like the very idea of trying is a joke.

"These children are lazy. They don't value education. There's no support at home. That's why they perform poorly on exams. I'm telling you, you can give them the answers, and they'll still fail."

She turns toward me, her voice softening into something that sounds almost maternal, if not for the edge behind it.

"You see, Mr. Connelly, you're new. I've been in this profession a long time. One day, you'll understand exactly what I mean."

No—I won't. Not now. Not ever. I believe in them too much to stop fighting for them, even if that makes me seem naïve in her eyes. Maybe that's why she talks to me like I'm a child—not a colleague, not an equal. And the way she looks down on the students? It's the same lens she uses on me. I take a breath, steady my voice, and respond.

"In all fairness, you gave them a test without reviewing what would be on it. How can you expect the students to do well when you don't even prepare them?"

Her smile fades. The warmth drops from her voice.

"Listen, Mr. Connelly. Don't tell me how to run my class. This is my classroom. And I don't appreciate being corrected in front of students. Even if there was a mistake, it's not your place to address it." She folds her arms.

"You want to earn your credentials, right?" She doesn't wait for a response. "Did I hear things didn't go so well at your last school?"

I offer no defense—just a small nod.

"Okay. Then, I need you to observe, learn, and let me run my classroom. I don't need any help. Understood?"

"Understood. And look, I'm sorry, I wasn't trying to step on your toes. I was just trying to help. From now on, I'll keep my thoughts to myself. I know I can't get my license without your support, so rest assured, you won't hear another word from me. Sorry again for the trouble."

"Okay, Mr. Connelly. I'll hold you to it."

"All right. I'll see you on Wednesday. I've got deliberate practice tomorrow."

"Okay."

I nod and head out. Thank God for deliberate practice. Every Tuesday, I get a "get-out-of-jail-free" card. In theory, it's for skill-building. In reality, it's a much-needed break. I showed up thinking Mrs. Srinivas might take me under her wing. Turns out she'd rather have me under her thumb. Relay might be my last shot at guidance because I'm not getting it here. But I didn't come this far to fold, so the beat goes on.

Chapter 17

Teacher's Anonymous

—

I ARRIVE AT RELAY HEADQUARTERS A FEW MINUTES before deliberate practice begins. The red brick building still shows its warehouse roots, but the sleek black trim and glass entryway hint at a recent transformation. I take it all in for a moment, then grab my book bag and hurry down the cobblestone path. Through the tall windows, I see a few colleagues gathered around an office table, heads down, deep in conversation.

I step into the industrial-chic lobby and make my way to the meeting room. The mood hits the moment I walk in—quiet, heavy, off. I say "Good morning," but all I get in return are lackluster nods and mumbled hellos. I expected everyone to be excited about missing class and spending the day "practicing."

Yeah . . . not the vibe.

Professor Hernández says we'll give the latecomers a few more minutes. She's a sassy New Yorker in a pint-sized frame, all charisma and confidence. She looks too young to be a professor, but her big-city bravado makes you take her seriously.

Still, it's five minutes past showtime, and I'm quietly losing it. I remind myself that the alternative is being bored to death in Mrs. Srinivas's class. So, I take a chill pill.

As I settle in, bits of conversation drift my way—gripes about students, admin, burnout. It takes me back to the start of my teaching journey. Boy, I don't miss that chapter. Though these days, I've got other Goliaths to slay.

Professor Hernández starts to speak. "Good morning, everyone. Let's get started. We'll begin by doing a check-in. Let us know how you feel, how things have been going, or if you have anything else you want to share. Would anybody like to get us started?"

Olivia raises her hand, her fingers trembling just enough to notice. "Hey, everyone." She clears her throat. "I'm sorry."

My colleague, seated beside her, gently places a hand on hers.

"It's okay," she whispers. "Take your time, girl."

Olivia nods, takes a breath, doing her best to hold it together.

"I'm just gonna be honest. I'm overwhelmed. Like, really overwhelmed. My class is out of control—fighting, cussing, not listening, refusing to do anything. And I feel like I have no support. My mentor teacher's already called out, like, four times, and every single time, I'm the one left holding the bag. It feels like I'm the lead teacher. Then I'm forced to cover other classes too—almost every day. It's exhausting. I'm just . . . I don't know. I'm tired. I'm frustrated.

"We're not even a month in, and I'm already at my breaking point. So, Professor Hernández, can you please tell me what I'm doing wrong or what I can do differently? Because this can't be it."

She falls silent, her pain still reverberating through the room. This is what it looks like when a new teacher starts to unravel. For a moment, no one speaks. The room holds its breath. Heads nod. Someone murmurs, "Same."

Olivia didn't just speak for herself, she gave voice to something sitting heavy in all of us.

Professor Hernández responds, "First off, thank you for keepin' it real. And girl, trust me—I feel you. That first year? Whew, baby! These kids will run you ragged, make you question your life choices, your degree, your hairstyle, everything. But let me tell you something: if you can survive this part? You golden. You hear me? Golden. So, keep your head up, boo-boo. We've all been there. Sometimes you gotta fake it till you make it, okay? But you gonna be all right—trust me. Now come on . . . let me see that gorgeous smile."

Olivia forces a smile, but it doesn't quite reach her eyes. The worry's still there, flickering beneath the surface.

Without missing a beat, Professor Hernández says, "It gets easier, I promise. Just give it time. That's all it takes—*time.*"

Yeah, right. Sure it does. Still, I've gotta admit, she's giving me that warm and fuzzy feeling, à la Robin Williams in *Dead Poets Society.*

But warm and fuzzy doesn't fix anything. I keep waiting for a proper solution, something tangible to actually make things better, but nothing.

Professor Hernández says, "Now, I won't even sit here and act like I've got all the answers, because I don't. But I'll tell you one thing: ten minds work better than one. So I want to open up the floor and have your colleagues weigh in. Has anybody tried something that's worked for you this year? Can you offer Olivia any advice?"

What? Are you kidding me? I don't expect you to have all the answers, but could I at least get one? I was hoping Professor Hernández would offer real strategies, not just throw the question back at us. We're not experts. Olivia doesn't need opinions; she needs real expertise. Practical tools. Classroom management techniques. Something she can actually use.

Instead, she gets empty platitudes, nothing that actually changes the reality she's dealing with. The next hour dissolves into a full-blown gripe fest. I just wish we spent half as much time on solutions as we do on problems. But honestly? I'm starting to wonder if Relay has any to offer.

Professor Hernández wraps up our group therapy session by commending us for being social justice warriors. "Disrupting systems of oppression is not for the faint of heart, but we have to remember why we chose to do this work."

Yeah, right. We're not disrupting anything. We might even be making things worse—even with the best of intentions. She continues, "Believe me, I've stood in your shoes before. I know exactly how it feels, but I promise you, it gets better. You just have to trust the process."

Oh, boy. More Kool-Aid. Goes down smooth, but leaves a nasty aftertaste.

Finally, Professor Hernández hits us with her most profound words yet: "That's a wrap."

I keep it cool, but inside, my inner child is moonwalking. She says we can hang around or return to school early. Instead, I go home. Mrs. Srinivas won't miss me. I would hate to have someone watching and scrutinizing every little thing I do too. So yeah, the space, it's healthy. Necessary, even. Maybe the absence will make our hearts grow fonder. I'm not holding my breath. But still . . . you've got to keep hope alive.

Chapter 18

The Lesson Wasn't for the Students

——

TWO MONTHS LATER, I PULL INTO THE BACK OF THE teachers' lot. The early birds have already claimed the front spots—no surprise there. It's five minutes before the bell. I kill the engine, grab my bag, and step into the crisp fall air—the kind that jolts you awake and slices through the morning fog. I rush inside and charge up the stairs. By the time I reach the top, my calves are on fire.

I swing open the heavy metal doors, and a wave of noise smacks me in the face. A swarm of students floods the hallway like a burst dam. You can always tell when multiple teachers are out; the halls swell with bodies and chaos, buzzing like a beehive without a queen. I weave through the crowd and reach Mrs. Srinivas's room with a minute to spare.

She's at the door, greeting students with that bright, polished smile she wears like armor. We exchange brief pleasantries. That's it. It's become a pattern, the same hollow routine every day. I head to the back and take my usual spot—corner desk, quiet and out of the way. I sit still, obedient, invisible. But inside, I'm boiling because I know I could be helping if only she weren't so frigging insecure. Like many teachers, she'd rather point fingers at the parents, at the students, than face the mirror.

To be fair, I agree with her . . . to a point. Still, she acts as if teachers have no influence on student outcomes—as if we're just bystanders in our own classrooms. I'm still waiting for her to try something different, explore a best practice—anything. But let's be real, I'll be waiting until the cows come home.

The problem is that many teachers conflate lecturing with learning. Instead of using objective data to confirm students' knowledge, they make assumptions based on how much they blabbed about a topic. Then, they unfairly administer tests without ensuring that the students truly understand the material. The test becomes the first opportunity to see what students know. But the test should be the final checkpoint, not the first.

How teachers can be okay with most students failing and not feel like failures themselves is beyond me. I guess it's hard to be disappointed when the expectations are in the Mariana Trench.

I try to act like I don't care, but it eats at me, especially in a place like Agape, where the students are respectful, well-mannered, and eager to learn. I can see they used the "magnet school" label to cherry-pick which students to accept. Many of them have the potential to excel at an advanced level, but they aren't given the chance. As the saying goes, "Talent is universal, but opportunity is not." Here I am, capable of rectifying that injustice, yet I find myself effectively silenced.

Some people are content collecting a paycheck for doing nothing, but it's draining the life out of me. I hate wasting time. It's the most valuable thing we've got. Every hour I spend here has an opportunity cost—and it's not cheap. If I'm going to pay that price, it better be for something that matters because I didn't come here to coast. I came to inspire, to spark change, to give students the education they deserve. But that's turning out to be a lot harder than I thought.

The first semester is slipping by faster than I expected, and with it, my chance to gather the evidence I need for my teaching license. By now, I should have videos, student work, and other data for Relay. On paper, I've got very little, but I haven't been idle.

Most days, I finish my homework in about ten minutes. Then, I dive into the suggested readings. Funny enough, they've taught me more than the professors ever did. After that, I start my daily rounds: MSN, The Atlantic, Drudge Report, AP, The New York Times, TMZ, Media Take Out. From my corner desk, I've practically become a global affairs correspondent.

Still, none of that counts here. Relay wants footage, proof that I'm leading the class, though nothing could be further from the truth. So far, I haven't had to video any assignments because I just switched schools, but my time is running out.

The final bell rings. Usually, I trail behind the students, but today I have no choice but to engage. I have to complete my midterm, and I can only do it if she gives me the green light.

I gather my belongings—and myself. I'm nervous, given how our previous conversations have gone. Still, I take a deep breath and go for it.

"Hey, Mrs. Srinivas, do you have a second?"

"Sure," she says.

"I need to complete my midterm, which requires me to record myself instructing. So, I wanted to know if you would be okay with me teaching a class or two."

"Mr. Connelly, I have no problem with that. Just let me know when you want to teach."

"Great. Would you mind sharing your lesson plans so I can see what standards you're focusing on?"

"You can teach anything you like," she says.

"Thanks. Though I was hoping to stick with whatever you're already covering, just so it fits with the flow of the class."

"Mr. Connelly, I don't have any lesson plans to give you."

"Got it. Any suggestions?"

"Just continue with photosynthesis."

"Okay, I'll teach on Monday."

"No problem."

"Have a good evening, Mrs. Srinivas."

"You too."

I bolt out of class like a man on a mission. As I make my way down the empty staircase, I run into the principal.

"Hey, Mr. Connelly, are you in a rush?"

"No, I've got some time."

"Can I speak with you for a minute?"

"Sure."

She leads me into her office and gestures to the chair.

"Have a seat. So, how are things going? And be honest. You can keep it real with me, okay?"

"Okay. Honestly . . . things could be better. For the most part, I don't do anything. I try to help the students, but Mrs. Srinivas gets upset. I've offered suggestions, but she always reacts defensively, so I'd rather just stay quiet."

She nods, lips pressed into a thin line.

"No, Mr. Connelly. We need you to be more involved."

"I'd love to, but Mrs. Srinivas has made that very difficult."

"Don't worry, I'll speak with her."

"Thanks. I appreciate it. To be fair, she did agree to let me teach on Monday, so I'm hoping once she sees what I can do, she'll be more open."

"Okay, good to hear."

"You're welcome to stop by and observe if you'd like."

She smiles.

"Most certainly. Just let me know what time."

"Third period works perfectly."

She reaches for her calendar.

"I'm putting it in now."

"Cool beans." I rise to leave. "Well, I appreciate your support—and I look forward to Monday."

"Same here, Mr. Connelly. Take care."

I spend the entire weekend designing an engaging lesson. I always begin by looking at the standards associated with the topic. The standards are my academic bible. It says:

"Use a model to illustrate how photosynthesis transforms light energy into stored chemical energy."

Nice!

THE FOLLOWING MONDAY, I arrive fifteen minutes early to set up my tripod. Everything has to be perfect. The principal and my advisor, Dr. Richardson, will be there. It's seconds before the late bell rings. The students come strolling into the class. Some light up at the sight of the camera.

Others get stoked when they realize I'm the one teaching. I tell them to ignore the camera and just act like it's not there. I hate to impose that on them. But it is what it is. Dr. Richardson and Principal Ross come walking into the class together just as we are about to begin. It's game time.

"Good morning, Mrs. Srinivas. Good morning, class. I want to welcome our guests, Principal Ross and my advisor, Dr. Richardson. It's a pleasure to have you ladies with us. We're going to get started. Can I have a volunteer read the objective, please? Damon?"

"Use a model to illustrate how photosynthesis transforms light energy into stored chemical energy."

"Thanks. By the end of class, if I do my job right, you'll be able to show how photosynthesis works using a model. In our case, we'll be using a symbolic model: the photosynthesis equation.

"But first things first: let's go over the Do Now. Can I have another volunteer, please? Diamante."

She reads confidently, "What would the world be like without plants?"

"Great job," I say, giving her a quick nod.

I start the five-minute timer on the smartboard. The students work quietly as soothing music plays with tropical drone footage displayed on the screen.

I make my rounds, checking in with each student. "Excellent work, Takara, four sentences already! Charmelle, great job writing the date and question." I praise the class for staying on task and tell them, "We have about two minutes left. Try to write at least three complete sentences."

I edit responses on the spot and push students to expand their answers. I ask two to share their work.

Kyaira says, "If there were no trees, it would be really bad. They give us air to breathe. They give us shade too."

I ask, "What's that air called?"

A few students shout out, "Oxygen!"

"Excellent. And without oxygen, can humans survive?" The class shakes their heads.

"So, no plants mean no what? Dahmir, what do you think?"

"No humans," he says.

"Exactly. No humans—and no animals either. Let's keep going."

Jyleem shares: "Without trees, it would be sad. Animals would lose their homes, and we would lose food. The world would be a dark place."

"Good job, Jyleem. What's an important point he made? Ralph?"

"Plants give us food?"

"Bingo. Now imagine a world without plants—what would cows, goats, and chickens eat? How would we replace our fruits and vegetables? Plants are the foundation of the food chain on Earth. So, no plants. No food. No oxygen—no life as we know it."

I give students a few minutes to revise their responses after posting a model answer on the board. Then I give them a quick five-minute brain break before we transition to the next part of the lesson: understanding the photosynthesis equation.

"All right, let's break down the process of photosynthesis together. What does a plant need to make its own food—or energy?"

Voices pop up from around the room.

"Carbon dioxide!"

"Water."

"Sunlight!"

I nod as I write each one on the board.

"These are the reactants. Now—what does the plant produce after photosynthesis?"

Without missing a beat, a couple of students call out— "Glucose and oxygen!"

"Perfect, these are the products." Then, I erase the parts of the equation and ask, "Does anyone think they can write the full equation from memory?" Porscha volunteers. She writes:

$$6CO_2 + 6O_2 + \text{Sun's energy} \rightarrow C_6H_{12}O_6 + 6H_2O$$

"Is this correct?" The class is divided.

"Who would like to respectfully disagree?"

Imani volunteers. She writes:

$$6CO_2 + 6H_2O + \text{Sun's energy} \rightarrow C_6H_{12}O_6 + 6O_2$$

"Would anybody like to disagree?" Nobody raises their hand. "Great, so we're all in agreement? Perfect." I erase the equation from the board.

"Now, let's have a little friendly competition. Everyone should have a set of cards showing parts of the photosynthesis equation—the chemical formula on one side and the full name on the other. It's time to see how much you guys were paying attention. We've got some candy on the line to spice things up a bit.

"When I say 'go,' you will arrange the cards correctly using the side with the chemical formula, like we just did on the board a second ago. The first three to finish will win some candy. Naomi, can you repeat the instructions for me, please?" She does so flawlessly.

"Are there any questions? Okay. On your mark, get set, go!"

The students get to work laying out their cards like puzzle pieces.

"Let's go! The first three to finish win!"

"Mr. C., I'm done," one student calls out.

"Let me check. Do plants release oxygen or carbon dioxide during photosynthesis?"

"Ah, man," she groans, laughing as she scrambles to fix her mistake.

Around the room, others are close behind, flipping cards, reviewing notes, locking in answers. I move from desk to desk, checking their work. Everyone nails it.

"Great job. Now, for round two, arrange the cards using the full names. Ready? Set! Go!"

The students work quickly. Principal Ross and Dr. Richardson give me a smile and thumbs up as they exit. They look impressed by the level of engagement.

I give the students one last task. "I'm passing out a worksheet to reinforce everything you've learned. It should only take ten minutes. Once you finish, you're done for the day.

"Great job today, class! I'm proud of y'all."

Their faces light up—grins, small nods, that quiet satisfaction of putting the pieces together. I walk by and check in with each student for a fourth and final time.

"That lesson was fire, Mr. C."

"Thanks, Tari."

"Man, why can't you take over the class? When you explain things, I understand them so much better," he says.

Mrs. Srinivas cringes.

"Chill," I say. "There's always something to learn when you stay open-minded."

Minutes later, Mrs. Srinivas says, "Mr. Connelly, can I speak with you for a second?"

"Sure."

I'm hoping she'll praise my lesson and offer me more opportunities to teach.

Instead, she says, "Mr. Connelly, you're not allowed to give out candy in school. God forbid one of the students has an allergy."

"Okay, thanks for the heads-up. Anything else?"

"No, that's it."

"Thanks."

I feel reinvigorated. Leading today's lesson was a beautiful reminder of why I became a teacher. I love seeing that spark in a student's eyes when something clicks. And the best part? The students were doing the thinking—not me. I didn't lecture or talk them to death. The lesson flowed like a well-rehearsed dance: graceful, responsive, and full of energy. I wish I had more opportunities like this. But as Proverbs 18:16 says, "A man's gift maketh room for him." So until that door opens, I'll be at my corner desk—doing the work, trusting that my gift will carry me when it's time.

Chapter 19

My Gifts Made Room

———

I**T'S FIVE MINUTES BEFORE PROFESSIONAL DEVELOPMENT** (PD) begins. The room is cavernous, with dull fluorescent lights casting a dreary hue over the space. Roughly ten round tables are neatly arranged at the front of the room. The back half is a total disaster. It must be the school's storage—where things go to die a slow death. I can only imagine what's back there, besides a bunch of taxpayer dollars wasting away. One thing's for sure: the mice are always throwing a party.

The teachers are spread out and clustered into their content cliques, chatting about who knows what. Usually, these occasions are the bane of my existence. But today, yours truly is running the show. The principal was so impressed by my photosynthesis lesson that she asked me to share my approach with all of my colleagues. I didn't tell Mrs. Srinivas I'd be leading the PD. She'll be horrified.

Now she has no choice but to be my student. Let's hope she behaves. I check the smartboard; the title slide's up. My heart's steady, but my mind's already a few slides ahead. Two minutes to takeoff. As I begin my spiel, Mrs. Srinivas enters the room with a coworker. Perfect timing.

"Good afternoon, everyone. We'll begin in a couple of minutes. When you're ready, please fill in these three tables. That way, we don't have to raise our voices too loud. Thanks."

Mrs. Srinivas stares at me in disbelief, trying to figure out what's happening. She connects the dots after reading "Backward Design Planning, presented by Tarique Connelly, inspired by the work of Wiggins and McTighe" on the smartboard.

Her body language says, *Lord have mercy, please give me strength.* Mrs. Srinivas isn't the only one drinking haterade. Some of my colleagues are in their feelings too. It's written all over their faces. They're clearly wondering—who am I to tell them how to do their job? I'm still a student teacher. What could I possibly know at this stage of the game? But as the saying goes, I can show you better than I can tell you.

The class is now in session.

I hand out three-by-five cards as my colleagues begin filling in the tables.

"Good afternoon again. I hope everyone's doing well today." I scan the room. Half look curious. The other half look like they're here against their will.

"Let's do a quick temperature check. On a scale of one to five—one being 'I feel horrible,' five being 'I feel incredible'—how are we doing today? On the count of three, hold up your number. One, two, three."

Everyone slowly raises their hand, glancing around to see how their colleagues are feeling.

Okay, we've got a few threes here, a few fives there. Surprisingly, no ones. Maybe they're not as jaded as I thought. We're averaging around a four—which, on a PD day, is basically a ten. Not bad. I click to the next slide.

"All right, now that we've checked in, quick show of hands—who thinks lesson planning is, *hands down,* the most time-consuming part of teaching?"

Nearly every hand goes up.

"Exactly. We've all got better things to do with our weekends, right? That's why I'm excited to share 'Backward Design'—a planning approach that can save you hours, streamline your lessons, and help you source content that actually sticks.

"If I had to sum it up in one sentence, it's this: Begin with the end in mind. If you take nothing else from today, take that. Most teachers start lesson planning by hunting for material that matches the topic. But Backward Design flips that. Instead of asking, *'What am I going to teach?'* you ask, *'What should students be able to do by the end of the lesson?'* So the focus shifts from just covering content to building skills students can actually use.

"It's called Backward Design because you start with the summative assessment—a final test, project, or performance task—and design each lesson to lead students toward that goal. That's the big picture. Don't worry, we'll break it down step by step.

"Can I have a volunteer read the objective, please? Mr. Ogugabunga?"

"Teachers will be able to apply Backward Learning Design by creating SMART objectives and standards-aligned key points."

"Thank you, sir."

I click to the next screen.

Key Points

1. What is Backward Learning Design? Why?
2. How to construct "SMART" objectives.
3. How to Use Key Points as a Classroom "Road Map."
4. TELL-SHOW-DO Method – Model of Backward Design.
5. Teachers will be able to apply Backward Learning Design.

"This is our roadmap. Our end goal is step five. But steps one to four are how we get there."

I click again. Now, it's time for the icebreaker.

"Please use the three-by-five card to complete the activity on the board. We'll regroup in five minutes."

Icebreaker: Arrange the following vacation to-do list in the correct order.

1. Catch a flight to Bora Bora
2. Relax beachside with a Piña Colada

3. Take a cab from the airport to the Four Seasons
4. Choose destination
5. Take a cab to PHL Airport
6. Book flights and hotel

I set a five-minute timer on my phone as the smartboard cycles through a loop of exotic landscapes with soft instrumental music playing in the background. Call it my attempt to make PD feel a little less like a root canal.

The timer chimes softly, pulling everyone back to center.

"Okay, let's get started. What's the first order of business—besides checking your bank balance? Mrs. Landry?"

"Choose a destination."

"Anyone disagree? Everyone on board?" Heads nod.

"Great job. We have to pick a destination first because everything else depends on it. Now, how is this like beginning with the goal of your lesson? Mrs. Smith?"

"You need to know where you're going before you plan how to get there."

"Exactly. Imagine driving for hours without knowing where you're going. That'd be a nightmare, right? Well, that's how students feel when they get work with no clear goal. They're on the road to learning, but without a destination, they'll never arrive at true understanding.

"So here's the real question: What are we asking of our students, and what are we preparing them for?"

I give the silence room to work. Then, I click to the next slide.

"Because how we plan doesn't just affect engagement—it affects cognition. If we never ask students to think critically, analyze, and create, we're not just missing the mark, we're holding them back from what they're truly capable of."

I let that sit too. Because sometimes, silence teaches more than words ever will.

Next, I draw them back in with a question.

"By a show of hands, how many of you are familiar with Bloom's Taxonomy?"

Most hands go up.

A pyramid appears on the screen.

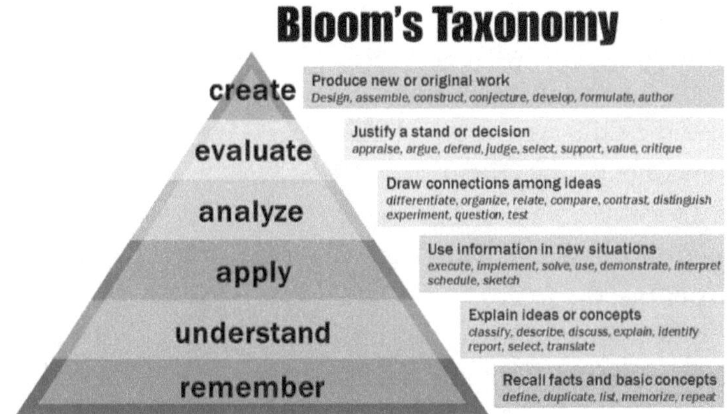

"Thought so. Most of us have seen this before. It breaks learning down into levels—from simple recall all the way up to critical thinking and analysis. Now think about your assignments. Where do they usually fall on this pyramid? Are we asking students to analyze? To evaluate? To create? Or are we keeping them stuck at the bottom—just remembering facts and filling in blanks?"

Silence fills the room. Teachers glance at one another, averted eyes and small movements betraying their unease. I let the pause linger. The truth emerges quietly—the kind that rarely appears because no one ever asks us to pause and truly face the realities of our teaching. The silence speaks louder than any data could.

"Many teachers question whether students can perform at these higher levels. But that's the wrong question. The real issue is: Are we giving them the opportunity? We say students are behind, but then assign busywork that demands no real thinking. That's not catching them up. That's holding them back. What's the cost of staying stuck on this lower level? Mrs. Dalembert?"

"They memorize. They repeat. And then they stop."

"Precisely. Imagine making it through high school without ever being challenged to read deeply, write clearly, or think critically. That doesn't just leave students behind in school—it leaves them behind in life.

"That's why this work matters. Every student deserves a real education—one that pushes them, prepares them, and equips them to navigate life with confidence, purpose, and adaptability. But that only happens when we're intentional: about the goals we set, the tasks we design, and the skills we choose to cultivate.

"I want to end with one of my favorite quotes, often attributed to Abraham Lincoln:

'Give me six hours to chop down a tree, and I will spend the first four sharpening the ax.'

"Just as a dull ax makes the work harder, a poorly planned lesson makes learning harder for both teacher and student. That's why sharpening our craft matters. When we do, we don't just teach better—we change lives."

For the exit ticket, I ask teachers to rate the session from 1 to 5 and write down one key takeaway.

Most give me a 5. Mrs. Srinivas gives me a 3—just enough to remind me she's still clinging to her throne. As people filter out, one teacher lingers near the door. "Great job," she says quietly. "That really made me think." I smile. "Thanks, I appreciate it."

Whether any of this sparks real change? That remains to be seen. You can light the way, but you can't force anyone to follow. Still, something in the air feels different. Like a current has shifted. And maybe, just maybe, I've not only become the change—I've become the proof that it's possible.

Download Bonus Items

You can download this presentation and access additional bonus content at:

TariqueConnelly.com

Chapter 20

A for Audacity

I ARRIVE AT BIOLOGY CLASS FIVE MINUTES AHEAD OF schedule, eager to prepare for the day. I say hi to Mrs. Srinivas as I walk into the room. Her response tells me she's not in the best mood. She's been irritated ever since she was forced to share teaching responsibilities with me. I imagine she's struggling with the same feelings of uselessness and boredom I battled for weeks, but that's her burden to bear. My only concern is that the students are learning. Everything else is inconsequential.

I'm halfway through wiping down the dry-erase board when Mrs. Srinivas cuts in: "I need you to finish today. You're taking way too long on this section."

"Okay, no problem. Let's discuss it after class because the students will be arriving shortly."

She totally ignores me and says, "You can give the test on Monday. And I'm taking the class back on Tuesday."

Before I can respond, I'm saved by the bell, and the students begin filling the classroom.

Thank God, because I'm one comment away from losing it. Sometimes, silence is the best response. I greet the students as they enter the class, doing my best to shift gears. But before the room even settles, Mrs. Srinivas repeats herself: "Tell them about the test on Monday." I have zero intention of giving them a test I haven't prepared them for, so I lower my hands and say, "Relax. We'll talk about it later."

"We have benchmarks to prepare for. We cannot spend a year on this unit. It's time to move on!"

The students can see me getting flustered. Her voice grates like nails on a chalkboard. She adds another comment, testing my patience. Finally, I respond firmly, "This is not the time to discuss it. Let's talk about it after class."

She slams her pen down, stands up, and bolts from the classroom. I have no idea where she's going, nor do I care. The students and I share side-eyes, but nothing is said.

Minutes later, she reenters the classroom accompanied by Mr. Young, the school-based teacher leader. God only knows what she's told him. He leaves after ten minutes when he sees everything is cool. The vibe's off, but we make it through the rest of class without any issues.

Mrs. Srinivas just needs to relax. I'm not trying to take over her class. If she wants control back so badly, she can take it. It's not that deep. Besides, I'm tired of fighting to teach a frigging lesson. So, I'll be the bigger person, bow out gracefully, and hand back the reins—only she beats me to it.

As the bell rings, she turns to me and says, "You don't have to worry about the test or teaching. I'm taking over immediately."

"That's fine. I'll just wait to hear that from Principal Ross first."

The next day, I arrive to find Mr. Young in the room, sent by Principal Ross to "make sure we play nice." I imagine he has better things to do than babysit us. There's no Do Now, no objective, nothing on the board. But that's no longer my concern. The students enter the classroom, glance around for the day's plan, and start asking what they're supposed to do.

Then, to my surprise, Mrs. Srinivas says, "Mr. Connelly, would you mind continuing to teach today?"

I want to say, *You have to be frigging kidding me. You can't be serious after all that ruckus you made yesterday.*

Instead, I respond calmly, "Unfortunately, I'm not prepared to teach today."

"Okay, no problem."

She wings it and instructs the students to work on their test prep questions, which is code for chill out because the answers are in the back of the book. Regardless, I'm over it. I have no fight left in me. I'll spend the rest of the year in the background. I have enough "data" to complete all my Relay work. I feel sorry for the students though. But I've accepted that I can't change much right now. I'll be able to make an impact once I have my own classroom, but I'll never get that chance if I can't make it through this year.

DAYS LATER, things are back to how they were before my photosynthesis lesson. I'm here physically, but mentally and emotionally I've checked out. I'm scrolling aimlessly on my laptop, half-watching the screen, when suddenly I hear Mrs. Srinivas arguing with a student. It snaps me out of my social media stupor. I act like I'm not paying attention as my eyes stay fixed on the screen. My AirPods are in my ears, but the volume is zero. Finally, Mrs. Srinivas yells at the student, "Get out! You are out of this class!"

"Fine!" The student grabs his things and jets out of the room.

I can't help but feel partially responsible for the altercation. Mrs. Srinivas has been on a rampage since getting her class back. I think she subconsciously takes her anger at me out on certain students, especially the ones I've built strong connections with. But it's all good. I have one mission now, which is finishing this school year. And I'm not about to let anyone stop me.

I continue to occupy myself, browsing the internet while subtly ear-hustling on conversations around me. Then, my ears perk up as I overhear Mrs. Srinivas discussing the expelled student with his classmates, which I find very unprofessional. She says, "He didn't deserve to be in this class. It's a privilege to be here." *Yeah, right, more like a handicap.*

That's when she lets it slip. "You girls are lucky—you're getting two grades for one class. That'll boost your GPA *and* help you get into college."

My heart skips a beat. What? Surely, I didn't just hear what I thought I did. I keep scrolling, eyes on the screen, as if I didn't hear a thing. But inside, my mind is racing.

Initially, I'd planned on waiting until after class to dig deeper into this revelation, but ten minutes later, I can't take it anymore. I start circling the room, pretending to check whether students need help. In the back, two girls are working together quietly. I glance over their shoulders as if I'm reviewing their work. Then I lower my voice.

"Ladies, I need to ask you a question. Keep your eyes on your paper."

They nod.

"How is this class listed on your report card?"

One of them answers without looking up. "AP Biology and Honors Biology."

"So, you're receiving two grades for one class."

"Yes."

"Okay, thank you."

OMG.

I walk back to my desk to digest what I just learned. I can't believe it. It's bad enough that students are deprived of a quality education, but nothing could've prepared me for discovering that they have a fake class on their report cards. I take a few deep breaths to slow my heart rate while staring at the computer screen in disbelief.

How are parents unaware of this? How does the school get away with it? I knew they were under pressure because they receive extra funding for advanced classes, but I couldn't have imagined they would resort to putting fake classes on students' report cards. That's beyond preposterous. It's criminal. For now, I'll put the info in my back pocket while I decide what to do with it.

Chapter 21

Breaking Point #2: Fights, Freakouts & Fiascos

———

A WEEK LATER, I'M SITTING AT MY DESK LISTENING TO music. Mrs. Srinivas asks a student to pass out review packets for the benchmark exam they'll be taking. I find this strange because she never reviews for tests, let alone comes up with an entire packet. Good teachers use benchmarks to pinpoint learning gaps, target instruction, and ensure students are prepared for the state exam in May.

For many others, it's just another box to check. I grab a copy of the review packet, curious and a little skeptical. At first glance, it's clear the teaching doesn't match the complexity of the questions. The students will be up a creek without a paddle. Furthermore, it includes material she hasn't even introduced yet, which makes parts of it seem random.

My curiosity gets the better of me, and I can't resist checking how closely the review aligns with the actual benchmark exam. It turns out it's a perfect match. Mrs. Srinivas just copied all the questions and answers freehand. It reminds me of what she said at the beginning of the year: "You can give them the answers, and they'll still fail."

So, I imagine it's par for the course. No wonder the students are lost in the sauce on test day. They've never learned the material. And Mrs. Srinivas fakes accountability by getting them to memorize answers.

Days later, when the students take the benchmark, their scores improve significantly compared to last quarter's dismal results. Of course, it's all a big fat fraud. But I don't say anything and put this in my back pocket too. Besides, who would I tell? They'll probably just sweep it under the rug anyway.

I SPEND MY LUNCH break meditating in my car, trying to wring a little peace from the day. I'm dying to go home, but lucky me—we've got PD, a true masterclass in wasting time. The sun warms the windshield. For a moment, the silence almost feels sacred. I set my alarm for ten minutes, and just as I settle in, "Pie Jesu" starts playing. Beautiful? Yes, but also my reminder it's time to suffer. My brain says go, but my body says kick rocks. I give myself a pep talk, then finally push the door open. Now, I'm late, but who cares? Let them start without me.

I make my way up the stairs to the third floor, each step heavier than the last. As soon as I exit the stairwell, the noise hits—screams, laughter, the kind that says something's spiraling out of control. Down the hallway, students are clustered together, phones held high, filming like paparazzi. I freeze, fighting the urge to retreat. Then—straight into the madness.

As I get closer, the crowd shifts, and through a gap, I finally see what's going on. Two girls are locked in a full-blown brawl—hair flying, fists swinging, while the mob circles them like it's Friday night at Madison Square Garden. Students shout and shove, jostling for a better view.

I spot the hallway lady hovering at the edge of the chaos, whistle in hand, trying to part the crowd. She lunges forward just as someone backs into her, and she goes down hard. Normally, I stay out of school fights. I'm not a referee, and I definitely don't get paid enough for combat duty. But I can't stand here and watch the little hallway lady get trampled on.

So I jump in, heart pounding, instincts on autopilot, and try to separate the two future UFC champs.

"Back up! Stop fighting! Somebody grab her!"

I'm standing between them, doing everything I can to keep them apart, but they keep lunging past me, trying to get at each other. There's still no reinforcement in sight.

"Back up! Get out of here!" I shout, scanning the crowd for help.

That's when I hear it: a deep, guttural snort, followed by a wet, disgusting launch. At first, I don't even realize it hit me. The loogie lands in my mustache. But then it creeps down, slow and sticky, sliding into the corner of my mouth.

That's when I taste the Doublemint gum the student was chewing. There's a beat of silence, just long enough for the shame to settle. Then it hits me: sharp, hot, instant. I explode. The girl clocks what she's done and bolts. The others scatter as well. And right on cue, backup rounds the corner.

"I can take it from here," one of them says.

I guess so. Mofo, you're two seconds too late.

I step back without a word and head straight to the teachers' lounge. I turn the faucet on full blast, scrubbing my face, rinsing out my mouth, over and over, like it'll somehow erase the fact that someone else's snot got in there.

My heart's still racing, clothes are a mess, and I can't shake the taste of that damn gum. I give myself five minutes to regroup. Lord knows I want to go home. But I've got to be on my best behavior if I want that license.

Ironically enough, the meeting is right next to where the fight went down. When I enter, they're already in the thick of things.

Principal Ross says, "You're late, Mr. Connelly."

"I'm sorry, but there was a fight in the hallway, and I had the honor of having someone spit in my face, so pardon my tardiness."

"Are you serious?"

"Yes."

Really? A royal rumble goes down right outside the door, and they're completely oblivious? No way. They heard it. They just chose to ignore it. And just like that, I'm right back at boiling point. But it's all good. I'll shut my mouth, sit quietly, and bounce after this meeting.

Principal Ross begins reviewing the benchmark results. She says, "I would like to acknowledge Mrs. Srinivas and Mrs. Alexander for the huge improvements in their benchmark scores." I roll my eyes and sigh.

"Their scores have increased by more than 50 percent compared to last quarter's results." The two ladies beam with pride, basking in all the praise.

I'm sitting next to another science teacher. She congratulates the ladies, but I can tell she feels terrible, given that her students' scores haven't improved much.

I quietly tell her, "Don't read too much into it. It's all bullshit. The scores only increased because she gave them the questions and answers beforehand."

Mrs. Alexander "ear hustles" and says emphatically, "We did not."

"I wasn't talking to you," I shoot back.

"But you're talking about me."

"Well, if the shoe fits, wear it."

The principal intervenes. "What's going on here?"

"He's insinuating that we cheated in the benchmark."

"Oh, I'm not insinuating," I say. "I'm telling you: it's a fact. I can prove it. We simply need to compare the review sheet with the actual benchmark."

I rush out of the classroom to find the review. Our students are on the same floor, so they'll be easy to locate. I spot them in no time. They have a substitute babysitting them—surprise, surprise. I give the sub a quick hello. Then, I ask the class if anyone has a copy of the review.

Of course, no one does. Why would they? I go to Mrs. Srinivas's class, hoping the door is open. It's not. I search through all my stuff to no avail. I return to the meeting and say I can't find the review, but I'll prove that they cheated once I do.

Then, Mrs. Srinivas says, "I have it right here."

"Great." Is she really giving me the shovel to bury her with? I stay quiet, open my laptop, and pull up the district's website to find the test. No theatrics. No grandstanding. Just facts—though I've completely hijacked the meeting at this point.

Meanwhile, they whisper among themselves, trying to downplay what's coming. Finally, Principal Ross cuts in, voice tight and composed. "That's enough, Mr. Connelly. You need to leave. Now."

"Oh, my pleasure. Have a nice day, everyone." I grab my bag and bounce. Thirty years later, and I'm still getting kicked out of classrooms. Some things never change.

I ARRIVE at Mrs. Srinivas's room the following Tuesday for first period. She's standing outside the door, guarding it like a sentinel. When I get within a few feet of her, she says, "You're no longer allowed in this class. You can go downstairs and speak with Principal Ross."

I turn around without saying a word and head to the main office to find out what's going on. I ask the secretary if I can speak with the big boss. She calls and relays my request, then hangs up the receiver.

"She's busy."

Of course she is.

I'm tempted to bail like I would have in high school. Instead, I patiently wait for an explanation for why I can't enter the classroom. One hour bleeds into two. I get the impression the principal is trying to avoid me. No worries. It's all love. I won't let the door hit me where the good Lord split me. I'm out. There's only an hour left of school anyhow. And I have a Relay class tonight, so it's better to go home and chill.

I TAKE LINCOLN DRIVE INTO GERMANTOWN and pull up to Dubois Charter School for my Relay class. After such a long day, this is the last place I want to be, but here we are. I walk into the building with a colleague. We take a second to commiserate before entering the classroom. I try to stay optimistic, to avoid slipping into cynicism, but this class just feels like a colossal waste of time.

As we take our seats, the familiar routine sets in: casual venting, surface-level chatter, nothing that resembles actual training. Any hope that Relay would strengthen my science skills is officially gone. We're just playing school. It's incredible how much my Relay experience mirrors what I see in the classroom: the same boredom, the same low expectations, and barely a shred of rigor. Different setting, same dysfunction.

I wish we could perform more experiments. We completed one at the start of the year, then never looked back once that box was checked. Instead of building real competency, the year has been dominated by emotional survival, with most classes resembling group therapy sessions, which I get. Teachers expend and absorb an enormous amount of energy. You have to do something with it. And venting is cathartic. It feels good. But it doesn't change anything.

It's a release valve, not a solution. But that's the trap. The system gives us just enough space to blow off some steam but never enough to ask why we're running on fumes in the first place. And that's no coincidence. Teachers and students alike are trained to comply, not to question, so it's no wonder they're both cheated: teachers out of real preparation, students out of real learning. It's all a charade, a performance that keeps tax dollars flowing and generations of students locked in wage slavery at best, entrenched poverty at worst.

The thought lingers as I glance at the clock, hoping an hour has passed. It hasn't. The day is dragging by slower than a tortoise trudging through mud. I feel restless, so I take a walk to get some fresh air and a sip of water. As I'm leaving the fountain, I look down the hallway and see Dr. Richardson. I smile and wave. She waves back, then gestures for me to wait.

"You were just the person I was looking for," she says as I start walking toward her. "Cool beans." I meet her halfway. "What's up, Dr. Richardson?"

She lowers her voice. "Unfortunately . . . I have some bad news for you. Today, I was contacted by the district. Mrs. Srinivas filed a harassment claim against you. She said you've created a hostile environment inside the classroom, and she no longer feels safe."

"That fucking bitch. It's complete bullshit. She's pissed because I caught her and another teacher cheating on the benchmark, and I exposed it during PD last week."

"Do you have any proof of that?"

"Absolutely. And I've already submitted the receipts to Harrisburg last Friday. Oh, but it gets better because Agape also fraudulently gives kids two grades for one class."

"What did you say?"

"The students have a fake class on their report cards. They receive two grades for one class: one for AP Biology and one for Honors Biology. And it's a complete fraud! I sit there every day, bored to death. I can assure you it's one crappy class."

"How's that even possible?"

"They get away with it by making AP Biology the real grade, but everybody gets an A or B in Honors Biology, depending on how much she likes you. The parents never question it. The students never question it. All they see is either the A or B.

"All the district sees is the inflated number of kids who are taking advanced classes, which keeps that 'magnet school' label and the tax dollars flowing. To add insult to injury, the class sucks! My eighth graders learned five times as much as these students."

"Okay, Mr. Connelly, take a deep breath." I take a second to compose myself. It feels like I just had a manic episode. My heart is still racing like a Lamborghini.

Dr. Richardson continues, "So you filed a complaint with Harrisburg last Friday?"

"Yes. Funny, their allegations came a week later. It's a counterattack. I was just in class with Mrs. Srinivas yesterday with zero issues. I just received the news today that I've been barred from the class. The principal wouldn't even talk to me. But I didn't see this coming."

"Okay. Calm down. Let's wait and see how all of this plays out. Both of you are part of the union, so they'll have to get involved at some point. Just keep me posted and let me know if I can assist."

"Thanks, I appreciate that. I'm sorry to drag you into this."

"No worries. Just take care of yourself."

I head back to the classroom, heart pounding. If they think I'm going down quietly, they've picked the wrong ninja.

The moment I walk in, my face says it all. My colleagues look up. "What's up, Rique? Are you good?"

"No!" I retell the entire story, expletives included. I'm so riled up that there's no coming down. I tell the professor I have to go. I grab my things and bail out of there.

THE NEXT DAY, I arrive at Agape and go directly to Principal Ross's office. She's not there. I check at the front of the school. She's not there either. I finally run into Dr. Bobbitt. He says, "The principal is out for the day." Of course she is. What am I supposed to do all day? And if they think I'm covering classes, they're smoking. I'll put in a personal day too. Instead, Dr. Bobbitt says to just hang out in the teachers' lounge.

Cool beans. Luckily, there's a smartboard that I can hook my laptop up to. Lately, I have been binge-watching *Survivor* and dreaming of becoming a contestant. I only have twenty more seasons to watch before my one-month trial ends, so that should keep me busy.

The following day, I return to Principal Ross's office.

She says, "Mr. Connelly, now is not a good time."

"Okay, well, you'll have to speak to me at some point. You can't just have me removed from class with no justification, and expect me to sit in the lounge all day."

"You'll receive something in writing soon."

"What do you expect me to do all day? Because I would love to go home."

"Mr. Connelly, you're not permitted to leave. You can wait in the teachers' lounge until further notice. Please excuse yourself."

I turn around and make my way back to the teachers' jail.

I hook up my laptop and continue watching *Survivor*. I've converted the lounge into my man cave. I turn off all the lights, put a few chairs together, prop my feet up, and chill out. I still can't help feeling like I'm in prison. Most of my colleagues notice that I'm stuck here all day. Frankly, it's infantilizing and flat-out idiotic, especially when there are classes upstairs with no teacher.

But the principal is trying to prove a point and flex her authority. Or better yet, she's trying to get rid of me altogether. Either way, I'm not bothered because I'm innocent. They were the ones caught with their hands inside the cookie jar, and this is retribution for my whistleblowing.

A week later, I'm still stuck in the teachers' lounge: no explanation, no recourse. At this point, we're beyond ridiculous. I've contacted the district, union, and Relay, but everything is in limbo during the investigation. So, what does one do in the most litigious land on earth?

You find a lawyer. I spend the entire day looking for representation. Most offices just have a paralegal take my info and say someone will be in touch—*if* they want to follow up. Which, of course, means if they see any economic potential.

But money isn't what I'm after. I want Mrs. Srinivas to answer for her bald-faced lies. I can't just let her get away with it. She needs to be held accountable.

God only knows how long that'll take. But one thing's for sure: I'm not sticking around to find out. I'd lose my mind.

So, you know what time it is, my friends? It's *travelerapy* time.

Tulum, Mexico—here I come!

¡Adiós, enemigos!

Chapter 22

Travelerapy: Tulum Edition

——

B Y NOON THE NEXT DAY, I'M BARRELING DOWN THE Yucatán coast, sweaty, wired, free . . . and still too pissed to relax. I lean against the glass and watch the world blur by: fruit stands, sun-faded ads for beach clubs, jungle creeping toward the pavement. Somewhere along the way, the fog in my head begins to lift, not completely, but enough to feel the tension melt.

Two hours later, I arrive at Lum, a hip hostel tucked a few blocks off Tulum's main drag. From the outside, it's nothing to brag about—a plain concrete box, windowless, and tagged with graffiti. Maybe the architect was going for "brutalist budget chic." I knock. The moment the door opens, I'm floored.

"Buenas tardes." ("Good afternoon.")

"Buenas."

"Bienvenido a Lum." ("Welcome to Lum.")

"Gracias."

The guts of the building are super chic, with polished concrete walls painted a light gray. There are tropical plants everywhere, contrasting with the white stones on the ground. All the windows and door frames are made of wood, which helps tie everything together. It's very feng shui. The splash of Mexican tiles adds some local flavor.

This isn't backpacking—we're flashpacking now, baby.

"You're staying for three nights?" the hostel worker says.

"Yes."

"*Bueno*. May I offer you a welcome drink?"

"*Por favor. Gracias.*"

The punch packs a delightful kick, perfectly countering the dry Caribbean air.

Luckily, the bed is ready, so I make my way upstairs. I'm staying in a six-person dorm. I have a top bunk, which should be fun to access. I stash my bags, grab a bike, and ride to the main strip because my stomach is growling more than the Cookie Monster. I stumble upon a quaint restaurant with four tables in the front.

Only one of them is vacant. I always judge how nice a place is by the crowd it draws. The patrons seem like locals as well. If it's good for them, it's good for me. I say, *"Buen provecho"* (*"Bon appétit"*) to the other guests in the restaurant.

They all respond with a friendly *"Gracias."* I love this part of Mexican culture. You never enter a restaurant without saying *"Buen provecho."* That would be blasphemy! The waiter leads me to my table. Moments later, he returns with the menu board and goes over the day's specials. I select the red snapper cooked Veracruz style.

As the aroma of garlic, onions, and tomatoes fills the air, my anticipation grows. Fifteen minutes later, the waiter arrives, skillfully balancing the sizzling dish. I say my prayers, then get down to business.

The fish is so fresh it practically melts in my mouth. The flavors don't whisper—they shout, igniting my palate like fireworks. The crisp wine with citrus notes seals the deal. I polish off my meal in record time. Moments later, the waiter returns with the dessert menu. Yes, they have my favorite. I smile, already tasting it.

"Tiramisu, *por favor*." The entire meal costs me less than $20. *Increíble*. It's the first time in months I feel full—in more ways than one.

In the days that follow, I dive into everything Tulum has to offer: cenotes, beach-hopping, parties with my hostel crew. Each adventure lifts the weight a little—one wave, one laugh, one dance at a time. I didn't realize how much the tension with my colleagues had been weighing me down. The road always brings clarity—space to let go of the noise and hear myself again.

I feel like a new person, lighter, stronger, unwilling to let anything or anyone drag me down. But it's easy to feel carefree when you're far from your problems. The real test is finding the beauty in the chaos back home. It won't be easy. Then again, nothing worth having ever is.

A COUPLE OF DAYS later, I'm back at school, still simmering with anger, but at least now I see it clearly. Change is impossible without awareness. The principal finally agrees to meet with me. She says, "The district and the union have concluded their investigation, and you will return to Mrs. Srinivas's class just for biology and work with small groups during the other periods. Okay?"

"Not okay. How do you expect me to work around this lady after the baseless allegations she made? We have yet to meet once to discuss this matter. Now, I'm supposed to carry on like nothing ever happened? Absolutely not."

"Very well, Mr. Connelly. So, you're not following my directives?"

"Not until the three of us sit down and talk because she's not lying on me again. But I'm fine working with the small groups."

"I'll be sure to give Relay that update."

"Please do. So, I'll return to the teachers' lounge."

"No, you can use the conference room behind the main office. That's where you'll be teaching your small groups." I go to check out my new digs. The space feels like a fishbowl. Everyone who passes by can see me. I still feel like I'm in prison. Before, I was in the cafeteria; now, I'm in the visiting room.

At least I have a landline to make calls. My phone gets the worst reception in this building. A few lawyers have gotten in touch with me. However, because I'm still employed with the district, there's little they can do. So, I'm between a rock and a hard place.

I'm stoked to start working with small groups soon. I'll do anything to relieve my ennui at this point. I receive a call minutes before the bell rings with a New York area code. It's probably one of those frigging tele-marketers. I debate whether I should pick up or let the person leave a message. But it's not like I have much else going on, so I answer the call.

"Hello."

"Hello, is this Tarique Connelly?"

"Yes, it is."

"Great! This is Angela. I'm a casting agent on the television show *The $100,000 Pyramid*. Do you have a second to chat?"

"Absolutely! Thank you so much for calling me!"

"Thanks for filling out the online application. The producers loved your energy. So, we're just following up to learn a little more about you. Our conversation should only take about ten minutes. Does that sound good?"

"Totally."

Angela asks me most of the questions from the online application. Why do I want to be on the show? What would I do with the money? And who are my favorite celebrities? For the celebrity question, I answer, "Oprah, Barack Obama, and Michael Strahan."

Gotta show the host some love—I mean, the guy made jumping from the gridiron to *Good Morning America* look effortless. Unfortunately, he's the host, so teaming up is off the table. The casting agent, bone-dry, adds there's a good chance Oprah and Barack will be busy too.

"Cool beans. Well, I'm open to playing with anyone."

After playing a few rounds of the game, she tells me she'll call if I advance to the next round.

Perhaps my fifteen minutes of fame will be extended!

It would be nice to fixate on something other than the absurdity of my situation at school. *Survivor* will have to be put on the back burner while I consume prodigious amounts of *The $100,000 Pyramid*. Mastering this game will become my new life's purpose.

Shallow, yes, but it's not every day you have the chance to win $150,000. I haven't been this excited about something since I began studying to become a teacher. I love being challenged and having things to look forward to. It's the best way to break the monotony of everyday life.

Then—just as I'm riding that high—an email comes in from a law firm. They want to meet on Monday to discuss my allegations.

Oh man, it's getting real.

A FEW DAYS later, I'm back in the fishbowl, this time with two lawyers. I'm not sure who they represent, but it's obvious they're not on the same team. My guess? One's with the union, the other with the district. They fire off questions, scribble notes, and ask for all my receipts, which I happily provide. I feel like David taking on Goliath.

Who knows if it'll even amount to anything? But at least I tried to make a difference by exposing the systemic racism that so often gets buried. The lawyers leave after my thirty-minute interview. As I sink into the office chair, a quiet sense of validation washes over me, but the feeling doesn't last long.

Through the window into the main office, I catch glimpses of concern on my colleagues' faces. There's tension in the air. I can't tell if it's because I spoke up or because of this new virus spreading across the country.

The threat feels serious. Everyone's on edge. Still, the idea of schools closing feels surreal. Technically, my school year ended weeks ago, but the idea of *all* schools shutting down? Unimaginable.

Two days later, on March 14, 2020, the hammer drops: schools are closing. Classes are moving online—effective immediately. No warning. No playbook. Just a system scrambling to reinvent itself overnight. But here's the kicker—we've got no clue how to pull it off. To make matters worse, many students don't even have internet access, but those are Mrs. Srinivas's issues, not mine. She spent the entire year icing me out. Now? I'm more than happy to sit this one out. I log on once to witness the drudgery—then, never look back.

Besides, I've got a game show to prepare for. It's official. I will be a contestant on *The $100,000 Pyramid. Woot! Woot!* I knew they would pick me after my third interview. The only question is when we'll tape the show, given that the world is shutting down. I'll tell you one thing: I'm not waiting around to find out. The funk is hitting the fan in the US. If I don't leave now, I'm afraid I'll be trapped here. I'd much rather be stuck on the beach in Mexico. So, it's time to bounce.

With that, sayonara, Agape. It's been real. I wish I could end on a happier note, but hey . . . *que será, será.* Here's hoping things go a little smoother with my next employer. Of course, this will be my fourth school in three years—but who's counting? Principal Ross definitely isn't inviting me back. That's fine. The feeling's mutual.

Still, despite all the drama, I made it. I survived. And somehow, I've come away with everything I need to secure my teaching credentials.

Sure, it came with some heartburn, but my students made every second of it worth it. Now I move forward with my head held high, knowing I did everything I could to make a difference. And that's something no one can ever take away from me.

Do I feel guilty for earning my license without jumping through all the usual hoops? A little. But I didn't write the rules; I just played the game. Hopefully, the path to my master's doesn't come with as many landmines. But I'll cross that bridge when I get there.

Right now, it's time to hit the reset button. *Beep!*

PART THREE

Chapter 23

Zoom and Gloom

——

THE CLOCK STRIKES SEVEN. NORMALLY, THAT'S MY cue to shake, rattle, and roll. But today, I'm still wrapped in blankets, soaking up the luxury of a slow start. In a twist I didn't see coming, the bigwigs decided to kick off the 2020/2021 school year online, turning my bedroom into a makeshift classroom. Luckily, the first two days are just for teachers, which gives me a little breathing room—especially since I missed day one.

While everyone else was shaking off first-day jitters, I was in New York, under the bright lights of *The $100,000 Pyramid*, trying my luck on national TV. After just twenty minutes in the hot seat, I walked away with a cool $11,110. Not bad for a day's work.

Now I'm back—new school, new format, new reality. Part of me is curious. Part of me is nervous. And all of me is flying blind. Back in the spring, when most teachers were earning their virtual stripes, I was barefoot, beach-hopping through Mexico.

Thanks to Mrs. Srinivas, my summer vacation started in March, which meant missing the entire remote learning kickoff. For months, she was a thorn in my side, but in the end, her sabotage became my salvation, giving me three unexpected months off during the most chaotic time in education.

And to top it off, the airline furloughed me with pay. And just like that, I went from 60-hour weeks to zero. Imagine getting paid in dollars while spending pesos, with nothing to do but rest, reflect, and recover. Jackpot.

But the real surprise wasn't the time off—it was what it revealed. I had spent so much energy fighting for students and clashing with colleagues that I barely recognized who I'd become. When the noise stopped, I could finally hear myself again. For the first time in years, I could step out of the fight mode I'd lived in for most of my life.

In that sense, it wasn't just a vacation—it was a reclamation of my time, my energy, and the joy I'd surrendered to constant conflict. In that quiet revolution, I reclaimed the part of myself I'd lost in the chaos. When the world stopped, I finally did too—and that changed everything.

Anyway . . . enough reflection for now.

Back to our irregularly scheduled programming.

Welcoming colleagues into my home feels strange, but at least my commute is down to zero. All I have to do is power up the laptop, log into Zoom, and voilà—class is in session. This year, I'll be working at the Innovation School. It's funny how life circles back.

Back in 2017, I was building my motivational speaking career and needed a demo reel, but I couldn't find a school willing to let me record it. I reached out to every high school principal in Philadelphia, offering my services free of charge in exchange for the chance to film. Out of fifty principals, only one replied: Jermaine Billingsley, principal of the Innovation School.

I joked about the lack of responses when we first met. I remember him saying, "I'm willing to try anything to get through to our students." I thought that was admirable and says a lot about him. Now, three years later, we meet again. It'll be interesting to see how he leads during these unprecedented times.

I roll out of bed with ten minutes to spare, feed Creamy, and brush my teeth. I don't have time to make my favorite sandwich, so I settle for a protein bar. It's five minutes until showtime. Thank God it's a staff-only day.

I quickly throw on a Polo fleece and basketball shorts. I set up my laptop with my bookcase as a backdrop. Most teachers will likely be freaking out about the students' arrival tomorrow—but me? I'm chillin' like a villain. Why, you might ask?

Well, for the second year in a row, I'll be working with a partner, still pulling full salary—and this time, with a raise. So, I'm getting paid more to do a fraction of the job. *How did I get so lucky? I swear it's karma.*

My official title is supplemental science teacher. It's the same position from the first year. However, this time, I'll actually be working in a supplemental capacity. I've been waiting for Principal Billingsley to pull the rug from under my feet and assign me other classes, but surprisingly, it hasn't happened.

Actually, I haven't heard from him at all. I wonder if he even realizes I'm the guy who spoke at Innovation years ago. I doubt it. He has a million other things to think about. But at some point, he'll have to tell me who I'm working with.

After all the drama last year, the last thing I wanted to do was work with someone else, but there weren't any biology positions available. Word on the street is that many teachers planning to retire or switch jobs decided to stay. Go figure. The district asked if I wanted an emergency permit in a different subject. I said absolutely not. Middle school? It'll be a cold day in hell. That's when they gave me the supplemental option. Perfect.

Now, don't get me wrong, I love my independence, but this arrangement feels like a godsend during these tumultuous times. Besides, it's only supposed to last until October. That's when the district does leveling and reshuffles teachers to where they're needed, but who knows what'll happen at this stage. For now, I'll just log in and play along.

I join the Zoom meeting with my camera on and mic off. The screen looks like a laptop version of *Hollywood Squares*. Principal Billingsley welcomes the staff. He says, "We'll start shortly." I look at all my colleagues and wonder which one I'll have the pleasure of working with.

Some let us peek into their bedrooms, clutter and all, while others float behind flawless digital backdrops, turning their homes into carefully curated illusions. I can't resist clicking on profiles to make up-close observations. The anxiety is written on everyone's faces. The first week of school is always nerve-wracking, but navigating it in a virtual setting during a pandemic is an entirely different beast.

Principal Billingsley says, "We're ready to get started." He's a cool cat with a clean cut and a calm demeanor. He seems to have an excellent rapport with the staff. After going through his spiel, he asks, "Are there any questions for the good of the group?"

Suddenly, a lady begins talking without realizing her mic is maxed out.

"Hello! Hello! Can you hear me?"

Principal Billingsley says, "Yes, we hear you loud and clear. Can you please turn your volume down?"

"Oh, sorry." She takes a second to lower it and adjust her camera. "How's that?"

"Much better," replies Principal Billingsley.

"My name is Ms. Holloway. I'm the new environmental science teacher. I could really use some assistance. I'm completely overwhelmed right now. I need help setting up my Zoom links and Google Classrooms. I also need a laptop because I'm working on my personal computer. I have tried contacting the district, but getting anyone on the phone is impossible. I have left several messages but have yet to receive a response. I'm also having trouble logging into the teacher's portal and . . ."

"One second, please," Principal Billingsley interjects.

I feel like I'm going to have a panic attack just listening to her. I want to say, breathe and take a chill pill, lady. It's not that deep. But that's easy for me to say.

Principal Billingsley says, "Your training included some of that information. Have you finished?"

"I have not."

"Okay, well, you want to start there. However, I will have our IT guy contact you to see if he can help. But he's swamped getting students started, so that might take a while."

"I appreciate any help that you can offer."

"No problem. Is there anything else for the good of the group?"

Everyone is panicking over anything and everything. I'm hearing the conversation but not actively listening. That changes when a colleague asks, "Hey, Billingsley, how do you feel about us working from the beach?"

He replies, "I have no problem with where you teach from, as long as it's presentable and doesn't impede learning. So, if you want to hashtag '#teachfromthebeach,' be my guest."

Oh really? That's wonderful to know. Realizing the questions are unending, Principal Billingsley says, "Everyone is free to go unless you have further concerns." I wish I could leave. I have some training to complete. However, I still have to figure out who I will partner with. My turn finally comes.

"Good morning, Principal Billingsley. My name is Mr. Connelly. I'm your supplemental science teacher."

"Welcome, Mr. Connelly."

"Thank you, sir."

"How can I help you?"

"I just need to know who I'll be working with."

"My apologies for not sending you a formal welcome letter. I only learned you were coming yesterday and completely forgot to reach out."

"No worries. You have your hands full."

"So, you're certified to teach biology, right?"

"Yeah."

"Let's pair you up with our biology teacher, Mr. Sanford. He'll be an excellent mentor. He has a ton of real-world and classroom experience. I'll inform him you'll be working with him. I'll also put his email address and Zoom links in the chat box."

"Cool beans. I appreciate you, sir."

"No doubt, brother. Welcome aboard. And don't hesitate to reach out if you need anything."

"Thanks."

Nice. Not only is my boss a guy, but my partner will be too. That's pretty ironic in a profession dominated by women. I email Mr. Sanford to introduce myself and offer to assist.

He responds minutes later. "Hello. I was unaware that I would be working with anyone this year, nor have I agreed to the arrangement. Principal Billingsley is in the process of clarifying things. You should hear something from him shortly." Shucks. Okay. I take it he's not too thrilled to have me on board.

I can't fathom why a teacher would pass up extra support. But I also can't expect everyone to think and act like me. If Mr. Sanford prefers to work harder than smarter, that's his problem. I'm not begging anybody to work. I saw how far that got me at Agape. If the district wants to pay me to twiddle my thumbs while they figure out how best to underutilize me, then so be it.

An hour later, Principal Billingsley follows up. "I apologize for the confusion. Mr. Sanford is a seasoned teacher and doesn't require any reinforcement. So, I will reassign you to the new environmental science and biology teacher, Ms. Holloway."

I cringe the moment I read her name. Don't tell me he's pairing me with the woman who was freaking out in the morning meeting? The email continues. "She's new to the school and district, so she could better use your expertise." *Damn it.* Why did Brother Sanford have to leave me hanging? Oh well, it is what it is. All I can do is take the cards I'm dealt and play them the best I can. Principal Billingsley includes all of Ms. Holloway's contact information in the email and encourages me to contact her.

The school day is almost over. I really don't want to reach out. However, I need the game plan for tomorrow. So, I email her, introduce myself, and encourage her to reach out if I can assist. Barely two minutes pass before she replies. "Hello, Mr. Connelly. I could really use your help. Please meet me at this Zoom link."

Okay, well, it feels good to be needed. I just didn't anticipate being needed so soon. I'm already shifting to after-work mode. Although, technically, I've been mentally checked out all day. So, I click on the Zoom link to meet up with Ms. Holloway.

"Hello. How's it going? I'm Tarique."

"Patty. Nice to meet you."

"Likewise. So, what's going on? Maybe I can give you a hand."

"Gosh, I would so appreciate that. I'm so stressed I don't know what to do with myself."

"What's up?"

"For starters, I can't set up these damn Zoom links. I'm trying to make them recurring events."

"Okay. Can you share your screen, please?"

"Yes."

"Scroll down."

"Right there, there's a box that says recurring meetings. You have to check that box and specify the dates."

"Oh my god. I feel so stupid. Thank you so much."

"No problem. That's what I'm here for. Two minds always work better than one."

"I agree. So, how long will I have you?"

"I'm not too sure. Hopefully, the entire year, but at the very least, you'll have me till the second marking period."

"Okay, so you'll be here for a while. Well, I need a huge favor from you."

"Shoot."

"I need you to manage the class this week, and I can pick things up from there."

"So, you want me to teach tomorrow?"

"Yes, please. I'm in a tough situation. I'm in the middle of a divorce and relocating from Maryland to Philly."

"Yikes. I'm so sorry to hear that."

"It's for the best. I'm just ready to move on at this point, but I have a lot to juggle over these next few days, so if you can help me, I will be forever indebted to you."

"No problem. Don't worry about it. It's a short week. I can handle things. You take care of yourself and do whatever you have to do."

"Thank you so much for being so understanding."

"No problem. I hope you have a smooth transition back to Philly."

"Thanks."

Just when I thought it was wine time, now I've got to put my teaching cap back on and prep a lesson for tomorrow. I can't help but wonder what Ms. Holloway would've done if I hadn't come along, but that's neither here nor there. We're a team now, and it's my job to support her. I wish I had more time to design an engaging lesson, but that's out of the question.

Now, I'm freaking out. I hate rushing and doing things at the last minute. It's not how I roll. But I remind myself that it's not about me. I'm part of a team now. So, get your boxers out of a bunch and get to planning.

It's the first day of virtual class. The only faces visible on the screen are Ms. Holloway's and mine. The students are all represented by black boxes with their names in white. Not one student bothers to turn their camera on. Well, one did for a millisecond but quickly retreated after realizing he was a lone ranger. They are all such copycats.

The administrators made students' camera usage optional. They don't want to embarrass students who may not have optimal living arrangements or, even worse, have no accommodations at all. This policy decision was made with the best intentions, but ultimately, it'll do more harm than good because there's no way to ensure that students are engaged. The only thing we see are names on the screen.

If students struggle to pay attention in the presence of teachers, you know they're not paying attention when we can't see them. It's too easy to get distracted at home, with a million things going on and your favorite vices at your fingertips. Shucks, I'm an adult, and I struggle with that. I can't imagine what it must be like for a kid.

Still, part of me wonders if virtual learning could be more of an opportunity than a setback. Students today live in an increasingly digitized world, yet their education rarely reflects it. Technology has transformed nearly every industry, but the education system remains stubbornly unchanged. For the most part, schools still look and function much like they did at their inception. Administrators could use this moment to modernize, but I'm not optimistic.

Either way, I'm already exploring cool websites such as CK-12, Padlet, EdPuzzles, and Kahoot! that I can integrate into class. I share these ideas with Ms. Holloway. She loves them. She's getting really comfortable chilling in the background and letting me do everything. I didn't mind taking over the first few days, but now she's milking it a bit, making it the perfect time to hand back the reins. I wait for all the students to log off at the end of class.

"Hey, Ms. Holloway."

"Hey, Mr. C. Are you ready to start your weekend?"

"I sure am, but only after I figure out the game plan for next week."

"Oh, I'm flexible. Feel free to do whatever you like. You're doing excellent."

"Thanks," I say. "I appreciate that. However, I would like to get you more involved. I had no problem taking over for the first few days but didn't intend to take over everything."

"Okay, so you no longer want to teach?"

"I'm okay with leading the class sometimes, but I don't want to teach all the time."

"How would you like to contribute?"

"I can start the class daily with a Do Now. That way, you'll have time to complete the attendance. I can also finish class with an exit ticket and complete all the administrative tasks like marking papers, grading tests, and test reviews. How does that sound?"

"Well, if that's all you are willing to offer, then that's what I'll take."

"Listen, I'm flexible and have no problem supporting you. I just don't want to be responsible for doing everything."

"Okay, I understand. So, from now on, you will start and end class. I'm okay with that."

"Perfect."

"So, what are your plans for this weekend?"

"I'm considering returning to Mexico. I'm going stir-crazy being locked in this house. I haven't left the country for months, and I'm long overdue for a detox."

"I hear you. I wish I could join you. So, Mexico?"

"Yeah, that's what I'm thinking. I don't have many options. I still can't believe Europe shut its borders. How about you? Any plans?"

"I'm spending some time with Dad, and my sister and I are having a date night."

"Cool beans. Are you making a new pasta?"

"Yeah, I found a smoked-mozzarella-and-spinach recipe. I'm going to take a stab at it."

"Sounds yummy."

"I'll let you know how it turns out."

"Awesome. Well, have a great weekend, and enjoy your time with the family."

"Thanks. Safe travels if you decide to bail."

"I appreciate it."

Ms. Holloway has been holding me hostage on Zoom every day after school. She's already told me her whole life story. Sometimes I feel like she's using me to fill the void her ex-husband left. But after months cooped up at home, I've grown antisocial, retreating further into my own quiet. Still, I keep up the small talk, pretending it doesn't drain me.

Even with her stories, I can't help but notice how calm this setup feels compared to the frenzy of in-person teaching. God, I don't miss the fights, the drama, or the endless tension with colleagues. After so much chaos, this solitude feels like a rare gift.

The peace is priceless. The only thing I cherish more is freedom— though lately, both feel fragile, as if the world is conspiring to take them away. Amid constant news alerts, social distancing, and the daily uncertainty of a mutating virus, this calm feels fleeting, always teetering on the edge of disruption. So with the walls closing in, there's only one escape for me: travelerapy.

Time to chase the sun—Oaxaca, Mexico, here I come!

Chapter 24

Travelerapy: Oaxaca Edition

———

THE DIRT ROAD CURVES TOWARD THE BEACH, THE ocean glinting under a low golden sun. As I near One Love hostel, the thick wooden doors rise into view—weathered oak, wide open, as if welcoming me back. I step through the entrance, and the beach falls away. I'm in the jungle now. Everywhere I look, it's green and verdant.

What were once saplings when I first arrived years ago have grown into a lush, untamed canopy. Leaves the size of my torso fan out overhead. Vines spill down from tree limbs like they're reaching. The air is warm and still, buzzing faintly with life. Cali, one of the hostel cats, lounges on a stone ledge, watching me with slow-blinking eyes. I exhale. I'm home.

I've booked the four-person dorm again—$15 a night. A private room is only $30, but I don't need it. Besides, wealth isn't about what you earn—it's about what you keep. Right? Anyhow, I'm just here to sleep.

I drop my bag off in the dorm and head straight for the terrace, where the breeze rolls in from the ocean and everything slows down. It's where I spend most of my time, usually in a hammock with a book, or just watching the palms sway. It's also where yoga is practiced each morning, and if you sit still long enough, you can almost feel the energy the yogis leave behind. I let myself sink into the stillness, not thinking, just being.

As the sky fades from soft pinks to purples, the hours slip by unnoticed. Eventually, I pull myself up and make my way back to the dorm. Luckily, no one else checked in while I was gone. After completing my nightly rituals, I slip under the covers and let the sound of distant waves carry me to sleep.

In the blink of an eye, morning arrives. I shake off the last traces of sleep and slide into the day's rhythm, setting up shop in the restaurant. Time to log into Zoom and get this environmental science class rolling. Inside the chat, I type "Good morning," add the date, and post the Do Now question: "How does water go from the hydrosphere to the atmosphere?"

Students' names begin popping up on the screen like a cell dividing.

"Good morning. I hope everyone is well. Let's get started in five minutes. Be sure to give me at least three complete sentences. Remember, don't just accept the first answer you find. Read the answer from at least three credible sources and then develop your answer using your own words.

"We have two minutes left. Place a one inside the chat if you're ready, or a two if you need some more time." About ten ones are posted in succession. The other students are probably still asleep.

"All righty, let's get this party started. Let's begin with our check-in. From one to five, where one is 'I'm feeling horrible,' and five is 'I'm feeling like a million bucks,' drop your numbers inside the chat.

"Shout out to Ms. Holloway, holding it down at a three. I see you, Markeira, with the five. Imani's cruising at a four, while Damian's repping at a three. And hey, Asia, we're here for you with that negative five. Remember, having a bad day is normal; nobody's always at five. It's better to embrace it all. But kudos to you for not letting it stop you from being here. Let's send her some love in the chat, class."

I continue reading the names until I acknowledge everyone. In meetings, most of my colleagues complain they can't get any participation. Yet, most students respond to the daily check-in. I start there because their well-being means more than their academic success.

As the saying goes, "Students don't care how much you know until they know how much you care." The check-in brings that idea to life. It enables me to personally acknowledge each of them and address how they feel. It also allows me to normalize mental health conversations.

Unfortunately, many teachers become so fixated on academics that they miss the opportunity to help students cultivate their emotional intelligence. I love starting class here because self-knowledge is the best kind of knowledge. Once you're aware of how you're feeling, you can do something about it—but awareness always comes first. After completing the check-in and the Do Now, I hand the reins back over to Ms. Holloway.

She says, "Stick around till the end of class because I have to ask you something."

"Cool beans."

The sun is starting to climb. The roosters are crowing loudly, heralding the break of dawn with their grating calls. I turn off my camera and listen in while watching the quaint beach town wake up. After class, I stay back to chat with Ms. Holloway.

"Hey, Mr. C."

"Hi, Ms. Holloway. How are you?"

"I'm okay. I'd be a lot better if I were in Mexico. And you?"

"I'm excellent."

"Great. Well, we need to give the students a project. Any ideas?"

"I'm unsure," I say. "There's no time left. We barely fit the test in."

She shrugs. "I feel the same. I'll just give them a random assignment and call it a project."

"Okay."

"Now, about the test—how do you think they did?"

"I imagine the first period did well."

"No," she says, raising an eyebrow. "I'm not talking about the first period. The last two."

"A quarter of the students didn't pass?"

"Yeah, right. More than that."

"Yikes. That's a bummer."

"How can they be so fucking stupid?" She scoffs. "We made the test so easy. I don't get it."

The "stupid" comment offends me, but I act as if I didn't hear it. Ms. Holloway has said similar things before, but I've swept it under the rug because I'm trying to be nonconfrontational and play nice.

Moreover, I wouldn't be living my best life in Mexico without her help, so I've been more than gracious in accommodating her ignorance. However, my patience is starting to wear thin. I don't want to be the angry Black guy. I have battled with colleagues at every school I have been to, and I realize I'm the common denominator in all these occurrences. Lord knows, I want to change, but she is one crass comment away from me checking her.

I respond, "Well, they're going through a difficult time. If it's hard for us, you know it's even harder for them."

"Tarique, that's bullshit! You're making excuses."

"It's called empathy and compassion. Remember, it's the same compassion you asked for in the first week of school when you were having a hard time. Maybe try offering some of that to them."

"I did! Do you know how much I had to resist changing the questions on the test because you made them so easy? And they still bombed! The answers were right on the test. Like, how fucking stupid can you be?"

"STOP SAYING THAT! THEY ARE NOT STUPID! I'm so tired of hearing you make comments like that. I haven't said anything because I'm trying to be Mr. Nice Guy, but that's it. I never want to hear you make a comment like that again. Otherwise, we'll be having this conversation with Principal Billingsley.

"And let me explain something to you: just because you read verbatim from some outdated PowerPoint you downloaded off the internet doesn't mean you're a great teacher. Teaching is not about what you know but the knowledge you transfer. I have to sit through your class every day, bored to death, and if I were them, I wouldn't come either. So, before you start throwing stones, here's a newsflash: you don't live in a glass house. You need to look at yourself in the mirror and reflect on the part you've played in their failure because you're the captain of this sinking ship."

An uneasy silence settles between us. She finally says, "Mr. C., I am so sorry for offending you. I wish you had told me earlier so I could've made it right. But I promise I won't say anything like that again. I truly am sorry for upsetting you."

"I accept your apology. And I'm sorry I snapped."

"No, no, no. It's okay. You had every right to."

"No, there's a way to disagree civilly. But next time, I'll say something immediately."

"Oh, don't you worry. There won't be a next time."

"I hope not. Let's just keep it moving."

Moments like this change everything. You can't unhear the comment or unsee what it reveals. Respect fractures, and it's hard to repair. The truth is Ms. Holloway isn't unique—she just makes visible the divide so many teachers carry into the classroom.

We talk a lot about learning gaps, but the real crisis is an empathy gap. And closing that gap requires more than good intentions. It begins with seeing students fully—without judgment, without assumption. It's tempting to feel sorry for them, but pity doesn't just build walls; it quietly lowers the bar before students even have a chance to reach it.

Over time, many shrink to meet the low expectations placed on them, forgetting just how capable they are. That quiet erosion of confidence, happening in classrooms everywhere, may be education's greatest tragedy.

And yet, every student carries a spark of brilliance, even when the structure of school and standardized tests keep it hidden. Their curiosity, creativity, and resilience may be stifled, but they remain. Our responsibility is to create classrooms where those strengths can flourish, where students are given the space, support, and encouragement to grow and reach their full potential.

To make this possible, educators must first let go of limiting assumptions—about intelligence, behavior, and even themselves. Only then can we unlock the full force of human potential and build a future that does more than tolerate difference. We can build a future that draws its greatest strength from it, shaped by the unique gifts of every learner.

Chapter 25

Plot Twist: We're Going Back

———

I'M CRAMMED INTO A COLECTIVO (SHARED MINIVAN) winding its way through the Oaxacan mountains, one sharp turn after another. The road coils like a serpent, each curve tugging my body to the side as we climb higher. Cool, damp air seeps through the cracked window, carrying the scent of pine and wet earth. Up front, a tiny screen plays a Spanish-dubbed *Bourne Identity*. I try to follow along, but the dialogue moves way too fast, and I can't keep up. Maybe that's a sign from the universe to keep my eyes on the road and focus on not throwing up.

Last night, the entire network in Puerto Escondido shut down—no internet, no signal, nothing. One moment I'm talking, the next I'm frozen mid-word, eyes half-closed, mouth hanging, like a screenshot no one meant to take. I'd been dreading this exact moment, but when it finally happened, I didn't panic. I felt surprisingly calm. Good thing Ms. Holloway jumped right in without missing a beat.

So, now I'm on my way to San José del Pacifico, praying that the internet will be better there. After four hours of hairpin turns and close calls, we finally roll into town just in time for sunset. The hills stretch out around me, blanketed in deep green. Trees crowd the slopes, their tops vanishing into a slow-moving mist that moves through the valley, like it has nowhere else to be. The whole place feels hushed, suspended in its own rhythm.

I'm staying at La Cumbre, one of my favorite hostels. For eleven bucks, I get a four-person cabin with a private bathroom and a view so majestic that I forget I came here looking for Wi-Fi. Of course, I risk having roommates. But I'll take that trade for the natural light, the space, and the peace this place always gives me. The night comes swiftly as the temperature drops by more than twenty degrees. I listen to the howling winds, branches falling on the roof, and dogs barking until they lull me to sleep.

The following day, I wake up before my alarm sounds. I tiptoe, but my steps drag heavily like feet made of lead. I set up my computer on the little wooden table. I'll have to use my Darth Vader voice to avoid waking my hostel mates in the other rooms. The walls are paper-thin—I know because they offered zero insulation last night. Still, it's an epic deal for eleven bucks. I log into Zoom, greet Ms. Holloway, and drop the Do Now in the chat. The students' names trickle in one by one, little black boxes blinking to life. It's showtime.

I launch into my spiel about the Water Cycle—evaporation, condensation, precipitation, all that good stuff. I'm hyping it up like it's a Marvel origin story when Ms. Holloway cuts in with the voice she saves for news I won't like.

"Mr. C., check your email."

"Cool beans." I try to play it off, but my stomach tightens. She never tells me to check my email mid-class. I keep going, rambling about runoff and collection, but my focus is already split. I return the reins and start digging through my inbox, half-expecting something minor.

Then I hear her say it.

"Students, I have some good news. Please don't quote me, but we might be returning to school soon."

Wait—what?

Did she just say *returning?*

I freeze for a second, then start clicking through my inbox, scrambling to find whatever email she's talking about. And there it is—an email dated May 6th, 2021.

After more than a year, it's happening—we're going back. In person.

Why now? There's only a month left. What's the point? Everyone knows the last stretch is a joke. Still, after being locked away for so long, I imagine the students are craving some sense of normalcy. The prospect of returning to a physical classroom feels surreal after a year behind screens, yet it's the commitment I signed up for.

My bond with my students pulls me back, despite the temptation to stay on the road. Even with our limited interactions, I've grown fond of them and would love to finally put faces to names. It's kind of funny—they've had eyes on us all year, but I've only caught glimpses of a few.

As stoked as I am to see them, I'm also a little sad to trade in the freedom of my current setup. Nonetheless, I'm grateful for the time I've had. Besides, summer will be here before I know it, and then I'll be free to hit the road again.

As we confront the challenges of returning to the physical classroom, a flame of hope burns within me. It's a hope for forging deeper connections with students, a hope for resuming some normalcy, and a hope for a brighter and more interconnected future after weathering these turbulent times.

The resilience displayed by educators and students alike fuels this optimism, reinforcing my belief that we possess the strength to surmount the obstacles that lie ahead. So, off to the concrete jungle we go. *¡Adiós México!*

AND JUST LIKE THAT, WE'RE BACK. It legit feels like the first day of school, even though it's early May. We're having a pep rally to welcome students. The energy in the building is anxious and festive. I arrive twenty minutes before the party starts. Upon entering the building, Assistant Principal Kittles greets me.

"Good morning, Mr. Connelly!"

"Good morning, Principal Kittles. It's nice to finally meet you in person."

"Likewise." She's taller than I thought, given her appearance on Zoom.

"I thought you would still be living *La Vida Loca* in Mexico."

"Nah, I wouldn't leave my students hanging like that."

"Are you from Philly, Mr. Connelly?"

"Yeah, I'm from West. And you?"

"I'm from Uptown."

"Okay, that's what's up. I went to Central and was up that way for a while."

"Nice, I graduated from Cheltenham."

"Cool beans."

"OMG, did you say 'cool beans'?"

"I sure did."

"Why did you steal my phrase?"

"What? Your phrase? We go back like babies on Similac!" We share a laugh. One of the hall ladies walks in.

"Well, hello, hello, hello! If it's not Mr. Tank-Top himself."

"Good morning."

She extends her hand to introduce herself. "Mrs. Smith."

"Nice to meet you, Mrs. Smith."

"The pleasure is mine."

She holds on to my hand, looks into my eyes, and asks sincerely: "Are you married?" The timing of the question catches me off guard.

"Stop playing. You don't see a ring on this finger."

"Well, my play daughter, Principal Kittles, is hardworking and owns her car and crib."

Kittles interjects, "Girl, go ahead and stop playing. You're always trying to hook somebody up. Mr. Connelly, I'm sure you have better things to do. Have a nice day. She's a mess."

Their morning shenanigans put a smile on my face. I peace out and head upstairs.

I say hello to all of my colleagues as they pass by. Many of them seem surprised to see me. It almost feels like I'm back in high school.

As I approach the classroom, I look inside and see Holloway sitting at the desk. I open the door and say, "Honey, I'm home."

"Good morning, Mr. C.!"

"Good morning, Ms. Holloway!" I walk over to the desk as she stands up to embrace me. Seeing her in person is weird after spending so much time with her online. She sounds the same, and her energy is as expected, but she is a little shorter than I anticipated. She probably feels the same about me. After a few minutes of chatting, the loudspeaker interrupts.

"All teachers report to the front for the pep rally. All teachers report to the front for the pep rally."

"Oh, gosh. Do we have to?"

Ms. Holloway says, "Come on, we have to go." She's like my work wife, but the divorce papers will be coming soon, and then daddy is free, baby.

We hustle downstairs for the pep rally. The bell rings. The students come streaming in. There's music playing, which you can barely hear. We try to scream for every child that comes through the door, but after the first few, I'm over it. The students have to go through metal detectors, which creates a bottleneck. The staff must also ensure students are here on their designated day. To limit the spread of the virus, each student is allowed on school grounds two days a week, with Fridays reserved for deep cleaning.

All the added protocols have slowed the initial stream of students to a trickle. To pump up the energy, the teacher leader turns up the music: "Dreams and Nightmares" by Meek Mill. It's an excellent choice, given he's one of Philly's own. The only problem is that it's the explicit version. Now, I love Meek, and I'm hyped at hearing his most iconic song, but the volume and expletives make the whole affair seem hella ghetto.

I know they were trying to check the cultural competency box, but there are better ways. Would they play the explicit version of this song anywhere else other than at an urban school in Philadelphia? I wonder if someone will notice the mistake and turn it off; they don't, so I join in and sing along. I can see the surprise on students' faces as they take in the spectacle. One girl in a mask comes up to us: "Hey, Mr. C.! Hey, Ms. Holloway!" We're looking at her, wondering who she is.

Seeing our confusion, she pulls her mask down and says, "It's Brazil."

"Oh, shucks!"

This happens several times over the next fifteen minutes. With everyone masked up, it's like we're all strangers at a masquerade ball—eyes familiar, but the rest a mystery. It feels like I'm meeting students for the first time. However, the pep rally is drier than the Sahara Desert, so I escape to our room, where Holloway joins me.

We arrive with only ten minutes to prepare for the students' arrival. I'm still thinking of a Do Now for the day. I log on to Zoom to open the virtual classroom for students. Five minutes before the class begins, they start streaming in like clockwork.

Surprisingly, most students still show up online. A whopping two students, bless their hearts, decide to grace us with their physical presence. Shucks, only two more bother to show up all day. It seems the students aren't so eager to come back after all. Can you blame them?

Even though the teachers and a handful of students are back in the building, things still feel anything but normal. Teachers are stressed because they're dealing with a heavier workload as they navigate the challenge of both virtual and in-person teaching.

But luckily, Ms. Holloway and I split the responsibilities. That keeps both of us from getting overwhelmed. Now that we're in person, she's brought me some of the salads she makes for her movie night with her sister. I return the favor by bringing her a piece of my famous seafood and spinach lasagna with lump crabmeat, salmon, shrimp, scallops, and artificial crabmeat to add sweetness.

She always asks me to stick around for lunch, but I would rather chill in the park. Going outside for lunch is a habit that dates back to my days at Columbia. And if I'm honest, there's still a part of me holding on to some resentment over her crass comments. Frankly, I have no desire to be her friend anymore. I just want to be cordial and make it to the finish line. Then she can find a surrogate husband elsewhere.

Chapter 26

Setting the Record Straight

—

IT'S THE LAST WEEK OF MAY, AND FOURTH-QUARTER grades are due. I'm sitting in the room next door to Holloway. It's my new private classroom. Our computers started creating a lot of feedback when we were both logged into Zoom. It gave me the perfect excuse to bail. I love having my own space. I'm sure she notices I'm a little distant, but I find it hard to be chummy in person. It's a lot easier online. The reality is she just isn't my cup of tea.

Maya Angelou said it best: "When someone shows you who they are, believe them the first time." Well, it took me five, but I finally got the memo.

I ask her, "Do you need any help entering the grades?"

"No thanks, I have it covered."

"Cool beans."

The day crawls like a snail through mud. It almost makes me miss the madness of my early days at Columbia. I can't believe how far I have come since then and how much the world has changed. Speaking of change, I just learned that I have to switch schools again next year. They're eliminating a general science and a physics position, and those teachers are taking the jobs that Holloway and I have now.

Interestingly, the positions still appear on the district's website, even though I know current employees have already filled them. How many other ghost jobs are there? I wish I could stay here. It's close to home, practically brand-new, and right next to a park I love. But the beat goes on.

I'm sitting in class bored while we are watching *Our Planet* on Netflix when an announcement over the loudspeaker reminds teachers that grades are due by midnight. Out of curiosity, I log into the teacher's portal to see if I can check the students' grades. Surprisingly, I have access. With nothing better to do, I begin analyzing them. The results? Shocking.

The students only need a 60 percent to pass. There are a ton of students with a 59. There was no extra credit offered, no calls made to parents, no grace extended to these children who had just endured a life-changing circumstance. A part of me thinks she gets off on failing kids. And the facts seem to back that up. I start examining the grades further and find all types of discrepancies.

For starters, students are supposed to receive a minimum of 50 on any assignment, and many students have zeros. I don't agree with that policy entirely, but I understand the logic behind it. Receiving a zero on a test or project is nearly impossible to bounce back from. Also, we are supposed to have several tests, projects, and assignments, which help to balance the grade. We haven't had half of that. Whenever I asked her about grades, she insisted that she was being considerate; in actuality, she was erring on the side of failing kids who could have passed.

I feel terrible because it's the last quarter, and the grades are cumulative. I should have been paying more attention. I feel played. I start to go next door to confront her, but then I realize who I'm dealing with. Instead, I don't say anything and act like nothing ever happened.

At the end of the day, I say, "I'm going home but feel guilty for not helping you with grades. Are you sure you don't want me to give you a hand?"

"No, I'm okay. I only have a few more to go, anyhow, but thanks."

"Okay, well, don't say I didn't ask. Have a good day."

"You too, Mr. C."

I wait until about eleven o'clock at night, when I'm confident that she's finished. Then I log on, and I change all the zeros to 50s. I know many people might disagree with this and consider it hypocritical, especially since I reported my colleagues at Agape for giving out fake grades that students didn't earn. Both actions are forms of grade inflation, but there are key differences.

First, setting a minimum grade is often a transparent policy communicated to all students and parents, whereas a fake grade on a report card is not disclosed and is deceptive. Secondly, minimum grade policies are consistently applied to all students, whereas fake grades are not.

Lastly, minimum grade policies aim to motivate students and keep them in school, whereas fake grades misrepresent a student's capabilities and are merely a ploy to make schools look good on paper. While both practices involve altering grades, the intentions and implications behind them differ significantly.

I work feverishly until quarter to twelve. I return to the screen after midnight to see if I can make additional changes. A screen pops up and says the grading system is locked. *Awesome sauce!* Changing the grades will take a herculean effort now, so I think we're Gucci. She'll be beside herself when she finds out.

I can't wait to see her face. I have to admit it feels good to give her the final finger. The following day, I arrive for class fifteen minutes ahead of schedule, as is my usual practice. Ms. Holloway's class is empty. Five minutes later, she bursts into my classroom.

"Did you change my grades?!"

"I sure did."

"How fucking dare you! You did not have the right to change my grades! They are my grades!"

"Well, for starters, they are not your grades. They are *our* grades. We're partners, remember?"

"Oh! Now we're partners, and you decide to care with weeks left of school. What about when you were in Mexico? What about caring then? Huh?"

"That's irrelevant. I did my job."

"You know what? You're full of shit."

"I'll be that, but I bet those grades won't change. And you know what, now that they're in, you don't have to say another word to me. Good riddance. Have a nice life. Goodbye, Ms. Holloway!" She bolts out of the classroom and slams the door behind her. Thank God I never have to speak to her again.

The remaining two weeks fly by, without us saying anything to each other. I sign into Zoom, go through my spiel, and swiftly exit. The light at the end of the tunnel is starting to blind me. The kids aren't even showing up to school anymore. On the last day, I go next door and ask Holloway if we can talk. She says, "Sure."

I start explaining my reasoning for changing the grades.

She says, "You know what, Mr. C., it's water under the bridge. What's done is done."

"Well, I'm sorry things had to end on such a sour note, but no hard feelings. I wish you all the best."

"You too, Mr. C."

"Come on, bring it in." She cracks a small smile and draws near for a side hug.

"You take care of yourself, Holloway."

"Bye, Mr. C."

And just like that, my third school year is over. Despite all the drama with Holloway, it was still my best year yet. I loved combining my love of traveling with teaching and making dollars while spending pesos. I even started looking into virtual teaching jobs, but most still require you to report to a building. So, if that's the case, I might as well just go back to school.

Still, part of me wonders if it's time for a new chapter. I don't have a job lined up. The world is still adjusting to a new rhythm—and maybe I am too. Everything feels up in the air. But like Mama Oprah said, "When you don't know what to do, do nothing. Be still." So I'll wait— not with fear, but with faith—that clarity will come when the time is right.

PART FOUR

Chapter 27

The Sequel No One Asked For

———

FAIRMOUNT PARK IS HANDS-DOWN MY FAVORITE PART of Philadelphia. It's sacred ground to me—a living cathedral where nature's grandeur softens the city's rough edges. Some of my fondest memories are of skipping school with my brother and cousins, wandering these trails for hours, as if they were made just for us. We'd watch deer dart between trees, spot foxes slipping through the brush, and listen to birdsong echo through the stillness—reminders that a wild, wondrous world was hiding right in our backyard.

These days, I don't roam the trails; I drive past them. The woods I once wandered are now landmarks on my daily commute. I never imagined teaching would bring me back, yet here I am. Once a playground of wonder, this forest now stands as a quiet witness to my full-circle return. Funny how life brings you back to familiar places in unfamiliar ways.

A few blocks away stands Thomas Sowell High School, my new assignment. I'm filling in as a supplemental science teacher. It's not the role I was aiming for, but it beats the last-minute gigs the district tried to throw at me.

"Middle school?"

"Nope."

"Different subject?"

"Pass."

"Special Ed?"

"How? I've had zero training. So—no."

Finally, they offered me another supplemental position. Score. I have no idea what I'm getting myself into, but it can't be any worse than working with Holloway.

A few blocks from school, I hit one of those chaotic five-way intersections. The light drags, but my pulse starts to pick up. I'm anxious, sure, but underneath it, something steadier flickers. Hope.

Still, it feels a little strange that school is fully back in session, especially after almost two years spent behind screens. I didn't realize how much the classroom meant to me until it was taken away. I missed the energy, the connection, the chance to turn a spark of curiosity into a fire. But more than anything, I missed the soul-to-soul moments, the in-person magic no screen could replicate. We lost our way these past couple of years, but for the first time in a long time, it feels like we might be finding it again.

I turn into the teachers' parking lot and fall in line behind a slow parade of caffeine-fueled cars. As I pull in, my eyes catch a familiar figure, and my heart skips a beat. A surge of disbelief rushes through me. What is she doing here? Oh, the universe's sense of humor strikes again—and guess who the punchline is?

Ms. Holloway.

I wrapped up the year with a happy dance, certain I'd seen the last of her. But lo and behold, she's back in all her glory.

I kill the engine and sit still for a moment, collecting myself. Then I walk over like it's any other morning. "Good morning, Ms. Holloway," I say, pleasant as ever.

She looks up, horror written all over her face. "What the hell are you doing here? Don't tell me you're working here too."

"Nice to see you too. Out of three hundred schools in Philadelphia, what are the odds we'd end up at the same one? What are you teaching?"

"I'm working in special education, supporting students individually."

"Makes sense."

I'm praying that means I won't have to see her. Having to deal with her for another year would be a special kind of torture.

She says, "There were no biology positions left."

"Don't I know."

"So, they offered me that. Look, I'm only three years from retirement. I just want to make it to the finish line. I don't care what I do at this point."

"I feel you," I say.

"How about you?"

"I'm working as a supplemental science teacher again. That's all they told me. I'll find out soon enough. Let me grab my things, and we can walk inside together."

After the initial shock fades, I have to admit it's nice to see a familiar face. Despite everything, I still care about Holloway and want the best for her. You can't spend five days a week with someone and not get attached. Well, at least I can't. That said, I'll keep it professional, but the friendship part is over.

The school rises in front of us—brick and silence, the kind that feels temporary, like the pause before a storm. In a few days, these halls will echo with voices, footsteps, laughter, and drama. But not today.

Today, it's just us.

She shuts her trunk, and we walk side by side across the lot toward the building.

"How's Dad?" I ask.

"He's hanging in there," she says. "Ninety-two and still kicking."

"Wow! That's amazing."

We reach the front doors. I pull one open and gesture for her to go first. Just inside, to the right, sits a small office where two women are stationed behind a desk.

"Good morning, ladies."

"Good morning. How can I help you?" one of them asks, her voice cold and robotic.

"Could you tell me where the main office is?"

"What do you need? And who are you here to see?"

"We're new teachers, and we're looking for the principal."

"I am the principal."

You could've fooled me.

"I'll have to deal with y'all later. I've got too much going on right now. Y'all can go to the lunchroom. We'll be meeting there shortly."

"Okay. Thanks."

Holloway and I exchange a look. So that's the principal. Great. We pass by the metal detectors and head down the long corridor toward the lunchroom. Most of the teachers are already inside, scattered across tables or chatting in small clusters.

The moment I step in, it hits me—there are *a lot* of men.

At my other schools, the staff has been about ninety percent women. Here, it looks almost evenly split. The difference is hard to miss. I hope the extra testosterone translates into a more orderly environment. Only time will tell. Holloway and I stand in the back. You can already see all the cliques forming.

The principal arrives and walks to the front of the room and hollers, "Uh, uh! Where is Mrs. Armstrong? Where is Mr. Baker? Call your colleagues and let them know it is not a virtual day! Today is a regular school day! Who's got Mrs. Howard's number?"

"I'll text her," someone responds.

Why are we doing this right now? It's her responsibility to manage staff, not ours. But what do I know? Shut up, mind.

She checks her phone as if she's cramming for a meeting she called. "I'm sorry. I should've said 'Good morning.'" *Ya think?* "I just have a few things to review, and then y'all can handle your business. Y'all been doing this long enough. Y'all know the routine."

Okay, what if I'm brand-new and haven't learned the routine?

She continues, "We lost a few teachers, and we still have openings, so if you know anybody looking for a job, please let me know. Make sure you complete all of your training and remember that we are being tested for COVID weekly unless you have an exemption.

"Also, the expectation is that teachers remain in their own spaces. Stay away from my office. I repeat: do not come to my office! Send me an email or a text. We are still in a pandemic. And I need y'all to act like it, so no unnecessary fraternizing. And wear your masks!"

Damn. The infantilizing. The micromanagement. Her aura's sucking the spirit right out of me.

"Are there any questions?" She waits a beat, then says, "Great. Have a nice day."

Holloway says, "Should we ask her what she wants us to do?"

"Do we have much of a choice?"

The principal is making a beeline out of the lunchroom. As she passes us, Holloway says, "Pardon me, what would you like us to do?"

She says, "Meet me in my office in thirty minutes."

I thought she didn't want any visitors. *Okay, so what am I supposed to do until then? Whatever. It is what it is.* I'll go with the flow. I tell Holloway I'll catch her later. I need to go to my car to woosah for a bit.

"Okay, see ya."

I go to the principal's office precisely thirty minutes later. I don't see Holloway, so perhaps she has already been helped.

"Good morning, Principal Jackson. Is now a good time to speak?"

The look on her face says, *Do I have to?* But she says, "Yes, you can come in. You're the long-term sub, right?"

"No, I'm the supplemental science teacher."

"What subject do you teach?"

"Biology."

"Okay, so you're filling in for Mr. Aziz. He's our biology teacher, but he's out on medical leave, and I have no idea when he'll return."

"Okay, no worries. I can handle things."

"I don't know where his keys are . . . so, for now, I'll just let you into the room."

"Thanks."

We walk to the room without a word. I can already tell that less is more with her. I break the silence to ask her if there are any materials.

She says, "I have no idea, but you can check inside the science closet. You can get the key from one of your colleagues."

I want to ask if it is one of the thirty keys she's lugging around. But I remind myself that less is more.

"All right, thanks."

She opens the door and walks away. No "Welcome to Sowell High." No "Let me know if you need anything." Nothing. She's got the social grace of a cinder block. Let's blame it on the pandemic.

I turn on the lights in the classroom. Boxes are scattered everywhere. This dude must've been a hoarder. Like, who needs this much junk? And better yet, what am I supposed to do with it? To add insult to injury, the class has no windows. Zero. So in the middle of a pandemic, we'll be stuck breathing stale, recycled air because there is no proper ventilation. Awesome sauce!

I'm on the verge of losing it. I need to find a seat and take a few deep breaths. But before I can exhale, the principal's voice erupts over the loudspeaker, slicing through the quiet like a siren.

If her voice grates in person, it's unbearable through the speakers. I jolt at the first word and then flinch again as she hangs up the phone, producing a jarring rattling sound.

Oh, dear heavens . . . have mercy on my nervous system.

I try to relax in the chair, but the clutter won't let me. My eyes scan the room, and suddenly, the mess feels louder than the intercom. Determined to reclaim a sense of calm, I start clearing space, if only to breathe.

That's when I realize this isn't just a messy classroom. It's the de facto storage room for the entire building—a dumping ground for everyone else's junk. As I make a dent in the chaos, I remember there's a storage closet nearby that might help. I head next door to ask the chemistry teacher for the key.

She comes from Kenya and exudes warmth and kindness. Her accent brings back beautiful memories of my time on safari in her rich homeland, hanging out with the Maasai Mara tribe. Witnessing the wildebeest migration stands out as one of the most awe-inspiring experiences of my life. Unable to contain my curiosity, I inquire about the principal's peculiar demeanor.

She chuckles and says, "Don't mind her; she doesn't mean any harm. You'll get used to it." She opens the closet door for me.

"Thanks."

"No problem. If you need anything else, just let me know. Welcome to Sowell."

"I appreciate you." Finally, someone with decorum.

As expected, the closet is bare, lacking any supplies I could use. However, it offers ample space to stow away all this junk. I start digging through the boxes, hoping for something to liven up the room. A couple of generic science posters surface first. Then, tucked beneath them, I spot faces—Oprah, Maya Angelou, Thurgood Marshall, Martin Luther King Jr. Not exactly biology-related, but they represent excellence that we can all aspire to.

Little by little, the space transforms. Sterile white walls give way to vibrant color, familiar faces, and bold messages. Oprah smiles from one corner. Maya Angelou's words stretch across another. Thurgood Marshall and Martin Luther King Jr. stand side by side, silent but unyielding, their presence grounding the room in a larger story.

These walls speak. I just hope the students hear what they're trying to say.

I could still use more science posters, so I go online and order a ton with subjects like photosynthesis, mitosis, and meiosis. I'm doing the most, but what can I say? Go big or go home, right? Ultimately, my room goes from a storage closet to a showstopper.

As the day winds down, my final task is to hang up some placards I found while digging through the boxes. They feature virtues I hold dear: courage, integrity, compassion, resilience, wisdom . . . Teaching and modeling these values is the real work. Biology is just the medium. As I affix each word, I pause, taking a moment to reflect on what it means.

One second I'm lost in a moment of Zen, the next—*bam!* An announcement from the principal blares through the speakers, and my whole body tenses.

"All teachers storing things in the science closet must remove them immediately! Again, all the teachers storing things in the science closet must remove them immediately! The closet is not your basement." *Click.*

I always feel this tremendous relief the moment she stops talking. Man, she is not good for my mental health, but what doesn't kill you only kills you slower.

On second thought, I don't have to let her energy dictate my day. Better to live according to the words of Rumi: "As if everything is rigged in your favor," even when it feels more like a punishment than purpose.

But maybe this is what favor looks like in disguise. Maybe discomfort is the tool life uses to surface what still needs tending. Maybe the universe sends you loud bosses when quiet wounds still need healing.

Then again, Rumi never had to work under *her.*

She's lost her mind if she thinks I'm lifting a finger to move one of those boxes. I know I put ninety-nine percent of them in there, but she doesn't know that—or does she? Regardless, I refuse to endure the daily grind of teaching amid a mess.

An hour later, she makes the same announcement but follows it with, "Mr. Connelly, please come to the main office. Mr. Connelly, please come to the main office." *Click.*

Here we go again. Time to dust off my 'I survived the principal's office' badge. I pause, take a few slow breaths, letting the tension settle. I remind myself—I don't have to match her energy.

I say a quick prayer, asking for strength. Then, with quiet resolve, I head to the office.

"Hey, how are you doing, Principal Jackson?" I say nonchalantly, like I'm oblivious to why she's calling.

"Did you place those boxes inside the science closet?"

"Yes, I put some of them in there."

"Well, I need you to remove them all immediately."

"Where do you expect me to put them? There's no room inside my classroom. I barely have space for the students."

"Mr. Connelly, I'm not asking—I'm telling you. You need to remove all the boxes from the closet. It's a fire hazard."

I feel myself tighten. I breathe through it and say, "Mr. Aziz's class was a mess. It took me an entire day to move those boxes. Most of it wasn't even biology-related, so I'm guessing other teachers just used the room as a dumping ground. It's not fair I have to move all that stuff again because the other teachers failed to store their things properly. I'm willing to remove Mr. Aziz's boxes, but the other stuff is the other teachers' responsibility."

"Okay, Mr. Connelly, thank you."

"You're welcome."

I turn and head out. *It's a miracle!* I got a "thank you" and some understanding. I was expecting her to say something entirely different. But maybe you really do catch more bees with honey. I remove nine boxes and leave the other ninety behind. I organize the closet as best I can. It's still a hot mess, but at least I can say I tried. The bell rings. It's time to shake, rattle, and roll. Come Monday, it's on and popping, and this time, the chaos better be ready for me.

Chapter 28

Icebreakers & Epiphanies

———

FINALLY, THE FIRST DAY OF SCHOOL, ONE I WASN'T
sure I'd ever walk into again. But here I am. The sidewalk pulses
with energy, kids pouring in from all directions, hopping off
SEPTA buses, spilling out of yellow buses, drifting in groups down
the block. I weave through the crowd, focused but relaxed, my mind
scanning faces and backpacks like I'm already in teacher mode. The air
buzzes with possibility. Whatever this year holds, it starts now, and I'm
ready to face it.

I step into the front office to sign in. It's a full-on sensory extrava-
ganza: bright lights, phones ringing, people scurrying around. Parents
crowd the front desk, filling out forms and trying to make sense of
the back-to-school frenzy. Nearby, five substitute teachers sit quietly,
waiting for their assignments.

I take it all in—the noise, the tension, the strange mix of nervous
energy and blank stares. But it's the row of substitutes that catches my
eye. It's a bittersweet sight. After nearly two years away, some students
will return to school only to be met by temporary replacements. Still,
I'm relieved I'm not the one doing the honors. When no subs show up,
that burden falls on us.

The line creeps forward. I punch in, slip out, and within seconds, I'm across the hall, where silence finally has a chance to speak. I take a deep breath, grateful for the calm that greets me. It feels good to have my own space again, where I can move on my terms and do things my way. I make a few final tweaks, straighten a stack of papers, and glance at the clock. Showtime.

The bell rings, and students file in. I'm at the door, all smiles. "Good morning! Welcome back!" Most just look at me like, *Why's this guy so hyped?*

The class is filling quickly. I have far more students than I have desks, but there are tables where I can group some of them. The late bell rings, so I go inside to take attendance. I apologize in advance for butchering names. God forbid I get a syllable wrong. Blasphemy!

I get through the list reasonably well. Now comes the real challenge: memorizing them all. My goal is to have every name down by the end of the week. I like to use the brain game of repeating a new name three times to help remember it. Typically, this strategy works for me. It's incredible how some teachers go the entire year without knowing how to pronounce students' names. Then again, some parents don't make it easy.

Remembering names is the first step in building relationships with students. I introduce myself and ask if anyone is taking biology this year. They all raise their hands. "Nice. I will see some of you later." The first-period bell rings. I say my goodbyes. A handful of students stick behind for class. I encourage them to get started on the Do Now on the board. It'll be nice for the other students to walk in and see them already working on day one.

The rest of the students begin making their entrance. Positioned at the door, I offer a warm welcome. This batch seems livelier than the first; perhaps the advisory period served as their morning wake-up call. I tell them, "I'm collecting the Do Now, and it will count as your first grade, so complete it." They are clearly surprised I'm expecting something from them immediately. The late bell rings. I start the ten-minute timer on the smartboard and take roll. The classroom undergoes a remarkable transformation, thanks to my calming background music.

The Do Now question prompts contemplation: "What excites you most about returning to school?" As some students stare off into outer space, I gently prod them to kick-start their responses. Suddenly, one student says, "Mister, I don't have paper or a pencil." Suppressing the urge to launch into a rehearsed tirade about the importance of preparing for class, I take a more practical approach. I hand him some supplies I unearthed during my classroom scavenger hunt. Suddenly, I'm hit with a barrage of supply requests, and my patience wears thin. It's time for a reality check.

"Listen up! Let me get everybody's attention." The sound of my voice reverberates off the concrete walls. "I need each of you to come prepared with at least a piece of paper and something to write with. Realize that school today is a warm-up for the life you'll lead tomorrow. What'll happen if you show up to work without the tools you need to be successful?"

A student enthusiastically chimes in, "You won't get paid!"

I nod. "Exactly. They are going to send you right home."

"Oh, so what are you saying? I can go home?" a girl playfully asks.

"Did you hear me say that?"

"No."

"Then, stop playing with me."

The seriousness of my tone takes everyone by surprise. I have found that if I don't establish my authority on day one, it gets increasingly more difficult, so I have to be a bit of a stickler from the start.

"We need to focus on being more responsible. While I'm assigned to teach biology, I really want to help y'all develop these qualities," I point to the virtues on the front wall, "because that's the true path to success. And we all want to be successful, right?" I get a mixture of nods and blank stares. "So, I got you today, but tomorrow I'm expecting everyone to come prepared. Understood? All right, we have five minutes left. Let's finish the Do Now, and then we'll have our first share-out of the year."

The class is remarkably quiet as the soothing music continues in the background. What a stark contrast to my first day at Columbia four years ago. The alarm goes off, signaling it's time to rock and roll. I allow a few students to share their responses. Most are excited just to leave the house, see friends, and escape their boredom.

We transition from the Do Now to the next act in our academic circus. I display the agenda on the smartboard. Our mission is to get to know each other. A hush falls over the students as they study the agenda, surprised by the idea of a class with direction. The realization sets in: this will be a structured start to a wild ride.

The first week of school is usually a masterclass in unproductivity. However, with the significant regression most students have faced because of the pandemic, there isn't the luxury of time to squander. Also, you have to start the year the way you want to finish it. After reviewing the roadmap, I give my formal introduction. A student raises his hand and says, "Mister, are you a substitute?" *Why does everyone mistake me for a substitute?*

"No, I'm a full-time teacher. Why do you ask?"

"Because my roster says a different teacher's name."

"Oh, that's a good observation. Mr. Aziz is the assigned teacher, but he's currently on medical leave. But don't worry, I'll be here for the foreseeable future, and I know my stuff, so you're in good hands. Okay, it's time for us to get to know each other. I want everybody to stand up." The students stare at me like deer in headlights.

"Am I speaking Polish? Stand up! Let's go, let's go, let's go! Time is money. You've been sitting on your butts long enough, so like James Brown, get on up! Let's go! It's time to get to work. We're going to complete a couple of icebreakers so we can get to know each other. For our first game, I want to test how well you guys communicate. By a show of hands, how many of you agree that communication skills are essential to success?"

Most hands go up, but a few students are still off in la-la land. It's all good though; we're about to liven things up.

"We are going to play the 'Line Up' game. I will give you a condition, and you will sort yourself accordingly. So, first, let me count and see how many students we have. Awesome! There's an even number, so I'll split the class in half. There are prizes involved, so I want to see some energy. First, is there anybody in the class with an allergy?" Nobody responds. "Great!" I show the students the prize bucket filled with Snickers, Reese's Cups, Butterfingers, Airheads, Mr. Goodbars, Skittles, Starburst, and school supplies from the dollar store. Their eyes light up with anticipation.

"When I say go, please organize yourselves alphabetically according to your first names, with those starting with A at the front and Z at the back. Does everyone understand the instructions?" Again, I get the deer-in-headlights look.

"What's your name?"

"Tori."

"Excellent. It's nice to meet you, Tori. Tori, please repeat the rules for the first round for me."

She does so flawlessly.

"Thank you, Tori. All right, let's get it. On your mark, get set, go!"

Tori's group quickly dives into the task, while the others seem unsure where to start. She's a natural leader.

"I see you, Tori."

"I want my candy!"

She asks everyone their names and single-handedly dominates the game like Kobe.

"Let's go! Let's go! Let's go!" I'm hyper than the Philly Fanatic after a quadruple espresso.

Suddenly, Tori screams, "We're done! We're done! Where is my candy?"

"Relax. First, I have to ensure everybody is in the correct order. Y'all could be capping." The students snicker, hearing me use their lingo. I have everyone say their names aloud, and they're arranged correctly. "Great job, Team 1. Here is your award, as promised." I can see the FOMO on the other group's faces as they devour their treats. Hopefully, that'll inspire them for the next round.

"Team 2, we have one more round, so you still have time to redeem yourselves. When I say go, you will arrange yourselves according to your birthdays. The earliest at the front, and the latest at the back. Everybody got it?"

"What's your name, brother?"

"My name is Nazir."

"Cool. Nice to meet you, Nazir. Nazir, can you please repeat the instructions?" He doesn't miss a beat. "Thanks. I appreciate it, Nazir."

"Okay, on your mark, get set, go! Now, we have a competition. Watching them scarf down those Snickers must have made the other team hungry because they are rolling now. There's a student who's still lost in the sauce. I ask him what month his birthday falls in.

He says, "November."

"Which day?"

"The sixth."

"Get out of here. We're birthday twins."

"For real?"

"Real rap. Where do you think you belong in the line based on our birthdays?" He starts making his way to the back. I'm trying to help Team 2, but now Tori is in her Jordan bag. They're still neck and neck, though.

The scene is chaotic and boisterous. I love it. This is what school should be like. Tori screams, "We're done!" Of course, they are. Team 2 shouts the same two seconds too late.

"Okay, let's make sure you guys are correct. I want everybody to state their birthdays." Everything is perfect until we reach the halfway point. That's where we find a discrepancy. Two students are out of place.

I shimmy over to the other side, like Steve Harvey strutting across the Family Feud stage to let the other team steal. They all state their birthdays. They are in the correct order. Score!

"Great job! See, it's not over until it's over." They all take their candy, pencils, sharpeners, and so on.

Tori says, "That was fun, Mister . . .? What's your name?"

"I'm Mr. Connelly, or you can call me Mr. C."

"Say less."

"Everybody, have a seat. The next game we'll play is two truths and a lie." I hand all the students a little piece of paper. I put my three statements on the board to demonstrate how the game is played.

My statements are:

- *I have visited over sixty countries.*
- *I have fraternal twins, a boy and a girl named Tarique Jr. and Tiana.*
- *I have been suspended over twenty times, expelled three times, and attended more than ten different schools.*

"Take a second to think about it, and then we will do a poll." Most students guess the last statement is a lie, as I was confident they would. Only one student thought my statement about the twins was a lie, despite not having one picture on my desk. Guess who? Of course, Tori.

I confess that the second statement is, in fact, a lie. "What, Mister? I don't get it. How have you been suspended and expelled but still became a teacher?"

"Well, because it's not how you start your journey. It's how you finish. I eventually went back to school and graduated."

"Why did you get into so much trouble?"

"Because I had anger issues and would fight a lot."

"Stop playing, Mister, you ain't got hands."

"What? Your boy was like Baby Mike!" I do a little shadowboxing to show them I still got it. The spark of amazement flickers in their gaze.

"Now, I'm not glamorizing violence, but I'm telling you this because how you start doesn't have to determine where you end up. No matter what you've been through, you still have time to choose better. But enough about me—I want to hear about all of you.

"Take five minutes to complete the assignment. Then I'll collect the statements, and we'll share them."

I set my five-minute timer on the smartboard. Once the bell rings, I ask students if they need more time. They say yes, so I slide them another five, and then we get it cracking. I always ask the students if they want me to read theirs. Surprisingly, most of them tell me to go for it.

The game gets serious in no time. Their level of honesty and vulnerability surprises me. One truth stands out the most. A student's mom was shot in the face by her boyfriend. We all picked that as the lie. We didn't want to believe it, but it was true. Thank God she survived.

Unexpectedly, the class transforms into a safe space where walls come down and truth finds its way in. My honesty and vulnerability gives students permission to open up, creating a profound moment of intimacy and connection. What was meant to be a ten-minute game stretches to thirty.

As the gravity of the moment sinks in, I become acutely aware of the deep trauma some students carry daily—trauma that often remains unspoken but still weighs heavily on them. Yet, there's also the immense joy of creating a space where healing can occur and authentic connections can be made.

As time slips away, I ask if anyone still wants me to read theirs. Two students volunteer—thankfully, their statements bring a lighter touch, lifting the mood and proving that not every truth has to hurt.

Finally, I hand out a word search puzzle for the remaining ten minutes of class. I catch the students staring at me with disbelief, their eyes practically saying, "Are you out of your mind? Why are you throwing more tasks our way?"

There's no way they'll finish it, but it's better to be over- than under-planned. I hype the assignment up by telling students, "This isn't just any word search puzzle. This puzzle is very special. Don't turn the papers over until I tell you to. I want somebody to tell me what's so special about them when you figure it out. Okay, now you can look."

Choruses of: "Oh my god!"

"What!"

"How did you do that?"

"He put all our names inside the word search!"

"I found you, Keisha! Here you go, Nazir!"

"Where? I still can't find my name."

Hopefully, I've hooked them for the rest of the year with that assignment. Now that I have their attention, I need to work hard to keep it.

It's funny how most students focus on finding their names first. The bell rings amid all the excitement. They are still sitting and completing the assignment. I gently nudge them out the door. I swear that was the quickest ninety minutes of my life. It had such a beautiful flow and enabled me to establish our little community, or even family, on day one. Lucky me, I get to do it two more times.

The second class sails by smoothly, but the universe has a trick up its sleeve for the grand finale. Riding high on the success of the earlier sessions, I welcome the last group with unbridled enthusiasm as they puzzle over my excitement. Surprise, not everyone in the school is jaded; some genuinely love what we do.

Suddenly, my upbeat mood takes a nosedive when a student strolls in with an unexpected companion. Drumroll, please—it's the illustrious Ms. Holloway, waltzing in like she owns the place and casting a shadow over the room. There goes the vibe.

She flashes a tight smile and says, "Looks like we'll be working together again."

"Cool beans. Welcome aboard," I reply, keeping my tone light.

The situation is beyond ironic, but I know everything happens for a reason. It's funny how we've swapped positions from last school year. I'm the head honcho now, though I'm not drunk on authority. However, it'll be nice to show her what good teaching looks like.

Despite this momentary setback, the students' energy lifts my spirits. The first day is officially over, and in the words of Ice Cube, "Today was a good day." I power down the smartboard, switch off the lights, and lock up my room. It's only one o'clock, but my last two periods are for preparation, so you can guess where I'm going. It rhymes with home.

Chapter 29

The Final Showdown

———

It's Friday afternoon, and my last class is just getting started. Students drift in with weekend grins. Jokes fly, backpacks hit the floor, and the room fills with the kind of noise that says school's already over. It's less a classroom, more a holding zone before freedom.

Of course, there's always one punctual attendee: Ms. Holloway, the epitome of consistency. Lovely. We exchange a quick hello, but it's clear she's not thrilled to be here. Working with individual students is probably driving her up the wall. Less responsibility, more monotony, but that's her problem, not mine. Meanwhile, my class is cruising along just fine. Sure, the heat in here could cook an egg, but we make it work.

I brought in fans from home, hoping for a breeze—just enough airflow to take the edge off. Game-changer? Not even close. But hey, it beats a blank.

As the complaints roll in, I lean on my usual defense: solidarity.

"Look," I say, wiping sweat from my forehead, "I'm dying up here, too."

They don't flinch. I may as well be talking to chairs. Their blank stares practically scream, *And your point is?*

I shake my head. "I honestly don't get why only three classrooms in this whole building have windows. It's mind-boggling."

Dominique chimes in, casual as ever, like she's tossing me the final piece of a puzzle I should've solved weeks ago. "For real, Mr. C.? You really don't know why there are no windows?"

I arch a brow. "No. Please enlighten me."

She shrugs, like it's common knowledge. "You didn't know this building was an asbestos factory?"

"What the . . .? What? Stop playing!"

"No, I'm serious."

"An asbestos factory? No way."

"I'm dead ass."

I give her the look.

"I'm sorry. Look, if you don't believe me, google it."

"Say no more." I return to my desk and search for the query: *"Is Sowell High School in Philadelphia a former asbestos factory?"* Lo and behold—it's true. The first hit is an article about a teacher who mysteriously fell ill while working here. This building really *is* a converted asbestos factory. Incredible.

Just when I think I've seen the worst this system has to offer, it outdoes itself. So not only do we have the pleasure of inhaling hot, stale, COVID-infused air, but we're also potentially ingesting asbestos particles. Great! Just great. If I'd known this, there's no way in hell I'd be working here. But ignorance is apparently both bliss and deadly.

Who in their right mind converts a former asbestos factory into a school? It's beyond absurd.

Once again, the allure of escape invades my thoughts. I was on a high, hitting my stride—but this? This is a game-changer. I'm not sacrificing my health for anyone. My health is nonnegotiable. I knew the discolored water from the fountains was off-limits. Yet nothing could've prepared me for the possibility that the entire building might be toxic. Time and time again, the system demonstrates just how little they care about us.

Suddenly, my thought process is interrupted by the disciplinarian entering the room. His job is to enforce school rules and manage student behavior. Good thing he's not paid based on his effectiveness. We greet each other, and then he lingers. He doesn't say anything. He simply watches the class for a minute, then leaves. It feels weird.

I think he's shocked by how well-behaved the students are in my class. You wouldn't guess it, considering they're the same ones turning the cafeteria into a boxing ring every afternoon. My secret recipe? Just three simple ingredients: building relationships, setting high standards, and crafting engaging lessons. That's it. After a month, I don't have to tell them to start the Do Now, transition to independent work, and so on. They know the game plan is always on the board, so they get right to it.

With the weekend just minutes away, the energy's a little higher than usual, but I don't mind the chatter. A little noise means there's still a pulse. That quiet? That's the sound of learning flatlining. Every now and then, I have to reel them in, but for the most part, they're chillin'.

Ms. Holloway drifts from desk to desk, checking in on students. Why? Beats me. Maybe she's just restless—trying to feel useful somehow. She circles once, then again, eyes darting like she's scanning for contraband.

She slows near one desk, nostrils flaring, fingers twitching like she's winding up.

Then—*boom!*

"Where's your mask, and why aren't you doing your work?"

"I'm doing my work, Miss!"

"Where's your pencil? There's nothing on your paper? Stop messing around."

"Yo, bro. She drawlin'. Like, you're not even the teacher."

"And—I'll still get you suspended."

She clearly doesn't realize that arguing with a child only brings you down to their level. To be fair, it took me a while to get that memo too. After two minutes of them bickering, with no end in sight, I finally intervene.

"Ms. Holloway, what's the problem?"

"He's swearing! He's not on task! He's not wearing his mask! He needs to be written up!"

The student says, "I just took a breather for one second. It's too hot in here. And I wasn't even talking to her. Like, why is she even in here?" He does have a point. I tell him to stop talking.

"You know the expectations. You have to keep your mask on. And I keep telling you to watch your mouth." I tell Holloway, "Don't worry about it. I'll handle it."

"No! That's the problem! You're not handling it! I will not get sick because your students can't follow directions. If you're unwilling to do something about it, I will."

She storms off like a petulant child having a temper tantrum. Is she really about to run to the principal and try to get me in trouble?

Minutes later, I get a call from the big boss asking what's happening. She has me on speakerphone so that the whole office can listen in. She reminds me of expectations that I'm well aware of. I sense my body tensing and my breathing becoming shallower. I hold the phone away from my ear to lessen the noise.

Everything sounds like "blah-blah, blah-blah-blah, blah-blah-blah-blah." I think she forgot she was addressing a grown man, not one of her students. It takes everything inside me to resist acquainting her with the dial tone. Instead, I focus on my breathing, determined to stay calm under the students' watchful eyes. I want to model grace under pressure for them. Still, it's infuriating that Holloway is stirring up problems that didn't exist a moment ago.

After the principal's rant, I explain that I didn't see the student without his mask or hear him using swear words. "Believe me, if I had, I would've said something. I told Ms. Holloway I would handle it. I tried to de-escalate the situation, but she kept pouring gasoline on it. Just because I don't jump when she says jump doesn't mean I'm sweeping it under the rug. I'll handle it."

"Well, Mr. Connelly, I need you to get control of your classroom. And you need to talk this over with Ms. Holloway."

"No problem."

"Thank you." *Click!*

I'm sure Ms. Holloway watched all of this unfold, smiling inside as I was reprimanded. When the bell rings, all the students get up to leave.

I ask Deandre, "What happened?"

He says, "Ms. Holloway was upset because I wasn't doing my work or wearing my mask. Then she kept picking on me but ignoring everyone else."

"Listen, you were wrong. When she's in this class, you give her the same respect you give me."

"But respect is a two-way street, Mr. C. She was spazzing for no reason."

"Look, you're not on her level; you're a child, and you need to stay in a child's place. You should've had your mask on. And how many times have I told you to watch your mouth? You brought that attention on yourself. If you play with fire, don't be surprised when you get burned. It's chillin' in here—we don't need her, the principal, or anybody else killing our vibe."

"All right, Mr. C. My bad."

"Go to class, man."

"I need a pass."

"Come on, I have to walk that way anyhow."

I drop him off at his class to make sure he gets there. Then, I immediately search for Ms. Holloway.

I find her in the Special Ed office she shares with four colleagues. I ask if we could step outside for a moment. I'm deliberately cool, calm, and collected.

Once we're in the hallway, I say, "Ms. Holloway, I know you mean well, and you were only trying to help, but I don't need your help to run my classroom. This isn't last year when we split the responsibilities. It's my classroom, and you never have to return if you don't like the way I manage it. Better yet, don't come back. You're no longer welcome. If you want to work with your student, you can pull him out of class and bring him here. But I don't want to see you in my class again."

"Gotcha."

And just like that, the thorn in my side is gone—once and for all.

Chapter 30

Raise the Bar, Watch Them Fly

———

IT'S FIRST PERIOD, AND THE STUDENTS ARE SETTLING in. Quiet and focused, they ease into the day while working on an assignment through CK-12, a free online platform I rely on for its interactive lessons and adaptive features.

CK-12 offers a wide range of content, from photography to physics, and it doesn't cost a thing. That alone makes it a game-changer, especially for educators in under-resourced settings. While it requires internet access, it remains one of the more accessible tools available, helping close the gap for students who might otherwise go without quality resources.

Some international students have even used CK-12 to earn full scholarships to US universities. Those results speak to the platform's potential. One of my favorite features is the ability to track student progress and adjust instruction in real time. I can see exactly where they're thriving and where they're struggling, which allows me to tailor my teaching accordingly. That kind of insight changes the game.

Still, insight is only useful if you apply it, and today's a good chance to do just that. Most of the class is locked in—calm and engaged. But one student is off-task, playing around on his phone. I'm cool with students chillin' once they've completed everything, but he doesn't fit the bill.

"Haneef, what's up? Why aren't you working on the CK-12?"

"I already finished it," he shoots back.

"Yeah?"

"Real talk!"

"Cool, come here; let's do a little data dive and see how well you performed. I want you to see how I determine how much effort you put into each assignment." I click on the student's name in the CK-12 teacher's portal. It provides me with a comprehensive report that includes the total reading time, an engagement score determined by the number of clicks on embedded elements in the text, and a comprehension score based on the accuracy of responses to the final adaptive learning questions.

"All right," I say, "let's see how you did. I want you to read the report and answer a few questions for me. You have all the information right here. How many minutes did you spend reading?"

"Two."

"How many of the videos did you watch?"

"None."

"How many of the diagrams did you click on?"

"None."

"How many questions did you answer correctly out of ten?"

"Two."

"Consequently, what's your overall engagement score?"

"Twenty."

"All right, so what does that mean?"

"I got some work to do."

"Exactly. It also means you lied to me."

"My bad, Mr. C. I didn't realize you could see all that."

"Now you know—and next time, move different. Because who you're becoming matters more to me than what you turn in. Ultimately, this assignment won't matter, but your character will."

"Facts."

"So, how are we going to improve these scores?"

"I'll read the entire article and watch the videos."

"All right, let's shake on it. The next time I call you up here, I expect to see some improvement. Do you understand me?"

"Yes, sir."

"Have a seat."

After reviewing hundreds of these reports with students, one thing becomes clear: higher engagement scores almost always lead to stronger comprehension. I stress this to my students as often as I can. The more you put in, the more you get out. That's not just true for class—it's a metaphor for life. And the data from CK-12 helps me drive that point home.

Minutes later, there's a knock on the door.

"Mr. C., you want me to answer it," says one of my students.

"No, it's all good. I got it."

I open the door. It's the assistant principal.

"Hi, Principal Campbell."

"Hey, Mr. C. Can I speak with you in the hallway, please?"

"Sure."

I really like her energy. She's classy, stylish, and married with two children. Bummer. Her presence is so calming. She's someone that the young ladies in the building could look up to.

She says, "I need to ask you a big favor."

"What's up?"

"Would you be willing to teach English?"

"No, I'm not certified to teach English."

"I know, but I'm sure you can do it. Come on, please?"

I take a deep breath to consider it. "I just can't. It goes against all of my morals. It feels like I'm robbing the kids by teaching them something I'm not confident in."

"I understand how you feel. We're trying our best to keep you here. We would hate to lose you."

"So, Mr. Aziz is coming back soon?"

"Yes, we're unsure when, but he is returning."

"Well, maybe they'll let both of us stay. I was supplemental last year, and they allowed me to work with my partner for the entire year."

"Okay, well, let's see. Think about it. If you change your mind, please let me know."

"No doubt."

"Thank you."

I enter the classroom feeling uneasy. Ayana picks up on it right away.

"What's up, Mr. C.? Everything okay?"

I pause, debating how to say it.

"Yeah . . . well, not really." I exhale. "I might be leaving. Sounds like Mr. Aziz is coming back soon."

"When?"

"I'm not sure. They want me to teach English, but I've never taught it. I don't want to teach something I'm unqualified to teach. So, they might send me to a different school if there's a biology vacancy."

"Oh, man. You're leaving us, Mr. C.?"

"I don't want to, but it's possible. Let's see what happens."

The bell rings, and the students head to lunch.

Normally, this would be my cue to pack up and head home. But today, I have to stick around for this soul-sucking PD. Fortunately, it's still happening over Zoom, which takes some of the sting out. I log on to the meeting. There's jazz playing while we wait for everyone to sign on. I love jazz.

The teacher leader begins by welcoming us. She says, "The focus of the PD will be reviewing the benchmark scores."

I hadn't even planned on giving the students the benchmark. What's the point? None of it will matter unless the next teacher builds on what I've already taught and keeps reinforcing it. And based on last year's results, I'm not holding my breath.

Even so, I was forced to give the test with zero preparation. The teacher leader said, "Just tell the students it's extra credit because we're running out of time. It's just a box to check. It's only for us to assess what topics we have to reteach." That's easy for her to say.

I agree begrudgingly, feeling like I'm setting the students up for failure. How do you give someone a test you haven't prepared them for?

And now we'll have the pleasure of spending the next hour reviewing the dismal results. She starts with the math and reading scores—and I'm shocked.

They look worse than the pre-pandemic results, and those were already on life support. It looks like the students are regressing. That's unfortunate, but I'm not surprised, given the challenges of virtual schooling. She continues, "And finally, for some good news!"

She pulls up the biology results. She says, "I want to congratulate Mr. C. because six percent of his students scored proficient on the benchmark." I immediately notice that she made a mistake. She continues, "Our biology goal is five percent proficiency, so you are already above the target. These scores are a vast improvement from last year's results. Would you like to say anything, Mr. C.? I always tell you I'm your biggest fan."

Yeah . . . just one quick correction. Actually, six percent of students scored advanced, forty-eight percent scored proficient, and the rest fell into the basic and below-basic category."

She reexamines the chart. Then she says, "OMG, I stand corrected! The students performed even better than I thought. Great job, Mr. C.!"

"Thanks."

Initially, I was aiming for at least twenty percent of students to land in the advanced category. Nevertheless, I'm content with the results—especially considering the lack of preparation. The impromptu test gave me something rare: a snapshot of what actually stuck.

Einstein is often credited with saying, "Education is what remains after one has forgotten everything learned in school," so it's rewarding to witness learning that lasts.

Of course, tests aren't perfect, but throwing them out entirely is a mistake. Unfortunately, more and more schools are doing just that, swept up in a growing trend to abandon common assessments altogether. And that worries me.

Without some kind of shared benchmark, it becomes too easy for teachers to do whatever they want, with no real way to track what's actually working. Sure, many educators complain about "teaching to the test," but that phrase is often used as a scapegoat. If an exam is well-designed and aligned to meaningful standards, then teaching to it isn't the problem—it's just good instruction.

At the end of the day, we're either helping students master content and build lasting skills, or we're not. The test isn't the enemy. Misusing it is.

I consider my students' results on the state biology exam my final report card. It gives me a concrete measure of how much they actually learned, independent of how well I think I taught them. While the benchmark only captures a fraction of the material tested in May, the outcome makes one thing clear: when expectations rise, students rise with them. Still, with almost half falling short of proficiency, there's more work to do, even if I won't be the one to finish it.

Chapter 31

The High School Shuffle

—

TWO WEEKS BEFORE WINTER BREAK, MR. AZIZ returns, and we hit it off immediately. He is well-read, well-traveled, and has an interesting history. Despite the decades between us, we have more in common than you'd expect. I've never encountered another brother who has traveled extensively, is bilingual, speaks professionally, and teaches biology. What's even more remarkable is that I've been dreaming about writing a book to share my teaching experiences, and Mr. Aziz has already published several. What are the odds?

He gave me one of his tomes today. Our meeting feels rife with synchronicity. We talk like best friends for hours, and the days fly by. He is like the grandfather I never had. He says, "Man, had I known you were here, I would have stayed home. I could've retired. We have to do something to make you stay. These kids love you, man. They need somebody like you who they can look up to."

"Thank you, sir. I appreciate it. It means a lot hearing you say that." Teaching can be a thankless job, so it feels good to be acknowledged. However, if staying means I have to teach something I'm not qualified to teach, I would be forced to leave, as much as I would hate it.

With winter break just days away, the school is descending into chaos. Fights are erupting nonstop, but our class remains a sanctuary. I've handed over teaching duties to Mr. Aziz, partly because I'm uncertain how much longer I'll be here, and partly because I'm intrigued by his teaching style.

While I'm in the back of the class catching up on emails, a message from the district pops up. The subject line sends a shiver down my spine: "New School Assignment." I click it open, my heart racing, and there it is in black-and-white—my time at Sowell is officially over. Effective immediately, I'm being reassigned to Noam Chomsky High School.

Wow. They actually did it. I knew it was coming, but it still lands like a punch. It taps into the pain of my students being taken from me at Columbia. It reminds me of being kicked out of the class and separated from my students at Agape. And it draws energy from the abandonment and neglect I felt as a child.

I feel like I'm letting my students down, but it's out of my hands. So, "God grant me the serenity to accept the things I cannot change." I must go where I'm needed if there's a biology vacancy elsewhere. I go to the front of the class to tell Mr. Aziz.

"Oh man, are you serious? Effective immediately?" The kids grow quiet, having overheard our conversation.

Najah blurts out, "Mr. C., you leaving us?"

"Unfortunately, I am."

There are choruses of "Ahh, man!" and "No!" filling the room.

"Mr. C., you can't go."

I wish it were up to me, but it's out of my hands. The class ends in three minutes. How do I sum up everything in three minutes? I take a breath, glance at the ceiling, and try to find a place to start.

"Man, it's been awesome working with all of you. I've seen y'all grow so much since the beginning of the year, and I couldn't be prouder. I wish it didn't have to end like this, but that's life—always changing, always moving. Just remember, each of you has something unique to offer the world, and with hard work and determination, you can achieve amazing things—I'm living proof. Don't let anyone tell you otherwise." I take a deep breath, feeling the weight of our last moments together.

"I'm really going to miss y'all. Real talk, I love y'all and wish all of you nothing but the best. So, take care of Mr. Aziz. And don't be cutting up—in the lunchroom or out in the streets. Be safe, all right? Peace."

The bell rings, marking the end of an era. One by one, the students come over to dab me up. I feel a wave of emotion rise, but like Mary J. Blige said, "I'm not gonna cry." Instead, I smile, soaking in the moment, letting their energy remind me why I do this.

This chapter is over. But the story? It's still being written.

And as always, I'll keep turning the page, ready for whatever comes next.

THE FOLLOWING MORNING, I check in at my new school. I can still ride through the park but have to drive deeper into the city. The area is nicer than I anticipated. It looks gentrified. I lock up my car, make my way up the large staircase, and enter the building. Immediately, I notice a childhood friend from my church. She's the security guard at the entrance.

"Hey, Sheree!"

"What? Boy, what are you doing here?" We hug.

"I'm teaching here now."

"Okay, that's what's up! We need more men in this building."

"I bet."

"Well . . . welcome to Chomsky. I'll see you around."

"Appreciate it—peace."

I make my way up the marble stairs. It's incredible how many schools in Philly are replicas of one another. This school's foyer is shaped precisely like the one in my middle and high school. I enter the office and let the secretary know that I'm here to see the principal. She says I can have a seat, and she'll be with me shortly.

"Shortly" becomes a half an hour later. I'm becoming impatient, so I start playing *Word Feud* on my phone to kill time. Out of nowhere, the principal enters the office with a student who's going ballistic.

"They keep bullying me! It's not going to stop. It's never going to stop."

"Come on, baby. Come on. It's going to be okay."

The principal gently holds and guides her into her office, offering comfort and reassurance as they move. I can feel her pain. She's really in distress. She must have hit a breaking point. I shouldn't have been so quick to judge the principal for being late. Clearly, she's juggling bigger issues behind the scenes. Fifteen more minutes crawl by before she finally calls me in.

"I'm so sorry for keeping you waiting. I'm sure you noticed the emergency."

"No worries. How is she doing?"

"She's okay. She calmed down eventually. She's at the nurse's office waiting for someone to pick her up."

"Okay, that's good to hear."

"So, I'm excited to have you come aboard. I can tell that you'll be perfect for this environment."

I want to ask—why? Because I'm a bald Black guy with a big beard? But that's not good enough. We need competent teachers too. I don't care what race they are. All I say is, "Thanks."

"So, tell me a little about yourself." I go through my spiel, and she gets even more excited to have me on board.

"The students will love you." Her excitement is almost scaring me.

She says, "I don't understand why your other school let you go. I can tell you're an asset. I bet the students are going to miss you." That statement unlocks a flood of emotions, and tears start streaming down my face.

"I'm going to miss them, too." The principal hands me a tissue. "But the beat must go on. At least here, I can teach biology, which I'm certified to teach."

The principal responds, "Initially, you'll be covering for our math teacher because he's out on medical leave for the foreseeable future."

"Math teacher? I thought I was teaching biology."

"Eventually, you will, but we need you to cover temporarily for Mr. Langston. The biology class already has a long-term substitute."

"Had I known I'd end up teaching math, I could've just stayed at my last school and taught English instead. They have about ten vacancies as well. We're robbing Peter to pay Paul. Besides, how am I supposed to teach math? I've never taught it a day in my life."

"Don't worry about it. We'll give you the resources you need to be successful." *Yeah, right. I've heard that before.*

"But what good are the resources if I don't have the training to use them?"

"Believe me, these students have had substitutes the entire year. They'll just be happy to have someone there consistently." *Great. Thanks for setting the bar so high.*

I reply, "Okay, well, it is what it is."

"Don't worry! You're going to do well."

She walks me to the front entrance. I thank her for her time and tell her I'll see her after winter break. I hug my friend Sheree and peace out. The principal looks surprised. She didn't realize Sheree and I go way back.

We tell her about our holy-ghost, fire-baptism, speaking-in-tongues church connection. I say *church*, even though it sometimes felt more like a cult. Go figure.

I leave smiling and rush to my car. Still grinning, I know exactly what I need to do. The moment I sit down, I call Sowell and ask to speak to the principal.

"Good afternoon, Principal Jackson. I think I have found a technicality we can exploit to get me back to Sowell. They hired me at Chomsky High to replace the biology teacher. In actuality, I'm covering for the math teacher. If that's the case, I might as well teach a different subject at Sowell and fill in one of the vacancies there."

"Perfect! I'm so glad to hear that. The students need you. And I need you back too. Let me get on the phone with my contacts and work my magic. Don't worry. You will be coming back to Sowell!"

"I hope so."

"I'll be in touch shortly."

"Thanks."

A surge of pride washes over me. For the first time, a principal is fighting for me instead of against me. I have always felt like a problem child, creating issues everywhere I go, but this proves that I am an asset. Less than an hour later, I get a call from Principal Jackson. She says, "Everything is all set. You are to report back to Sowell after the break. You will take over for the French teacher."

"Great! Thank you!"

"No, thank you! We're excited to have you back."

"Me too. Take care and enjoy your break!"

This is the best Christmas gift ever. I can already picture the students' faces when they walk through the door. Technically, I'm supposed to be teaching French. But I don't speak French, and I refuse to stand in front of a classroom and fake it. I do speak Spanish, though. So that's what I'm going to teach.

To celebrate, I journey to the jungles of Ecuador for an Ayahuasca retreat. There, beneath the canopy's hush and the rhythm of the rain, I feel an anchoring—a quiet affirmation that I'm exactly where I'm meant to be.

The retreat mirrors my journey as both teacher and seeker: first, a deep unearthing of pain, then a lightness that feels like grace. It reminds me that brilliance is born from contrast—that it's the dance between shadow and light that gives each its meaning.

Life, after all, is a symphony. Every note, harsh or sweet, shapes the whole.

And now, I don't just hear the music; I move with it. I no longer resist the beat.

I dance, fully alive, to whatever life plays next.

Chapter 32

The Last Lesson: Joy

———

WINTER AIR BRUSHES AGAINST MY SKIN AS I return to Sowell—this time, by choice, not by chance. It's our first day back from break, but for me, it feels bigger than that, more like a homecoming, the kind you have to fight for. There's that familiar déjà vu, like I'm walking into the first day of school all over again. And in a way, I am, because nothing says fresh start like teaching a whole new subject—Spanish, of all things. It's a stretch, sure, but after everything I've weathered, it almost feels poetic.

I walk past the lunchroom and spot a few of my students.

"Yo! What's up, Mr. C.? You back?!"

"Yeah, I'm back."

"That's wassup! We missed you, man!"

"I missed y'all too."

Before I know it, the rest of my students are spilling out of the lunchroom to dab me up and welcome me back. It feels like a family reunion. I smile, soak it in, and then wave them off. "All right, all right—get back in there. I've gotta find my new classroom."

I make the trek, pop the door open, and flip on the lights. The space isn't bad. It's got potential—it just needs a little love.

Word spreads around school that I'm back, and all my students come by to see me. Before I know it, there are fifty students chilling in my room. It feels good to be home.

One asks me, "You're going to teach us French?"

"No, I'm going to teach y'all Spanish." A few students start complaining that they don't want to learn Spanish.

"Well, the alternative is having a parade of substitutes and learning nothing. Besides, what do you think is more important in our society, Spanish or French?" Most agree that Spanish is more important.

"Mr. C., can you really speak Spanish?"

"Claro que sí. No te preocupes. Y tú también vas a hablar español." ("Of course I do. Don't worry. And you're going to speak Spanish too.")

"How many of you buy things at the Papi Store?" The entire class raises their hands.

"Cool. You'll be able to talk basic Spanish with them by next week."

Most of the students are excited about learning Spanish. Hopefully, I can light the language spark for them. It takes no time to get everyone back on board. They know the routine. As soon as the late bell rings, they get started on their Do Now, which is two Duolingo lessons.

I still use the same crossword puzzles, fill-in-the-blanks, word searches, and word scrambles to teach essential vocabulary. For assessments, I test their ability to have basic conversations. They've also put together Google Slides presentations—one focused on Spanish-speaking countries, the other on famous Hispanics. I'm enjoying the challenge of teaching a new subject. However, I do miss biology; but it's a small price to pay to be back home.

As the school year winds down to its final week, only the diehards are still showing up, the ones who'd attend classes year-round if given the chance. With teachers burning through their last sick and personal days, the students are left to run amok. So I just let them chill in my room, watching movies and playing PS5 on the smartboard. At least they're safe and staying out of trouble.

I feel like the school's unofficial substitute, but I'm honored to create a space students actually want to be in. I've come full circle. I'm finally back to the chill, grounded version of myself I was before teaching tried to harden me.

One of my students turns to me and says, "You know what, Mr. C.?"

"What's up?"

"You're my favorite teacher."

"For real?"

"I'm serious. I wish I had you next year too."

"It's all good. Whoever you get, there's always something to learn."

"That's true."

"Now, I know you said I'm your favorite teacher, but do you know who your greatest teacher in life will be?"

She tilts her head. "Who?"

"Life itself. Every experience is trying to teach us something. The real question is whether we're willing to learn those lessons. As the saying goes: 'A wise man learns from the mistakes of others, an average man learns from his own, and a fool never learns at all.'"

She nods slowly, letting it land.

"The key is to stay a student—always."

ON THE LAST DAY OF SCHOOL, the same kids come back to hang in my room. But the crowd of thirty has dwindled to a loyal handful. We spend the day listening to music, shooting hoops on the mini basketball court, and passing around the virtual reality headset.

Many slipped away without a goodbye—quiet exits for a loud year. I'd planned a pizza party just for my students, but with only fifty kids left in the building, I thought: *Why not feed them all?*

I order twenty pizzas and sodas. A few lunch ladies chip in, grabbing twenty McDonald's burgers and slicing them in half. One of them eyes me and says, "You better grab a slice before it's all gone."

"Nah, I want to make sure the kids eat first."

"Stop playing and get yourself a slice," she says, grinning.

I give in. Mmm. Greasy, but it tastes like victory. The party is the perfect ending to an imperfect year.

The final bell rings, and the students scatter like a spilled bag of marbles. Some leave without a word, yet in the silence, a quiet love lingers, a truth I carry in my bones.

This was the hardest chapter of my life—and the most transformative.

It cost me blood, sweat, and a lot of tears. But I wouldn't trade a single step.

As I step forward, I carry the laughter, the heartbreak, and the grit. I walk with gratitude, and I rise with strength, because this wasn't just survival.

This was alchemy.

And now, no matter what comes next, I remain what I've always been: a student of life, eyes open, heart steady.

The final bell may have rung,
but class is still in session—
life's classroom never closes.
The lessons don't end; they evolve.
And so do I.
Still learning.
Still growing.
Still turning pressure into diamonds.

Woosah.

ACKNOWLEDGMENTS

First, I want to thank my family and friends for their unwavering support. Your encouragement, spoken and unspoken, helped me stay grounded through every twist in this journey. Thank you for holding space for me when I needed to process, disappear, vent, or dream out loud.

To my students: you were the spark, the fuel, the reason I kept going. This isn't just my book—it's ours. Your energy, your questions, your stories live in these pages.

To my fellow educators: thank you for the solidarity, the vent sessions, and the quiet nods of understanding. Sometimes knowing you're not alone is enough to keep going.

A special thanks to Sharif El-Mekki, who first planted the seed that I could become an educator. And to all my former teachers—especially Barbara Winokur, who was the first to tell me my writing was special. That moment stayed with me.

To Tiago Pereira, who designed a cover as bold and layered as the story itself. Thank you for your patience. Your care brought the vision to life.

To my editors, Hugh Grant and Michael McConnell—your feedback, precision, and patience helped shape this manuscript into the book I envisioned. And to Valerie Franz, who walked beside me throughout the entire journey. Your early read, your belief in the book, and your consistent encouragement helped lay the foundation and carry it forward. I'm also grateful to Jennifer Myers for your thoughtful input during the final stretch.

Finally, to my soul family—my tribe—the travelers and backpackers I've met along the way: thank you for listening, for encouraging, and for letting me talk your ears off about this book. Your curiosity, kindness, and nomadic wisdom have left their imprint on these pages.

You reminded me that learning doesn't just happen in classrooms—it happens everywhere.

From the bottom of my heart: thank you all.

ABOUT THE AUTHOR

Tarique Connelly was born in Philadelphia in 1983. He earned his BM from New York University and worked for The Ritz-Carlton, Delta Air Lines, and Comcast/NBCUniversal before turning to public education. His experiences teaching in public schools and traveling internationally inform his perspective on learning, resilience, and human growth. *A Teacher's Odyssey* is his first book.

TariqueConnelly.com
Instagram.com/TariqueConnelly
Email: info@montevistapublishers.com

Thank you for joining me on this journey. I hope this story has given you insight into the realities students and teachers face every day and shown what's truly at stake in our schools. Please join me in the fight to reimagine public education —your voice matters.

Leave a Review on Amazon

Your review helps others discover this story and join the mission to challenge the status quo in our schools.

Stay Connected

Sign up for my newsletter at **TariqueConnelly.com** for updates, bonus content, and more from my work in education.

www.ingramcontent.com/pod-product-compliance
Lightning Source LLC
Chambersburg PA
CBHW050031110726
47973CB00033B/289/J